Karen Brown's
France

Charming Inns & Itineraries

Written by
KAREN BROWN, JUNE BROWN, and CLARE BROWN

Illustrations by Barbara Tapp
Cover Painting by Jann Pollard

Karen Brown's Guides, San Mateo, California

Karen Brown Titles

Austria: Charming Inns & Itineraries

California: Charming Inns & Itineraries

England: Charming Bed & Breakfasts

England, Wales & Scotland: Charming Hotels & Itineraries

France: Charming Bed & Breakfasts

France: Charming Inns & Itineraries

Germany: Charming Inns & Itineraries

Ireland: Charming Inns & Itineraries

Italy: Charming Bed & Breakfasts

Italy: Charming Inns & Itineraries

Portugal: Charming Inns & Itineraries

Spain: Charming Inns & Itineraries

Switzerland: Charming Inns & Itineraries

All my love to my family,
Rick, Alexandra, and Richard
I always look forward to coming home

The painting on the front cover is of Résidence Hôtel Le Pontot in Vézelay

Editors: Karen Brown, June Brown, Clare Brown, Kim Brown Holmsen, Iris Sandilands, Lorena Aburto.

Illustrations: Barbara Tapp; Cover painting: Jann Pollard; Web designer: Lynn Upthagrove.

Maps: Susanne Lau Alloway—Greenleaf Design & Graphics; Inside cover photo: W. Russell Ohlson.

Copyright © 1977, 1981, 1985, 1986, 1988, 1990, 1992, 1994, 1996, 1997, 1998, 1999, 2000 by Karen Brown's Guides.

This book or parts thereof may not be reproduced in any form without obtaining written permission from the publisher: Karen Brown's Guides, P.O. Box 70, San Mateo, CA 94401, USA, e-mail: karen@karenbrown.com.

Distributed by Fodor's Travel Publications, Inc., 201 East 50th Street, New York, NY 10022, USA.

Distributed in the United Kingdom, Ireland and Europe by Random House UK, 20 Vauxhall Bridge Road, London, SW1V 2SA, phone: 44 20 7840 4000, fax: 44 20 7840 8406.

Distributed Canada by Random House of Canada Limited, 2775 Matheson Blvd. East, Mississanga, Ontario, Canada L4W4P7, phone: 905 624 0672, fax: 905 624 6217.

Distributed in Australia by Random House Australia, 20 Alfred Street, Milsons Point, Sydney NSW 2061, Australia, phone: 61 2 9954 9966, fax: 61 2 9954 4562.

Distributed in New Zealand by Random House New Zealand, 18 Poland Road, Glenfield, Auckland, New Zealand, phone: 64 9 444 7197, fax: 64 9 444 7524.

Distributed in South Africa by Random House South Africa, Endulani, East Wing, 5A Jubilee Road, Parktown 2193, South Africa, phone: 27 11 484 3538, fax: 27 11 484 6180.

A catalog record for this book is available from the British Library.

Library of Congress Cataloging-in-Publication Data

Brown, Karen, 1956.
   Karen Brown's France: charming inns & itineraries / written by
Karen Brown, June Brown, Clare Brown; illustrations by Barbara Tapp; cover painting by Jann
Pollard. - - [Totally rev. 12th ed.]
     p. cm. -- (Karen Brown's country inn series)
   Includes index.
   ISBN 0-930328-89-2 (pb)
   1. Hotels—France—Guidebooks. 2. France--Guidebooks. I. Brown,
June, 1949- . II. Brown, Clare. III. Title. IV. Series
  TX907.5.F7B76 2000
  647.9444'01—dc21
                      99-15253
                      CIP

Contents

Introduction

Yes, you can fly to Paris, eat hamburgers, stay in a generic chain hotel, and return home with stacks of snapshots or you can follow our regional itineraries and venture into the ever-changing French countryside. You can eat, sleep, and drink France, enjoy lovely scenery and unusual sights, mingle with the French, and return home with special memories as well as snapshots to recall them. To further tempt you, we have selected magnificent places to lay your head each night: elegant châteaux, cozy inns, scenic mills, and refined manors owned and managed by warm and fascinating people. Many of these were designed and built centuries ago as private residences and are set in beautiful surroundings. As travelers, you can take full advantage of this opportunity to live France every minute, twenty-four hours a day.

PURPOSE OF THIS GUIDE

This guide is written with two main objectives: to describe the most charming, beguiling lodgings throughout France and to "tie" them together with itineraries to enable travelers to plan their own holiday. The aim is not simply to inform you of the fact that these places exist, but to encourage you to go and see for yourself: explore towns and villages not emphasized on tours and stay at hotels that truly reflect the French lifestyle. This book contains all of the necessary ingredients to assist you with your travel arrangements: easy-to-follow driving itineraries and one train itinerary that take you deep into the lovely French countryside, and, most importantly, a selective listing of hotels that we have seen and enjoy. It might be an elegant château dominating a bank of the River Loire or a cozy mill tucked into the landscape of the Dordogne Valley, but there is a common denominator—they all have charm, enticing location, and comfort. Our theory is that where you stay each night matters: your hotels should add the touch of perfection that makes your holiday very special. The memories you bring home should be of more than just museums, landmarks, and palace tours. Such sights are important, but with this guide you can add a romantic element to your trip: traveling the enchanting back roads of France and staying in picturesque hideaways.

If you also enjoy traveling the "bed and breakfast way," we suggest you refer to our companion guide *France: Charming Bed & Breakfasts*. Bed and breakfasts, reasonably priced, are a fantastic value and offer charming accommodation with a more intimate experience—you are a guest in a private château or romantic farmhouse and often have the opportunity to dine with your hosts. An itinerary incorporating stays at bed and breakfasts as well as country inns can result in a wonderful and memorable trip.

We encourage you to buy new editions of our guide and throw away old ones because in each new edition we add new listings, update prices and phone and fax numbers, and delete places that no longer meet our standards. This thirteenth edition proudly boasts 172 hotel recommendations, and 11 wonderful driving itineraries and one marvelous train itinerary that weave a journey through the landscape of the French countryside.

CLOTHING

France stretches some 1,200 kilometers from Calais on the north coast to Nice on the Riviera in the south, so there is a great range of weather conditions, regardless of the season. For winter bring warm coats, sweaters, gloves, snug hats, and boots. The rest of the year a layered effect will equip you for any kind of weather: skirts or trousers combined with blouses or shirts that can be "built upon" with layers of sweaters depending upon the chill of the day. A raincoat is a necessity, along with a folding umbrella. Sturdy, comfortable walking shoes are recommended not only for roaming the countryside and mountain trails, but also for negotiating cobbled streets. Daytime dress is casual, but in the evening it is often appropriate to dress up for dinner at your hotel.

CREDIT CARDS

When a hotel welcomes plastic payment, the type of card is identified by the following abbreviations: AX: American Express; MC: MasterCard, VS: Visa; or simply, all major. Also, conveniently and wonderfully, credit cards are now widely accepted at most gas stations and can be used for paying tolls on the autoroutes. Previously it was necessary to ensure that you always had enough francs in hand to pay for gas and toll, both French currency guzzlers!

CURRENCY

The unit of currency is the French franc, abbreviated to F (1F = 100 centimes). It is generally best to cash travelers' checks at a bank with a *bureau de change* desk—

remember to take your passport for identification. Be aware that there can be quite large variations in exchange rates and service charges offered by banks even on the same street. *Bureaux de change* are open 24 hours a day at the Paris Charles de Gaulle, Le Bourget, and Orly airports, and are normally open from 7:30 am to midnight at major railway stations. Some hotels will exchange money as a service to their guests, but they will approximate the exchange in their favor to guard against daily currency fluctuations.

Since 1999, 11 European countries (Austria, Belgium, Finland, France, Germany, Ireland, Italy, Luxembourg, Netherlands, Portugal, and Spain) have their currencies fixed to the new unit of European Monetary Union (also referred to as the EMU) currency, the euro dollar. No bills or coins will be issued immediately. For the first three years the euro will be the internationally traded currency, though local currencies will remain in circulation. Then, during a six-month period beginning January 1, 2002, the euro will be phased in and local currencies will be phased out. Both types of currencies will be valid during this period. Finally, on July 1, 2002, local currencies will be removed from circulation. We still reference room rates in French francs.

BANKS: Banking hours vary, but in most large towns and cities banks are open Monday to Friday, 9 am to 4:30 pm. In small towns, many banks close between noon and 2 pm. Banks close at midday on the day before a national holiday and all day on Monday if a holiday falls on Tuesday. In small towns banks are often closed on Mondays instead of Saturdays.

CURRENT

If you are taking any electrical appliances made for use in the United States, you will need a transformer plus a two-pin adapter. A voltage of 220 AC current at 50 cycles per second is almost countrywide, though in remote areas you may encounter 120V. The voltage is often displayed on the socket. Even though we recommend that you purchase appliances with dual-voltage options whenever possible, it will still be necessary to have the appropriate socket adapter. Also, be especially careful with expensive equipment such as computers—verify with the manufacturer the adapter/converter capabilities and requirements.

DRIVING

BELTS: It is mandatory and strictly enforced in France that every passenger wears a seat belt. Children under ten years of age must sit in the back seat.

CAR RENTAL: Readers frequently ask our advice on car rental companies. We always use Auto Europe, a car rental broker that negotiates with the major car rental companies to obtain the lowest possible price. They also offer motor homes and chauffeur services. Auto Europe's toll-free phone service from every European country connects you to their US-based, 24-hour reservation center (ask for the card with European phone numbers to be sent to you). Auto Europe offers our readers a minimum of a 5% discount, and occasionally free upgrades. Karen Brown readers can also obtain a free car phone with rentals of 7 days or more. You will be responsible for the activation fee ($30), cost to ship the phone to your home ($30), and charge for time used. Be sure to use the Karen Brown ID number 99006187 to receive your discount and any special offers. You can make your own reservations via our website, www.karenbrown.com (select Auto Europe from the home page under Travel Center), or by phone (1-800-223-5555).

DRIVER'S LICENSE: A valid driver's license from your home country is accepted in France if your stay does not exceed one year. The minimum driving age is 18.

GASOLINE: Americans are shocked by the high price of gasoline in Europe, especially when they realize published prices are for liters—only one fourth of a gallon. At some self-service stations you must pay in advance, before using the pumps (credit cards such as MasterCard and Visa are now often accepted). "Fill her up, please" translates as *"Faîtes le plein, s'il vous plaît."*

PARKING: It is illegal to park a car in the same place for more than 24 hours. In larger towns it is often customary that on the first 15 days of a month parking is permitted on the side of the road whose building addresses are odd numbers, and from the 16th to the end of the month on the even-numbered side of the road. Parking is prohibited in front of hospitals, police stations, and post offices. Blue Zones restrict parking to just one hour and require that you place a disc in your car window on Monday to Saturday from 9 am to 12:30 pm and again from 2:30 to 7 pm. Discs can be purchased at police stations and tobacco shops. Gray Zones are metered zones and a fee must be paid between the hours of 9 am and 7 pm.

ROADS: The French highway network consists of *autoroutes* (freeways or motorways), *péages* (autoroutes on which a toll is charged), and secondary roads (also excellent highways). Charges on toll roads are assessed according to the distance traveled. A travel ticket is issued on entry and you pay the toll on leaving the autoroute. The ticket will outline costs for distance traveled for various types of vehicles. It is expensive to travel on toll roads, so weigh carefully the advantage of time versus cost. If you have unlimited time and a limited budget, you may prefer the smaller highways and country roads. A suggestion would be to use the autoroutes to navigate in and out of, or bypass large cities and then return to the country roads. Credit cards are now accepted as payment at tollbooths.

SPEED: Posted speed limits are strictly enforced and fines are hefty. Traffic moves fast on the autoroutes and toll roads with speed limits of 130 kph (81 mph). On the secondary highways the speed limit is 90 kph (56 mph). The speed limit within city and town boundaries is usually 60 kph (38 mph). Keep a lookout for the *gendarmes*!

HOTELS

HOTEL DESCRIPTIONS: In the third section of this guide you will find a selective listing of hotels referenced alphabetically by town. Every hotel recommended has been personally visited by us. It is impossible to revisit every hotel on a research trip as there are always new hotels to investigate, but we try to check up on as many as possible. We also rely on feedback from readers, follow up on any complaints, and eliminate hotels that do not maintain their quality of service, accommodation, and welcome. People who seek personal experiences and unforgettable accommodation rather than predictable motel-like rooms will appreciate our recommendations—we include château-hotels, hôstelleries, hotels, old mills, manors, country inns, and restaurants with rooms. As the accommodation varies from luxurious to country-cozy, we have tried provide an honest written appraisal of what each hotel has to offer so that you can make a choice to suit your preferences. However, no matter how careful we are, sometimes we misjudge a hotel's merits, or the ownership changes, or unfortunately sometimes hotels just do not maintain their standards. If you find a hotel is not as we have indicated, we would greatly appreciate your comments.

HOTEL RATES: We quote **high-season**, **2000** rates as provided by the hotels. The rates given are for the **least** expensive to the **most** expensive rooms inclusive of tax for **two persons**, **excluding breakfast**. Breakfast is priced per person. If a range of rates is given for breakfast, it generally differentiates between a Continental or more lavish buffet. Please **always check prices and terms** with hotels when making reservations.

HOTEL RESERVATIONS & CANCELLATIONS: Whether or not you opt to secure reservations in advance depends on how flexible you want to be, how tight your schedule is, during which season you are traveling, and how disappointed you would be if your first choice were unavailable. Reservations are confining and usually must be guaranteed by a deposit. Refunds are difficult should you change your plans—especially at the last minute. In France a hotel is not required by law to refund a deposit, regardless of the cancellation notice given. Although reservations can be restrictive, it is nice not to spend a part of your vacation day searching for available accommodation, particularly during the peak summer months and holiday periods.

Should you decide to secure reservations in advance, several options are discussed below and on the following pages. However, in each case, when making a reservation be sure to state clearly and exactly what you want, how many people are in your party, how many rooms you require, the category of room you prefer (standard, superior, deluxe), and your date of arrival and departure. Inquire also about rates—which might have changed from those given in the book—and deposit requirements. In any written correspondence be sure to **spell out the month** since Europeans reverse the numerical month/day order—to them 9/6 means June 9th, not September 6th as interpreted in the USA. It is also wise to advise them of your anticipated arrival time; discuss dining options if so desired; and ask for a confirmation letter with brochure and map to be sent to you.

When making your reservations be sure to identify yourself as a *"Karen Brown Traveler."* We hear over and over again that the people who use our guides are such wonderful guests. The hotels appreciate your visit, value their inclusion in our guide, and frequently tell us they take special care of our readers.

E-MAIL: With each edition of our guide, more and more hotels are becoming computer literate and providing us with their e-mail addresses. Rather than individual addresses, a number of hotels have given an e-mail address in connection with a particular organization, such as Relais & Châteaux Hotels, with which they are affiliated.

FAX: Faxing is a very quick way to reach a hotel. If the hotel has a fax, we have included the number in its listing. As you are communicating with a machine, you also don't have to concern yourself with the time of day or worry about disturbing someone's sleep.

LETTER: Although most hotels can understand a letter written in English, for ease of communicating, on the following page is a template of a reservation request letter in French and English.

SAMPLE RESERVATION REQUEST LETTER

Madame/Monsieur:

Nous souhaiterions réserver/ We would like to reserve

_____ *chambre(s) à deux lits simples/* (number) room(s) with twin beds

_____ *chambre(s) avec un grand lit/* (number) room(s) with double bed

_____ *chambre(s) avec un lit supplémentaire/* (number) room(s) with an extra bed

___ *avec toilette et baignoire ou douche privée./* with a private toilet & bathtub or shower.

Pour _____ *nuits, /* for (number) of nights,

du _____ *au* _____/ from (arrival date) to (departure date) inclusive,

au nom de M ou Mme _____/ under the name of Mr. or Mrs. (your last name).

Note: To avoid confusion, reference date spelled out by month and day or day/month/year.

Merci de nous confirmer cette réservation en nous communicant le prix de la (des) chambre(s), et le montant des arrhes que vous souhaitez./ Please confirm the reservation, rate or room (s) and deposit required.

Dans l'attente de votre réponse nous vous prions d'agréer, Madame, Monsieur, l'expression de nos salutations distingués.

Please advise availability, rate of room and deposit needed. We will be waiting for your confirmation and send our kindest regards.

Your name & address

TELEPHONE: A very efficient way of making reservations is by telephone—the cost is minimal and you have your answer immediately—so if space is not available, you can then choose an alternative hotel. If calling from the United States, allow for the time difference. (France is five hours ahead of New York) so that you can call during their business day. Dial 011 (the international code), 33 (France's code), and then only the last nine digits of the ten-digit number. The '0' in the regional prefixes is dropped (it is used only when dialing from within France).

HOTEL RESTAURANTS: French cuisine is incomparable in creativity and price—it is not uncommon to pay more for dinner than for a room. Where hotels are concerned, the price you pay for your meal is usually a reflection of the price you pay for your room: that is, expensive hotels usually have expensive restaurants. We do not discuss restaurants in depth but we note whether a hotel has a restaurant. Some of France's most charming hotels are actually "restaurants with rooms," principally restaurants that offer rooms to patrons of their restaurant. Restaurants often have a tourist menu or menu of the day; set meals, which usually include specialties of the house, are good value for money, and offer a meal where the courses complement one another. Restaurants known for their gourmet cuisine often offer a *menu dégustation* (tasting menu) so that on one visit you can sample a selection of the chef's many artful creations. Many hotels prefer overnight guests to dine at their restaurant. To avoid misunderstandings, inquire about a hotel's dining policy when making your room reservation.

INFORMATION

Syndicat d'Initiative is the name for the tourist offices (symbolized by a large "I") found in all larger towns and resorts in France. Tourist offices are pleased to give advice on local events and timetables for local trains, buses and boats, and they often have maps and brochures on the region's points of interest. They can also help with location and availability of local hotels and bed and breakfasts. The offices often close for two hours for lunch in the middle of the day.

In Paris the main tourist office is located at 127, Avenue Champs Élysées, near the George V Métro stop. (*Open all year, 9 am to 8 pm, tel: 08.36.68.31.12.*) They also now have a website: www.paris-touristoffice.com.

There are also 45 regional *Accueil de France* (French Welcome) offices that will make reservations at hotels in their area no more than eight days in advance. A list of regional offices is available through the French Government Tourist Office.

Assistance, information, and free brochures can be obtained before you leave for France by calling the new hotline, "France on Call": (410) 286-8310 from 9 am to 7 pm EST. You can also visit their website at www.francetourism.com where you can obtain contact information for all the individual, regionalized tourist offices throughout France.

It is also possible to obtain information free of charge by contacting the following French Government Tourist Offices:

AUSTRALIA
  BNP Building, 12th fl., 12 Castelreagh St. Sydney, NSW 200 Australia, fax: (292) 218 682

GREAT BRITAIN
  178 Piccadilly, London W1V OAL, England, fax: (020) 7493-6594

CANADA
  1981 Avenue McGill College, Suite 490, Montreal, QUE H3A 2W9, fax: (514) 845-4868

UNITED STATES
French Government Tourist Office Headquarters, e-mail: info@francetourism.com
  444 Madison Avenue, 16th Floor, New York, NY 10022, fax: (212) 838-7855

Los Angeles Office, e-mail: fgtola@juno.net
  9454 Wilshire Boulevard, Suite 715, Beverly Hills, CA 90212, fax: (310) 276-2835

Chicago Office, e-mail: fgto@mcs.net
  676 North Michigan Avenue, Chicago, IL 60611, fax: (312) 337-6339

ITINERARIES

Eleven driving itineraries and one train itinerary are included in this guide to help you map a route through the various regions of France. Depending on your time and interests you might want to patchwork together a trip encompassing a couple of itineraries. An overview map that shows all 12 itineraries is on the facing page. At the beginning of each itinerary we suggest our recommended pacing to help you decide the amount of time to allocate to each region.

MAPS

Each itinerary is preceded by a map showing the route and each hotel listing is referenced on its top line to a map at the back of the book. To make it easier for you, hotel location maps are divided into a grid of four parts, a, b, c, and d as indicated on each map's key. All maps are an artist's renderings and are not intended to replace detailed commercial maps. We very much enjoy the *Michelin Motoring Atlas of France,* a book of maps with a scale of 1:200,000 (1 cm = 2 km) and use highlight pens to outline our route. We also find the yellow Michelin maps very useful and we state which Michelin 200 series map each hotel's town is found on in the hotel description. While the atlas and yellow maps are invaluable, we find them too detailed for getting an overview of our trip and rely upon a one-page map of France to outline our journey. French hotel maps in this book can be cross-referenced with those in our companion guide, *France: Charming Bed & Breakfasts.*

POST OFFICES

Post offices are open in most towns from 8 am to 7 pm Monday to Friday and from 8 am to midday on Saturdays. There is a post office in Paris that is open 24 hours a day, located at 52, Rue du Louvre, 75001. In addition to the standard services typically provided by post offices, domestic and international telephone calls can be placed at the post office, efficiently and relatively inexpensively.

Itinerary Overview

Auto routes
Rail route

Rouen

Champagne

Reims

Épernay

Alsace

Strasbourg

Mont St. Michel

Caen

Normandy

PARIS

Colmar

St. Malo

Rennes

Brittany

Quimper

Angers

Tours

Orléans

Vézelay

Dijon

Burgundy

Beaune

Nantes

Châteaux Country

Brantôme

Les Eyzies

Sarlat

Dordogne & Lot River Valleys

Lyon

Gorges du Verdon

Conques

Moustiers Ste. Marie

Trigance

Cahors

Vence

Ste. Enimie

Avignon

Millau

Gordes

Nîmes

Arles

Grasse

Nice

Aix

Gorges du Tarn

Hilltowns of the Riviera

Carcassonne

Provence

TRAINS

Our itinerary for exploring France by train originates in Paris and travels to the Loire Valley, the Dordogne, Provence, Burgundy, and Alsace. It highlights some of France's most popular destinations, and towns have been selected as being truly representative of a given region. France does have an excellent train system serving major towns and cities, but it is often necessary to supplement your travel arrangements with either taxi or car rental to reach small countryside towns and isolated inns. If you decide to travel by train, be aware that, in addition to point-to-point tickets, a variety of travel passes and packages involving car rental and airline tickets is available. Information, reservations, and tickets are discussed in greater detail in the train itinerary and are available by contacting your travel agent or Rail Europe, tel: (800) 438-7245 or (800) 848-7245 from the United States, and (800) 361-7245 from Canada. It is now also possible to simply check schedules and fares directly by calling (888) 382-7245 or through their website, www.raileurope.com.

WEBSITE

We are constantly changing and updating the Karen Brown website with the aim of providing an enhanced extension of our guides and supplying you with even more information on the properties and destinations that we recommend. Many hotels that we work very closely with are featured on our website—their web addresses are detailed on the description pages. In 2000 we will continue to add photos for as many properties as possible and you will be able to link directly to the hotels' individual websites, if available, for their personal photos and more information. On our site we share comments, feedback, and discoveries from you, our readers, and keep you informed of our latest finds, current updates, and special offers. We want our website to serve as a valuable and added dimension to our guides. Be sure to visit our website at www.karenbrown.com.

Normandy

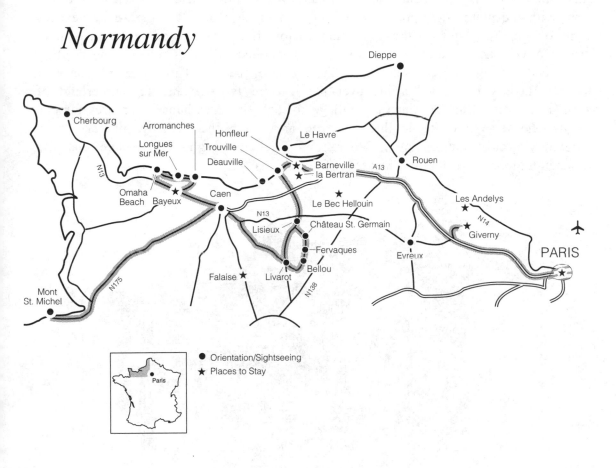

Dieppe

Cherbourg

Arromanches

Longues
sur Mer

Honfleur

Trouville

Deauville

Le Havre

Barneville
la Bertran

A13

Rouen

Omaha
Beach   Bayeux

Caen

Le Bec Hellouin

Les Andelys

N13

N13

Lisieux

Château St. Germain

N14

Giverny

Fervaques

Evreux

PARIS

Falaise

Livarot

Bellou

N138

Mont
St. Michel

N175

● Orientation/Sightseeing
★ Places to Stay

Paris

Normandy

This itinerary heads north from Paris to Monet's wonderful gardens at Giverny, on to the coast with the picturesque port of Honfleur, and to the world-famous D-Day beaches where on June 6, 1944 the Allies made their major offensive, reinforcing the turnaround in World War II. Decades have passed but abandoned pillboxes remain, the floating harbor endures, and museums document the events of the war. Turning inland you visit historic Bayeux to marvel at its over-900-year-old tapestry and the hinterland of Normandy with rolling farmland and villages of half-timbered houses—an area famous for its cheese. We conclude this itinerary, and begin the Brittany itinerary, with Normandy's most famous sight, Mont Saint Michel, a sightseeing venue that has attracted legions of visitors for hundreds of years.

Giverny

Recommended Pacing: While you can use Honfleur as a base for this itinerary (except for visiting Mont Saint Michel), our preference is to spend one night near Giverny, two nights in Honfleur, and a minimum of one night in the region of Bayeux.

Follow the Seine north out of Paris (Porte d'Auteuil) on the A13 and exit at Bonnières sur Seine. Travel a scenic route following the N15 north along the Seine to Vernon. As you cross the Seine with the village of **Vernonette** sitting at the crossroads, you see the remains of a picturesque 12th-century bridge and an ancient timbered dungeon. Just a few kilometers upstream lies the village of **Giverny**, a name synonymous worldwide with artist Claude Monet who came to live in the village in 1883.

Monet converted the barn into his studio, where he loved to paint, smoke, and reflect on his work. Now it's visitors' center and gift shop selling all things Monet from posters of his masterpieces to key-rings. The walls are hung with reproductions of some of his larger canvases and photos of the famous artist at work. Monet's sun-washed peach stucco home with green shutters is decorated much as it was when he lived there—the walls hung with Japanese-style paintings and family pictures. From the striking blue-and-yellow dining room with its matching china, through his bedroom, to the cozy tiled kitchen, you get a feeling for the home life of this famous artist.

The magic of a visit to Giverny is the gardens, a multi-colored tapestry of flowers, meandering paths shaded by trellises of roses, and the enchanting oasis of the water garden, whose green waters are covered with lily pads and crossed by Japanese bridges hung with white and mauve wisteria. Monet loved to paint outdoors and it is memorable to search out just the spot where he stood and painted a masterpiece. There is only one problem: you are not alone in your endeavors—Giverny attracts a multitude of pilgrims. However, the influx of tourists also means that this tiny village has a surprising number of facilities, including cafés, restaurants, and gift stores. (*Open April to October, 10 am to 6 pm, closed Mondays.*)

Another wonderful highlight and attraction just a couple of hundred yards from Giverny, is the **Musée d'Art Américan** which is dedicated to the appreciation of American art, focusing on the historical connection between French and American artists throughout the Impressionist and other 19th- and 20th-century periods. During the time of Claude Monet many American artists made pilgrimages to France to partake of the cultural and artistic fever of the time and be inspired by the beauty of the French countryside. If you desire a private tour, it can be scheduled directly through the museum: Musée d'Art Américan, 99, Rue Claude Monet, 27620 Giverny, tel: 02.32.51.94.65, fax: 02.32.51.94.67. (*Open April to October, 10 am to 6 pm, closed Mondays.*)

If you have let an entire day slip by in Giverny, you might want to consider accommodation in the orchards just above the artist's home. **La Réserve** is newly built to resemble a Normandy villa. Old windows, doors, and wood floors effect an ambiance of old but all the conveniences provide welcome modern comforts. This is a gorgeous inn—a destination to rival Giverny.

If you want to venture farther on to the coast, return to Vernon and from there follow signposts for Rouen, then Caen along the A13. Exit the autoroute at Beuzeville and travel north on the D22 and then west on the D180 to Honfleur. **Honfleur** is a gem, its narrow, 17th-century harbor filled with tall-masted boats and lined with tall, slender, pastel-wash houses. Narrow cobbled streets lined with ancient timbered houses lead up from the harbor. Cafés and restaurants set up tables and umbrellas outside so that customers can enjoy the sun and the picturesque location. Small wonder that this pretty port has inspired artists, writers, and musicians. Markets are held every Saturday on Saint Catherine's Square with its unusual wooden belfry, a tall bell-tower and bell-ringer's home, standing apart from the nearby church. Just off the square, farther up the hillside, on Rue de l'Homme de Bois, is the interesting **Eugène Boudin Museum** with its impressive collection of pre-Impressionist and contemporary paintings by Norman artists: Boudin, Dubourg, Dufy, Monet, Friesz, and Gernez. There are also displays of Norman costumes and paintings depicting life in 18th- and 19th-century Normandy. (*Closed noon to 2 pm and all day Tuesdays, tel: 02.31.89.23.30.*)

Just by the harbor, in a former church, the **Musée Marine** traces the history of the port of Honfleur. Nearby the ancient timbered prison is now the **Musée d'Art Populaire**, consisting of 12 rooms depicting the interiors of Norman houses including a weaver's workshop and a manor-house dining room. (*Closed Sundays in winter, open 9:30 am to 7 pm, tel: 02.31.89.23.30.*) In addition to having quaint shops and inviting fish restaurants, Honfleur is a haven for artists and there are a number of galleries to visit.

We recommend four hotels, one in, and three on the outskirts of Honfleur (one referenced in Barneville la Bertran). Our advice is that if you visit Honfleur, you stay for the night because this will give you the opportunity to enjoy this scenic town without the hordes of daytime visitors.

For a contrast to the quaintness of Honfleur you may choose to visit her two famous neighbors, Trouville and Deauville. **Trouville** has set the pace on the *Côte de Fleurie*

Honfleur

since 1852. A stretch of water divides it from its very close neighbor, **Deauville**, a much ritzier resort where row upon row of beach cabanas line the sands and well-heeled folks parade the streets. The casinos are a hub of activity, and if you visit in the late summer, you will experience the excitement and sophistication of a major summer playground for the rich and famous. For a few weeks each August there is the allure of the race tracks, polo fields, glamorous luncheons, and black-tie dinners. Celebrities and the wealthy international set come here to cheer on their prize thoroughbreds.

From Honfleur dip south into a region of Normandy referred to as the **Pays d'Auge**, a lush region sandwiched between the Risle and Dives rivers. Here quaint villages of timbered and some thatched houses cluster on rolling green hillsides grazed by cows or planted with apple orchards. It is a region to experience by driving along its quiet country roads. The drive we suggest is a leisurely half-day outing beginning at **Lisieux**, the region's commercial center. If you are fortunate enough to arrive on Saturday, enjoy the town's colorful farmers' market where stalls offer everything from live chickens, vegetables, and cheese to underwear and shoes.

Leave Lisieux in the direction of Vimoutiers (D579) and travel for just a few kilometers and take a left turn down a country lane to **Saint Germain de Livet**, a hamlet at the bottom of the valley. Here you see a picture-postcard timbered farm, a couple of cottages, a church, and the adorable 15th-century **Château Saint Germain de Livet**. This whimsical little château with pepper-pot turrets and pretty pink-and-white-checkerboard façade sits in geometric gardens behind a high wall. The interior contains some attractive furniture and some paintings and frescoes. (*Closed 11 am to 2 pm and all day Tuesdays, tel: 02.31.31.00.03.*) Leaving the château, follow signposts for Vimoutiers (D268) till you reach the D47 which you follow into Fervaques, a picturesque village in a green valley. Drive past its château, a vast 16th-century stone building, to the village with its timbered cottages set round a quiet square. Here you pick up signposts for **Route de Fromage**, a tourist route that guides you through this cheese-producing region.

Follow the well-signposted Route de Fromage into **Les Moutier Hubert**, a hamlet of farms along the road, up to **Bellou** with its large brown timbered manor house, and on to Lisores with its little church, ivy-covered houses, and farms in the valley. Regain the main road heading towards Livarot (D579) and travel for a few kilometers before being directed right by the Route de Fromage onto a back road that brings you by a more scenic route into the heart of the attractive old town of **Livarot**, home of the cheese that bears the same name. Leave town in the direction of Caen to see the **Musée du Fromage** in the basement of one of the town's grand old homes. Here you watch a video on the production of Livarot, Pont l'Eveque, and Camembert cheeses, and tour a replica of an old dairy farm with its traditional cheese-making shop and old-fashioned dairy (*Open 10 am to 6 pm in summer, closed noon to 2pm in winter, tel: 02.31.63.43.13.*)

As you continue on to Caen (40 kilometers), the countryside is pancake flat. **Caen**, one of Normandy's largest cities, is situated on the banks of the Orne, which lost nearly all of its 10,000 buildings in the Allied invasion of 1944. A large port, it is also the city that William the Conqueror made his seat of government. Your destination in Caen is the **Memorial** (Memorial to Peace). The museum is well signposted and has its own exit off the autoroute. Displays, films, tapes, and photos cover the events that led up to the outbreak of World War II, the invasion of France, total war, D-Day, the Battle of Normandy, and hope for lasting world peace. A good look round takes several hours, an in-depth visit all day. (*Open all year, 9 am to 9 pm, tel: 02.31.06.06.44.*)

A 15-minute drive down the N13 brings you to **Bayeux**, a lovely old town where inviting shops and honey-colored stone houses line narrow streets. **Saint Patrice** square is filled with colorful market stalls on Saturday and Wednesday mornings (**Hôtel d'Argouges** is found here and the beautiful **Château de Sully** lies just a few kilometers to the north of the city). There has been a town on this site since Roman times: it was invaded by the Bretons, the Saxons, and the Vikings, but thankfully escaped the allied bombers. It's a great place for shopping and serves as a convenient base for visiting the landing beaches.

Apart from the town itself, your premier destination in Bayeux is the **Musée de la Tapisserie**, which displays the famous tapestry that Odo, Bishop of Bayeux, had the English embroider following the conquest of England by his half-brother William the Conqueror in 1066. The color and richness of the tapestry make the little stick figures look as if they were stitched just yesterday, not 900 years ago. With the aid of earphones the intricately embroidered scenes come alive. We found we needed to go past it twice— once quickly to appreciate its enormous proportions and the second time to hear the story it tells. (*Open all year, 9 am to 7 pm, closed 12:30 to 2 pm except in summer, tel: 02.31.51.25.50, fax: 02.31.51.25.59.*)

Bayeux Tapestry

Next to the cathedral, the **Musée Baron Gérard** has some lovely examples of porcelain and lace manufactured in Bayeux. (*Open all year, closed 12:30 to 2 pm except in summer, tel: 02.31.92.14.21.*) On the main ring-road around the old town is the **1944 Battle of Normandy Museum** with its exhibitions of tanks, guns, and armored vehicles used in the Battle of Normandy. (*Open all year, closed 12:30 to 2 pm except in summer, tel: 02.31.92.93.41.*)

A ten-minute drive north brings you to **Arromanches** and the D-Day beaches. Arromanches is a lively seaside town whose broad crescent of golden sand was one of the D-Day landing beaches. In June, 1944 a huge floating harbor was erected in a gigantic U in the bay. Designed by British engineers, the harbor was comprised of massive concrete blocks, floating pier-heads, and 10 kilometers of floating pier "roads." It was towed across the Channel and erected here, enabling the Allies to unload half-a-million tons of materials in a three-month period. After 50 years of Atlantic storms much of the harbor is still in place and you can get an up-close look at several enormous sections marooned on the beach. Beside the beach is the **D-Day Museum** with its displays of models, photographs, and films of the military operations of June, 1944. (*Closed January, and 11:30 am to 2 pm except in summer, tel: 02.31.22.34.31.*)

Follow the **Route de Debarquement**, a route that weaves you through little gray-stone villages whose tall walled farmhouses and barns form their own little fortifications amongst the fields. **Longues sur Mer** is the only naval artillery battery on the Normandy coast that still has its guns. Farther on is the section where the American troops landed, just west of the lovely **Omaha Beach**: the Pointe du Hoc was captured on June 6, 1944 by American Rangers. All along this stretch of coast are military cemeteries—the final resting place for the Americans, British, Canadians, Polish, and Germans who died. Above Omaha Beach, set in manicured parklike grounds, are row upon row of white crosses, memorials to over 9,000 Americans.

This itinerary concludes at Mont Saint Michel, a 120-kilometer drive from Caen (about two hours). Straddling the border of Brittany and Normandy, **Mont Saint Michel** is France's most visited tourist attraction. Joined to the mainland by a narrow strip of roadway, Mont Saint Michel, initially a place of pilgrimage, then a fortress, and in the 19th century a prison, clings to a rock island and towers 150 meters above sea level. Depending on the tide, it is either almost surrounded by water or by marshes and quicksand. Wander up the narrow cobblestoned streets to the crowning 12th-century abbey and visit the remarkable Gothic and Romanesque complex, culminating in the glories of the *Merveille* (Marvel)—the group of buildings on the north side of the mount. Saint Michael, the militant archangel, is the saint for the beaches you have just seen.

From Mont Saint Michel you can return to Paris, join the *Châteaux Country* itinerary, or continue on the following itinerary into *Brittany*.

Brittany

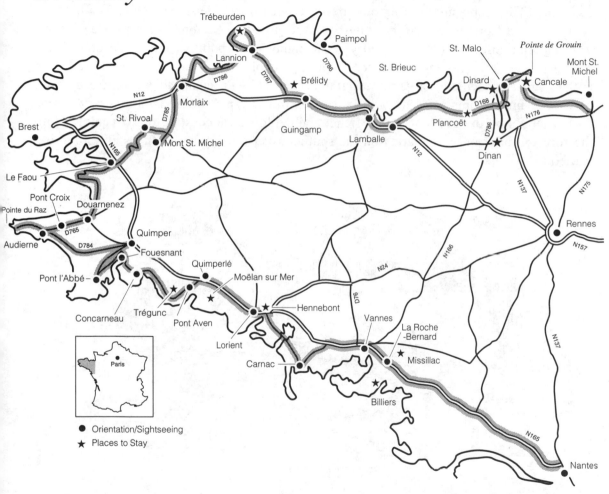

- Trébeurden
- Paimpol
- Lannion
- St. Malo
- Pointe de Grouin
- St. Brieuc
- Brélidy
- Dinard
- Mont St. Michel
- Morlaix
- St. Rivoal
- Cancale
- Brest
- Mont St. Michel
- Guingamp
- Plancoët
- Le Faou
- Lamballe
- Dinan
- Pont Croix
- Douarnenez
- Pointe du Raz
- Rennes
- Audierne
- Quimper
- Fouesnant
- Pont l'Abbé
- Quimperlé
- Moëlan sur Mer
- Concarneau
- Trégunc
- Pont Aven
- Hennebont
- Vannes
- La Roche -Bernard
- Lorient
- Missillac
- Carnac
- Billiers
- Nantes

N12, D786, D767, D786, D785, N165, D765, D784, N24, D76, N166, N137, N157, N175, N176, N137, N168, D786, N165

Paris

- ● Orientation/Sightseeing
- ★ Places to Stay

Brittany

Brittany is a rugged region of beautiful forests bounded by nearly 1,000 kilometers of coastline. This peninsula, jutting out from the northwest side of France, was for many years isolated from the rest of the country and regarded by Bretons as a separate country. The regional language is Breton and you see signposts in both French and Breton. Most of the houses are fresh white stucco with angled blue-gray roofs. *Crêpes* filled with butter, sugar, chocolate, or jam, *gallettes* (wheat crêpes) enhanced with cheese, ham, onions, or mushrooms and cider are Brittany's culinary specialties. This itinerary begins on Brittany's border at Mont Saint Michel and explores the coast before it ventures into the forested interior, culminating on the southern coast at Vannes with its charming old walled town.

Breton Coastal Village

Recommended Pacing: Select a location in northern Brittany for the northern portion of the itinerary and one on the southwestern coast for the southern portion. Two nights in each spot should give you ample time to explore the peninsula.

While **Mont Saint Michel** is technically in Normandy, it is geographically in Brittany. Mont Saint Michel is France's premier tourist attraction, and although it is wonderful, we think it best to warn our readers that the effort of pushing your way uphill through teeming crowds, past souvenir shops, to reach the abbey at the summit is not enjoyable. The appearance of the town is that of a child's sand castle, with narrow, cobblestoned streets winding up to the 12th-century abbey and lovely Romanesque church, dedicated to Archangel Michael. Depending on the tide, the mount is either almost surrounded by water or by marshland and quicksand. Travel across the paved causeway that joins the mount to the mainland, park in the massive car park, and explore on foot.

Leaving Mont Saint Michel, take the D976 to Dol. Follow signposts for Saint Malo across the flat farmland to **Cancale** whose beachside port is full of lobsters, mussels, oysters, and clams, and whose attractive little town is nestled on the cliffs above. Follow signposts for *Saint Malo par la Côte* to Pointe du Grouin, a windswept headland and promontory. Rounding the point, you are rewarded by vistas of coastline stretching into the far distance.

Saint Malo corsairs, who menaced British seafarers during the 16th century, were pirates with royal permission to take foreign ships. With its tall 13th- and 14th-century ramparts facing the sea and enormous harbor (the terminal of ferries from Portsmouth and the Channel Islands), the town is almost surrounded by water. Within the walls are narrow streets lined with interesting shops and small restaurants. Much was destroyed in battle between Germans and Americans in 1944 but it has all been magnificently restored. Walk round the walls (stairs by Saint Vincent's gate), visit the courtyard of the 14th-century castle (now the town hall), and sample *crêpes* or *gallettes*.

Following the D168, cross the *barrière* (low pontoon bridge) over the bay to **Dinard**, a popular beach resort. Once a sleepy fishing village, its confusion of one-way streets and seafront hotels (blocking views) discourage you from leaving the main highway. Just south of Dinard there is a wonderful small hotel for an overnight stop—the **Manoir de la Rance**, outside the village of Pleurtuit, overlooking the water.

Approximately 25 kilometers south of Dinard is the wonderful walled town of **Dinan.** Embraced by medieval ramparts, it is a charming city with cobbled streets, half-timbered houses, a historic convent, and castle ruins. It is a great place to spend an afternoon exploring the maze of streets, from its picturesque port to the encircling ramparts. Known as "the city of art history," Dinan has intriguing stores, a multitude of art galleries, and inviting sidewalk cafés. If you use Dinan as a base, **L'Hôtel d'Avaugour** offers charming accommodation on the edge of the old town.

A 45-kilometer drive through Plancoët brings you to **Lamballe**. (Nearby is the **Manoir de Vaumadeuc**, a 15th-century manor house that is now a welcoming hotel.) At the heart of Lamballe's industrial sprawl are some fine old houses on the Place du Martrai, including the executioner's house that is now the tourist office. The traffic is congested.

Join the N12 bypassing Saint Brieuc and Guigamp (the town where gingham was first woven) and take the D767 northwest to Lannion. **Lannion** is an attractive town beside the fast-flowing River Léguer with some fine medieval houses at its center, near the Place Général Leclerc. Follow signposts for Perros Guirec then **Trébeurden** that bring you to this attractive seaside resort. A small sheltered harbor is separated from a curve of sandy beach by a wooded peninsula, and overlooking the beach you find **Ti Al-Lannec**, one of our favorite hotels. Make your way back to Lannion along the beautiful stretch of coast and take the D786 towards Morlaix. At Saint Michel the road traces a vast sandy curve of beach and exposes vistas of succeeding headlands. Just as the road leaves the bay, turn right following signposts for *Morlaix par la Côte,* which gives you the opportunity to sample another small stretch of very attractive coastline. At Locquirec turn inland through Guimaéc and Lanmeur to regain the D786 to Morlaix.

Morlaix is a central market town whose quays shelter boats that travel the passage inland from the sea. You do not have to deal with city traffic as you follow the N12 (signposted Brest) around the town for a short distance to the D785, (signposted Pleyben Christ), which leads you into the **Regional Parc d'Amorique**. After the very gray little towns of Pleyben Christ and Plounéour Ménez the scenery becomes more interesting as the road leads you up onto moorlands where rock escarpments jut out from the highest hill. A narrow road winds up to the little chapel high atop **Mont Saint Michel** (an isolated windswept spot very different from its famous namesake). Return to the D785 for a short distance taking the first right turn to **Saint Rivoal**, which has a **Maison Cornic**, a small park with an interesting collection of old Breton houses.

Following signposts for Le Faou, you travel up the escarpment to be rewarded by sky-wide views of the distant coast. Travel through Forêt du Cranou with its majestic oak trees to Le Faou where you continue straight (signposted Crozon). The route hugs the Aulne estuary and offers lovely vistas of houses dotting the far shore, then gives way to wooded fjords before crossing a high bridge and turning away from the coast.

Breton Women in Traditional Dress

At Tar-ar-Groas make an almost 180-degree turn in the center of the village and continue the very pleasant drive following signposts for Douarnenez, a large fishing port that you skirt on the D765 following signposts for Audierne. **Pont Croix** is built on terraces up from the River Goyen. Leading to the bridge, its photogenic narrow streets are lined with old houses. **Audierne** is a pretty fishing port on the estuary of the Goyen where fishing boats bring in their harvest of lobsters, crayfish, and tunny.

Your destination is **Pointe du Raz**, the Land's End of France. Thankfully it is less commercial than England's, but it is certainly not isolated. Uniformly sized white holiday cottages dot the landscape and a large café and grotesque museum lie at road's end. If you can ignore the commercialism, you will find the views across the windswept headlands spectacular. This journey is not recommended in the height of summer when roads are congested.

An hour's drive (60 kilometers on the D784) brings you to the large town of **Quimper**, set where the Odet and Steir rivers meet. Park by the river, wander the town's pleasant streets and visit the **Musée Henrist**, with its displays of attractive regional pottery. *(Open mid-April to end-October, Monday to Saturday, 10 am to 6 pm, tel: 02.98.90.12.72.)* If the name of Quimper pottery is not familiar, it is, however, likely that you will immediately recognize the endearing figures painted in warm washes of predominantly blues and yellows that are now appreciated and recognized worldwide. The paintings on the pottery depict country folk in the old traditional dress and costume of Brittany.

This itinerary now explores Brittany's southern coast. The individual towns are very attractive but we were disappointed not to find more scenic countryside between them. Your first stop is **Pont l'Abbé**, set deep in a sheltered estuary. The squat castle contains a museum, **Musée Bigoudin,** of costume and furniture, with some fine examples of the tall white lace coifs that Breton women wear on their heads for festivals. *(Open March to end-September, closed noon to 2 pm.)* A pleasant park borders the river and the town square has a large covered market.

Cross the high bridge that spans the River Odet and catch a panoramic view of **Benodet**. If you go into its crowded streets, follow signs for the port, which bring you to its yacht harbor—from here the coast road weaves past sandy bays and holiday hotels to the casino. In summer do not tackle the crowded streets; we recommend that you just admire the town from the bridge.

Ten kilometers away lies **Fouesnant**, a traditional center for cider production. Its pretty port, **La Forét Fouesnant**, with its harbor full of yachts and small arc of golden sand, lies just a few kilometers away.

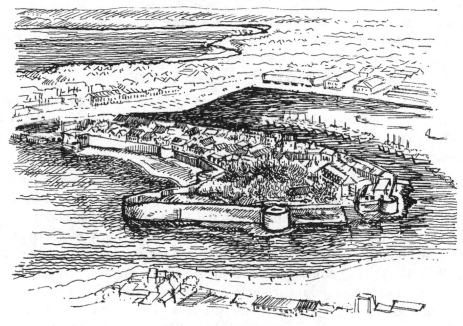

Concarneau, Ville Close

Leaving the village, follow signs for *Concarneau par la Côte* that quickly take you on a scenic back road into town.

Ignore **Concarneau's** bustling town, and park by the harbor as close as possible to **Ville Close**, the 14th-century walled town which sits amidst a vast harbor of colorful boats varying from sleek yachts to commercial fishing trawlers. The old town, with its narrow streets and old houses full of crêperies and gift shops, is fun to explore. Visit the interesting **Musée de la Pêche** covering all things nautical inside and with three old fishing boats tied up outside of what was once the town's arsenal. (*Open all year, closed 12:30 to 2:30 pm except July and August, tel: 02.98.97.10.20.*) Climbing the walls gives you good views of the inner harbor where fishing boats unload their catch.

From Concarneau it is just a few kilometers farther to the nondescript village of **Trégunc**. Secluded in its own park on the edge of town is a simple, country hotel that has a delightful restaurant as well as the fame of its own *menhir* (standing stone), Le Menhir de Kerangallou—**Les Auberges des Grandes Roches**.

The D783 brings you to **Pont Aven**, a pretty resort by the River Aven made famous by Gauguin and his school of artists who moved here in the 1890s. Gauguin with his bohemian ways was not popular with the locals and he soon moved on. There are a great many galleries and in summer it's a colorful and crowded spot.

Turning inland, the D783 brings you to **Quimperlé** (20 kilometers) where the rivers Ellé and Isole converge to form the Lafta. One of the town's central streets is cobbled and lined with old houses. From here head through the large town of Hennebont for the 27-kilometer (D9 and D781) drive to the rather dull seaside town of **Carnac**. In the windswept fields on the edge of town are over 2,700 standing stones (*menhirs*) arranged in lines (*alignements*). The stones, believed to have been erected between 4,000 and 2,000 B.C., consist of three groups each arranged in patterns of 10 to 13 rows. The area is somewhat divided by country roads but the site is large enough that you can meander around and enjoy the groupings unhindered by the milling crowds and ticket barriers that impede your enjoyment of the British counterpart, Stonehenge. The **Musée de la**

Préhistoire will help you interpret the stones. (*Closed noon to 2 pm and all day Tuesdays, tel: 02.97.52.22.04.*)

If you decide to settle between Quimperlé and Vannes, we have two wonderful hotels to choose from: Les Moulins du Duc and the Château de Locguénolé. **Les Moulins du Duc** is an enchanting complex of 16th-century stone buildings and little mills, nestled on a river just inland from the coast on the outskirts of **Moëlan sur Mer**. **The Château de Locguénolé** outside the town of **Hennebont** is a very regal home surrounded by lush wooded acreage. A member of the prestigious Relais & Châteaux hotel chain, it sits on a hillside of lawn and enjoys a secluded setting and view of the bay.

Leaving Carnac, follow signposts to **Vannes**, the region's largest city, complete with all the traffic and navigation headaches that plague so many downtown areas. The old walled town grouped around **Saint Peter's Cathedral** is delightful. The cathedral was built between the 13th and 19th centuries and has a great mixture of styles. The nearby parliament building has been converted to a covered market for artists, leather workers, metalworkers, and crêperies. There is a maze of old streets with beautiful timbered and gabled houses. Market days are Wednesdays and Saturdays on the Place des Lices.

If you are not quite ready to leave Brittany, the **Domaine de Rochevilaine**, **Billiers**, perched on a rocky promontory, serves as a dramatic and wonderful base from which to explore Brittany's rugged south coast or simply enjoy a last night in the region. The hotel is located on the tip of Pointe de Pen Lan, approximately 20 kilometers southeast of Vannes.

From Vannes the N165 whisks you around Nantes and onto the A11 which brings you to Angers, a convenient point to join our *Châteaux Country* itinerary.

Carnac

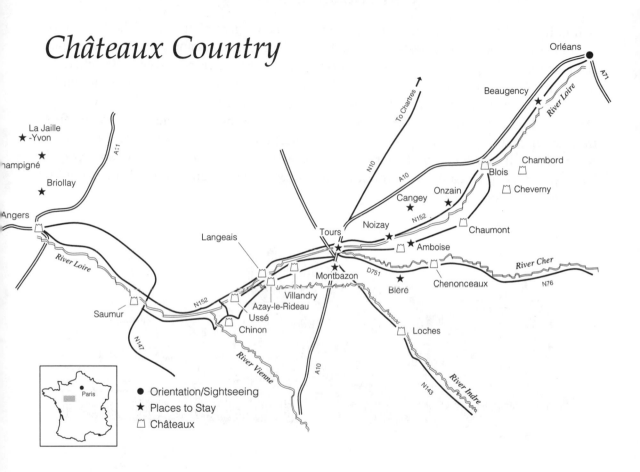

Châteaux Country

La Jaille
-Yvon ★

★ hampigné

Briollay ★

Angers

River Loire

Saumur

N152

N147

River Vienne

A10

N143

Langeais

Villandry

Azay-le-Rideau

Ussé

Chinon

Montbazon

Tours ★

Noizay ★

Cangey ★

Onzain ★

Blois

Chambord

Cheverny

Chaumont

Amboise

Bléré ★

Chenonceaux

River Cher

N76

Loches

River Indre

D751

To Chartres

N10

A10

N152

Beaugency ★

River Loire

Orléans

A71

A71

Paris

● Orientation/Sightseeing

★ Places to Stay

⌂ Châteaux

35

Châteaux Country

A highlight of any holiday in France is a visit to the elegant châteaux of the Loire river valley. This itinerary suggests a route for visiting the châteaux based on a logical sequence assuming Paris as a point of origin or finale. There are over 1,000 châteaux along the River Loire between Nantes and Orléans, and over 100 are open to the public. For the purposes of this itinerary, the Châteaux Country stretches from Angers to Orléans. Most of the châteaux were built for love, not war, and they range from traditional castles and grandiose homes to romantic ruins: we try to paint a picture of what you will see when you tour each château. In our opinion the best are Azay le Rideau and Chenonceaux. Be forewarned that in July and August you will be caught up in a crush of visitors.

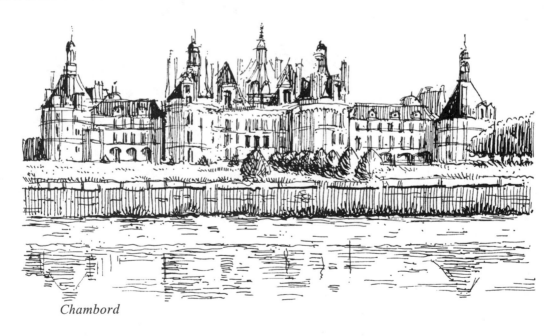

Chambord

Recommended Pacing: Any hotel from Map 7 makes an ideal base for exploring the châteaux country. Please do not try to visit all our châteaux sightseeing selections—it would be just too many for one holiday. Rather, read our descriptions and choose those that appeal most to you. As we do not tell you how to get from château to château, we recommend Michelin Map 64 with a scale of 1:200,000 (1 cm = 2 km) for outlining your route. Three nights in the region should give you all the time you need—one can visit only so many castles. Allow more if you are an avid fan of French furniture, French gardens, or the like, and want to explore properties in depth.

Many visitors spend time in Paris before coming to the Loire Valley and an excellent sightseeing venue on the way is **Chartres**, about an hour and a half southwest of Paris (97 kilometers). **Chartres Cathedral** towers high above the town and stands proud on the horizon. Three 13th-century stained-glass windows dapple the inside of the church with color and light. It's a magnificent edifice and on most days you find the redoubtably British Malcolm Miller describing the history and design of this marvelous cathedral, his knowledge of Chartres giving an added dimension to any visit. If you would like to arrange a personal tour, you can write to him care of Chartres' Tourist Office, Place Cathédrale, 2800 Chartres, France, tel: 02.37.21.50.00. The old city surrounding the cathedral has been lovingly restored and it's delightful to explore its old winding streets.

From Chartres the N10 takes you to Tours (130 kilometers, about a 2-hour drive). Located at the junction of the Cher and Loire rivers, Tours is a convenient starting point for our itinerary.

Begin your adventures in the Loire Valley by a visit to **Langeais**, one of the region's smaller châteaux. Remarkably, it has not been altered since it was built between 1465 and 1471 for Louis XI as a defense against Bretons. It is beautifully furnished and wax figurines commemorate the royal wedding of Charles VIII and Anne of Brittany which took place on a cold December morning in 1491. On a nearby ridge are the ruins of a 10th-century stone *donjon* or keep, one of Europe's first. This was a stronghold of the notorious Fulk Nerra the Black, Count of Anjou. (*Open all year, closed noon to 4 pm and all day Mondays November to mid-March, tel: 02.47.96.72.60.*)

Angers was the former capital of the Dukes of Anjou and is now a city full of factories with an old city and its 13th-century fortress at its heart. During the 16th century many of the 17 massive towers were dismantled, on royal command, to the level of the wall-walk. The castle has some spectacular displays of tapestries, including the Apocalypse tapestry, the longest ever woven in France, displayed in a special gallery. It was originally 164 meters long but during the Revolution it was thrown over the walls into the street and citizens snipped bits off. In 1843 the bishop managed to repiece two-thirds of it and about 100 meters are on display. (*Open all year, closed noon to 2 pm except July and August, tel: 02.41.87.43.47.*)

Saumur lies on the edge of the River Loire. Rising from the town are the walls of Saumur castle, a 14th-century fortification built atop a sheer cliff. There are spectacular views from the walls and an interesting museum of ceramics and horses. Lovely tapestries hang in the church. In 1811 Laurence Ackerman, who hailed from Alsace, showed the locals how to put *mousseux* (sparkle) in their wines. It's an enjoyable local drink but no substitute for champagne. (*Closed Tuesdays, and noon to 2:00 pm except mid-June to mid-September, tel: 02.41.40.24.40.*)

Chinon is a huge crumbling fortress set high above the River Vienne, with a medieval town and tree-lined boulevard at its feet. Henry II of England died here, his son Richard the Lionheart owned it, King John lost it to the French, and Joan of Arc came here to plead with Charles VII for an army. It is an interesting walk around the skeleton of this fortification, but be prepared to fill in large chunks of the interior with your imagination. There is an interesting museum celebrating Joan of Arc. (*Open all year, closed noon to 2 pm November to March, tel: 02.47.93.13.45.*)

Ussé overlooks the River Indre and is everything you expect a château to be with turrets, towers, chimneys, dormers, and enchantment. The house is completely furnished in period style, illustrating the way things were in the 16th and 17th centuries, complete with wax figurines dressed in period costume. Magnificent Flemish tapestries grace the Great Gallery, and while you are waiting for your guided tour (narrated in French with English description sheets), you can climb the tower whose turret rooms are furnished with scenes from *Sleeping Beauty*. Conjecture has it that Ussé was the château that inspired Perault to write the famous fairy tale. (*Closed November to mid-February, and noon to 2 pm in winter months, tel: 02.47.95.54.05.*)

Azay le Rideau and its elegant Renaissance château are not far from Ussé. Azay le Rideau's graceful façade is framed by wispy trees and is reflected in its lake and the River Indre, from whose banks it rises on one side. It was built by Gilles Berthelot, the treasurer to Francis I between 1518 and 1527. Francis accused Gilles of fiddling the nation's books and confiscated this ornate château. It was not until the 19th century that it was completed. You can accompany a knowledgeable guide on a detailed tour or explore on your own, walking from one showpiece room to the next, admiring the fine furniture and tapestries. This is one of our favorite châteaux. (*Open all year, closed 12:30 to 2 pm November to March, tel: 02.47.45.42.04.*)

Azay le Rideau

Châteaux Country

Villandry is known for its formal, geometric French gardens—even the paths are raked into designs. While you can tour the house, the real reason for visiting Villandry is to spend time in the gardens wandering along the little paths between the neatly clipped box hedges. Even the vegetable garden has been planted to produce geometric patterns. Be sure to capture the bird's-eye view of this colorful quilt of a garden from the upper terrace. (*Gardens open all year, house open mid-February to mid-November, tel: 02.47.50.02.09.*)

Southeast of Montbazon is the town of **Loches**, found in the hills along the banks of the Indre, and referred to as the "City of Kings." The ancient castle is the "Acropolis of the Loire"; the buildings around it form what is called *Haute Ville*. It was a favorite retreat of King Charles VII and here you will find a copy of the proceedings of Joan of Arc's trial. The king's mistress, Agnes Sorel, is buried in the tower and her portrait is in one of the rooms. (*Open all year, closed noon to 2 pm except July and August, tel: 02.47.59.07.86.*)

Chenonceaux

Châteaux Country

Chenonceaux almost spans the River Cher and is without a doubt one of the loveliest of the Loire's châteaux. This château owes a great deal to each of its six female occupants. Catherine Briconnet built Chenonceaux as a home, not a fortification, and sexy Diane de Poitiers, the mistress of Henry II, added a garden and the bridge between the house and the banks of the River Cher. When Henry died, his jealous wife, Catherine de Medici, took Chenonceaux back and consigned Diane to Château Chaumont. Catherine had the gallery built on the bridge, laid out the park, and held decadent parties. She bequeathed her home to Louise de Lorraine, her daughter-in-law who, after her husband's death, retired here and went into mourning for the rest of her life. In 1733 it passed to Monsieur Dupin whose intellectual wife was so beloved by the locals that it escaped the Revolution unscathed. In 1864 it was bought by Madame Peolouze who made it her life's work to restore her home. The château is now the home of the Menier family. Chenonceaux merits a leisurely visit: you want to allocate at least two hours for wandering through the park, gardens, and its elegant interior. The grounds also contain a wax museum with scenes from the château's history. (*Open all year, 9 am to 6 pm, tel: 02.47.23.90.07.*)

Just a few kilometers north of Chenonceaux is the striking castle of **Amboise**. A tour of this large property will fill you with tales of grandeur, intrigue, and gruesome history. Francis I loved to party, reveling in grand balls, masquerades, festivals, and tournaments. He invited Leonardo da Vinci here and the artist spent his last years at the neighboring manor **Clos Lucé**. You can see his bedroom, models of machines he invented, and copies of his drawings. Catherine de Medici brought her young son Francis II and his young bride Mary, later Queen of Scots, to Amboise when the Protestants rose up after the Saint Bartholomew massacre. The Amboise Conspiracy of 1560 involved a group of Protestant reformers who followed the royal court from Blois to Amboise under the pretense of asking the king for permission to practice their religion. However, their plot was betrayed to the powerful Duke of Guise (Scarface) and upon arrival they were tortured, hung from the battlements, and left twisting in pain for days—the court and the royal family would come out to watch them. (*Open all year, 9 am to 6 pm except July and August, tel: 02.47.57.62.88.*)

From Amboise follow the Loire to **Chaumont**, a château that has more appeal viewed from across the river than up close. Catherine de Médici was reputedly living here when her husband Henry II was killed and she became regent. She supposedly bought the château so that she could swap it with Diane de Poitiers (her husband's mistress) for Chenonceaux. Diane found it did not match up to Chenonceaux and left—you can understand why. Later Benjamin Franklin paid a visit to sit for an Italian sculptor who had set up his headquarters in the stables. Approached across a drawbridge, the château has three wings—the fourth side was pulled down in 1739—opening up to a fine view of the Loire Valley. You can tour the apartments and the stables. (*Open all year, 10 am to 4:30 pm, tel: 02.54.51.26.26.*)

Blois sits on the north bank of the River Loire. The Chamber of the States General and part of a tower are all that remain of the 13th-century fortification that occupied this site. Much of the magnificent edifice you see today is due to Francis I's trying to keep his brother Gaston d'Orléans (who was always conspiring against him) out of trouble. In 1662 he banished him to Blois and gave him the project of restoring the château. Gaston hired the famous architect Mansart. The château has its stories of love, intrigue, and politicking, but its most famous is the murder of the Duke of Guise. In 1688 the powerful Henri de Guise called the States General here with the intention of deposing Henry III and making himself king. Henry found out about the plot and murdered the Duke. Who did what and where is explained in great detail on the tour. The most interesting room on the tour is Catherine de Médici's bedchamber with its many secret wall panels, used in the true Médici tradition to hide jewels, documents, and poisons. (*Open all year, closed 12:30 pm to 2 pm October to mid-March, tel: 02.54.90.33.33.*)

Ten kilometers from Blois lies **Cheverny**, a château built in 1634 for the Hurault family. It is smaller than Blois and Chambord and more interesting to tour because it still has its 17th-century decorations and furnishings. The Hurault family has carefully preserved their inheritance with its exquisite painted woodwork, tapestries, and furniture. The kennels in the grounds are home to 70 hounds and watching them patiently line up for dinner is a popular event. (*Feedings: April to mid-September except Saturdays and*

Cheverny

Sundays 5 pm, otherwise 3 pm except Tuesdays and weekends.) In another outbuilding is a collection of 2,000 deer antlers, the family's hunting trophies. (*Open all year, closed noon to 2:15 pm except June to mid-September, tel: 02.54.79.96.29.*)

Standing on a grassy expanse amidst vast acres of forest, **Chambord** is enormous. Francis I built Chambord as a hunting lodge, but he believed that bigger was better so the vast edifice has 440 rooms and 80 staircases. Francis spent only 40 days at his huge home which now has far less furniture than many other properties and is owned by the state. Apart from its impressive size and isolated location, Chambord's most interesting feature is the double-spiral staircase in the center of the building. (*Open all year, except May 1 and December 25, tel: 02.54.50.40.00.*)

The last stretch along the Loire takes you to the lovely old town of **Beaugency** with its historic church, **Nôtre Dame**. A magnificent bridge with 22 arches spans the river. The French blew it apart in 1940 to delay the Germans, but it has been completely restored (the central arches are original) and provides an ideal viewpoint for looking at the river and this delightful little town with its narrow medieval streets.

Orléans is a modern town rebuilt after World War II destruction. This was the scene of Joan of Arc's greatest triumph, when she successfully drove the English from France in 1429. There is little left for Joan of Arc fans to visit except her statue in Place Martoi.

From Orléans it is a 120-kilometer drive on the autoroute A10 back to Paris.

Dordogne & Lot River Valleys

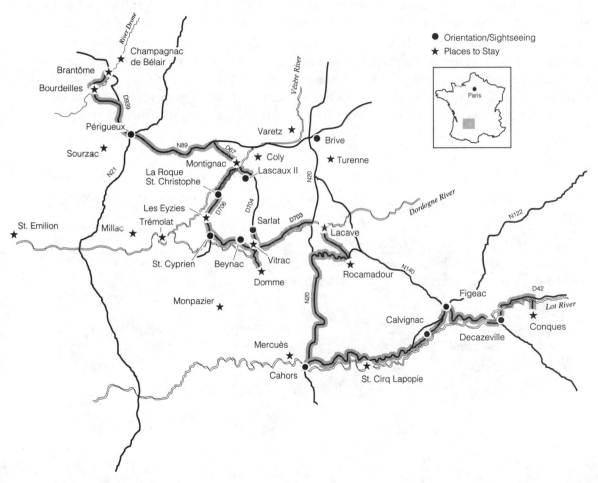

Orientation/Sightseeing
Places to Stay

River Drone
River Drône
Champagnac de Bélair
Brantôme
Bourdeilles
D939
Périgueux
Sourzac
N21
N89
D67
Montignac
La Roque St. Christophe
Les Eyzies
Trémolat
D706
D704
St. Cyprien
Beynac
Domme
Vitrac
Sarlat
D703
Coly
Lascaux II
Varetz
Vézère River
Brive
Turenne
N20
Millac
St. Emilion
Monpazier
Mercuès
Cahors
N20
St. Cirq Lapopie
Lacave
Rocamadour
N140
Dordogne River
Calvignac
Decazeville
Figeac
D42
Conques
Lot River
N122

Paris

Dordogne & Lot River Valleys

The lazy Dordogne and Lot rivers wind gracefully through some of France's most picturesque countryside past villages dressed with grand castles, through peaceful meadows dotted with farms, beneath towering cliffs, and into pretty woodlands. However, this itinerary is more than just traveling along river valleys, for the region is France's prehistoric capital: the Cro-Magnon skull was discovered at Les Eyzies; colorful 15,000-year-old paintings decorate the Lascaux, Font de Gaum, and Les Combarelles caves; and man occupied the terraces on the cliffside of La Roque Saint Christophe as long ago as 70,000 B.C. Visit Rocamadour, an ancient village that tumbles down a rocky canyon, and Conques, a medieval village on a dramatic hillside site.

View of Dordogne River Valley from Domme

Recommended Pacing: You could happily spend a week in the Dordogne, venturing along the river valley then adding unscheduled meanderings up little side roads to country villages. For the purposes of this itinerary, base yourself a night or two in the northern region, two to three nights close to the river itself (more if you make reservations at several of the caves), at least one night along the River Lot (optional), and a night at the hillside village of Conques. Should you opt for the lovely scenic detour north from Rocamadour before traveling south to the River Lot, I would recommend an additional night in the village of Turenne.

In the northern region of the Dordogne, **Brantôme** is a delightful little town on the banks of the River Dronne with narrow winding streets and a riverside park that leads you across the famous 16th-century elbow bridge to the old abbey, nestled at the foot of a rocky cliff. Founded by Charlemagne in 769, the abbey was reconstructed in the 11th century after it was ransacked by the Normans. The church and adjoining buildings were constructed and modified between the 14th and 18th centuries. Also beside the ancient bridge is the delightful **Le Moulin de l'Abbaye**, which offers elegant accommodation within the walls of an historic mill.

Follow the River Dronne for 10 kilometers on the D78 into the very pretty village of **Bourdeilles**. A little bridge takes you across the river to its 12th-century castle which the English and French squabbled about for years. Sharing the bridge is a charming country hotel, **Hostellerie des Griffons**, where you might choose to overnight or dine on their riverside terrace. From Bourdeilles country roads direct you to the D939 and on to Périgueux.

Périgueux changed allies twice in the 100 Years' War, eventually opting for France. It's a pleasant large market town with an interesting domed cathedral resplendent with little turrets. From Périgueux follow signposts towards Brive (D47) and at Thenon take the D67 to Montignac (40 kilometers).

Montignac is a popular tourist town because on its outskirts are the wondrous **Lascaux Caves** with their magnificent 15,000-year-old paintings. In 1963 these caves were closed to the public because the paintings were being damaged by the rise and fall in temperature as hordes of visitors came and went. It took ten years to construct an exact replica—**Lascaux II**. Except for the even, non-slip floor you will not know that you are not in the real Lascaux. The bulls, bison, and stags appear to be moving around the cave—so skillfully did the artists utilize every feature of the rocks that bumps appear as humps, cheekbones, and haunches. In July and August the quota of 2,000 tickets a day go on sale at 9 am at the *Syndicat d'Initiative* (Tourist Office) in Montignac. Tickets are not available in advance. For the rest of the year tickets are sold at the site on a first come, first served basis, so you may arrive at 11 am and find that you are offered a 4 pm tour. Tours are given in English and French. If you want to be first in line for tickets, you might want to look into overnighting at the nearby, elegant **Château de Puy Robert** or the charming **Manoir d'Hautegente** in nearby **Coly.**

Leaving Lascaux II, watch for signs that will direct you to Le Thot along the D65. The admission ticket for Lascaux includes admission to **Le Thot** where you can see a film of the building of Lascaux II and displays of large photos of the many prehistoric paintings found in caves in the valley. The grounds also have a park and a re-creation of a prehistoric village.

Leaving Le Thot, follow signposts for **La Roque Saint Christophe**. As the road winds by the river, a sheer cliff rises to a deep natural terrace before continuing upwards. As long ago as 70,000 B.C. man took advantage of this natural terrace for shelter and by medieval times it was home to over 1,000 people. The thousands of niches that you see today were used to hold up supporting beams for the houses and the rings you see carved into the rock were used to hang lamps and to tether animals. (*Open all year, 10 am to 6 pm, tel: 05.53.50.70.45.*)

Following the winding River Vézère, the D706 brings you into **Les Eyzies**. The caves in the cliff that towers above the town were home to prehistoric man who took shelter here during the second Ice Age. People lived here for tens of thousands of years. Archaeologists have uncovered flints, pottery, jewelry, and skeletons that have been identified as those of Cro-Magnon man found in the cave behind the hotel of the same name. Visit the **Musée National de la Préhistoire** in the 11th-century castle set high on the cliff beneath the overhanging rock, guarded by the gigantic sculpture of Cro-Magnon man. (*Open all year, closed noon to 2 pm, Tuesdays, tel: 05.53.06.45.45.*) On the edge of town, next to the train stop, is a lovely, family-run hotel, the **Hôtel Cro-Magnon,** with its charming restaurant and comfortable accommodation.

Nearby, the **Font de Gaum** cave has prehistoric wall paintings of horses, bison, mammoths, and reindeer with colors still so rich that it is hard to comprehend the actual passage of time. The caves are a bit damp and dark and entail a steep 400-meter climb to reach the entrance. The grotto is deep, winding, and narrow in parts. There arc some 230 drawings, of which about 30 are presented and discussed. Displayed in three tiers, some drawings are marred by graffiti, others are not clearly visible as the walls tower above the floor of the cave. Entrance is limited to 200 people per day but you can make reservations in advance by calling the booking office in Les Eyzies, tel: 05.53.06.90.80. There is a small additional charge for advance booking. With the closure of more caves each year, it is uncertain how much longer the opportunity to visit Font de Gaum will continue. (*Open all year 9 am to noon, 2 to 5 pm, closed Tuesdays.*)

A short distance from Font de Guam is **Les Combarelles**, a cave discovered in 1901. The entrance is about a 100-meter (level) walk from the car park. The cave is a winding passage with engravings of mammoth, ibex, bears, reindeer, bison, and horses—and man in the last 70 meters. Entrance is limited to 140 visitors per day and the cave is closed every Wednesday. Advance booking and hours of opening are identical to Font de Gaum.

From Les Eyzies follow the scenic D706 to **Campagne** with its abandoned château sitting behind padlocked gates. From Campagne take the scenic D35 to **Saint Cyprien**, an attractive town just a short distance from the Dordogne. It has more shops and cafés than most small towns in the valley, making it an attractive and interesting place to break your journey.

Through pretty countryside follow the Dordogne river valley, just out of sight of the river. As you approach **Beynac,** you are presented with a lovely picture of a small village huddled beneath a cliff crowned by a 12th-century fortress before a broad sweep of the Dordogne. The castle, while its furnishings are sparse, is well worth visiting for the spectacular views. *(Open all year, 10 am to 6:30 pm.)* On the water's edge is **Hôtel Bonnet**, recommended not for its accommodation, but as a very scenic and excellent choice for lunch under vine-covered trellises.

The Fortress of Beynac above the Dordogne River

Have your cameras ready as you approach **La Roque Gageac**. The town, clinging to the hillside above the River Dordogne and framed by lacy trees, is a photographer's dream. There's a grassy area on the riverbank with a few picnic tables and an inviting path, following the curves of the river, tempts you farther.

Just upstream cross the bridge and climb the hill to **Domme**, a medieval walled village that has for centuries stood guard high above the river and commanded a magnificent panorama.

Dordogne & Lot River Valleys

The town itself is enchanting, with ramparts that date from the 13th century, and narrow streets that wind through its old quarter and past a lovely 14th-century **Hôtel de Ville**. At the town center under the old market place, you find access to some interesting stalactite and stalagmite grottos. However, most visitors come to Domme for its spectacular views—the best vantage point is from the **Terrasse de la Barre**. Very near to *la Barre*, facing the church, is **Hôtel de l'Esplanade**, an ideal place to stay if you want to enjoy the village after the crowds have departed.

Because it is more scenic on the north side of the river, retrace your steps across the bridge and continue down river on the D703 to **Château de Montfort**, a majestic castle shadowing a wide loop in the river. Built by one of the region's most powerful barons, this intimate, restored castle, furnished like a private residence, rises out of a rocky ledge. The **Cingle de Montfort** offers some delightful views of the river.

When the D703 intersects with the D704, take a short detour north to the city of **Sarlat**. Sarlat has a delightful old quarter with narrow cobbled streets that wind through a maze of magnificent gourmet shops. The church and the Episcopal palace create a roomy space along the narrow bustling streets. Sarlat bustles with activity and color on market day.

After visiting Sarlat return to the banks of the Dordogne and continue east once again along its shore, this time in the direction of Souillac. When the D703 comes to an end, travel south (right) in the direction of Cahors. As you leave houses behind you, turn left on the D43 (rather than crossing the river) and begin a very picturesque stretch of the valley. As you cross a single-lane wooden bridge spanning the Dordogne, take note of the picture-postcard **Château de la Treyne,** one of our favorite hotels in the region, perched above the riverbank. **Lacave** is also known for some spectacular geological formations in its caves which you can tour on a diminutive train.

As you climb out of Lacave towards Rocamadour, the fields are filled with bustling geese being fattened for *foie gras* and you get a picturesque view of a castle sitting high above the distant Dordogne. A scenic country road winds to where the ground disappears into an abyss and the village of **Rocamadour** tumbles down the narrow canyon. Our preference is to park in the large car park adjacent to the castle, but if it is full, head for the valley floor and park in one of the grassy car parks. A stairway leads down from beside the castle to the chapels, houses, and narrow streets that cling precipitously to the rock face to the little chapels and the large basilica that incorporates the cliff face as one wall of the building. From the 12th century onwards Rocamadour was a popular pilgrimage site. There are lots of tourist shops and, thankfully, cafés providing a spot to sit and rest after climbing up and down the staircases. If steep climbs are not for you, buy a ticket on the elevator that goes up and down the hillside. If you want to experience Rocamadour in the early morning or late afternoon in order to avoid the busloads of daytime visitors, we recommend a wonderful hotel, just a 45-minute walk along a footpath, called the **Domaine de la Rhue.** (It is, of course, also possible to drive.)

From Rocamadour you can either travel directly on to the Lot river valley to the south or take a scenic detour of approximately 100 kilometers north to some enchanting and picturesque villages. This is a loop I discovered a few years ago, when I detoured to visit a charming hotel, La Maison des Chanoines, in the village of Turenne. If you opt for this northerly loop, I would also consider using Turenne as an overnight base before continuing south to the Lot.

For the scenic loop north, from Rocamadour travel east on D673 for just 4 kilometers, cross the N140, and continue on D673 as it winds through the village of Alvignac and then on to Padirac. At **Padirac** detour off on the D90 to **Gouffre de Padirac**. A *gouffre* is a great opening in the ground, and this wide circular chimney of Padirac was formed by the hollowed-out roof of a cave falling in. This impressive grotto leads over 100 meters underground to a mysterious river where the visitor can negotiate a stretch of some 500 meters by boat to discover the sparkling *Lac de la Pluie* (Lake of Rain) and its huge stalactite, the immense Great Dome room with its vault rising up 90 meters. The roof lies quite near the surface and it is almost inevitable that it too will one day collapse to form another chasm. (*Open April to October, 9 am to noon and 2 to 6:30 pm, summer 8 am to 7 pm. Allow approximately 1½ hours for a guided tour, tel: 05.65.33.64.56.*)

MAP OF SCENIC LOOP DETOUR:

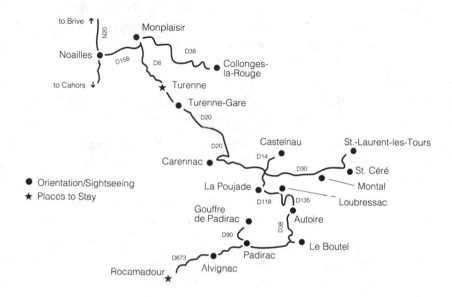

Retrace your trail back to Padirac and then wind along the D38 traveling east and then north in the direction of Autoire. This scenic drive winds down a hill to expose the beautiful village of **Autoire** set in a rich green valley shadowed by majestic, towering limestone cliffs. Autoire is lovely with its old stone houses topped with slate roofs clustering together along the narrow alleyways. Windowboxes overflow with flowers to provide a profusion of color against the mellowed stone of the buildings.

From Autoire, travel the few short kilometers to the picturesque village of **Loubressac**. Crowning the mountaintop, Loubressac appears dramatically on the horizon—another charming village, with a picturesque main square.

From Loubressac you enjoy gorgeous views across the river valley to the medieval fortress of **Castelnau** on the opposite bank in the town of **Bretenoux**. Impressive from a distance, the long façade of the fortress dominates the village skyline. Colored in the rusty red of the regional rock, the castle is remarkably preserved and impressive from the massive wooden portal to splendid interior furnishings. (*Open all year, 10 am to noon and 2 pm to 5 pm, closed Tuesdays and holidays, tel: 05.65.10.98.00.*) Crossing back to Loubressac, wind down to the river and then detour east to the Renaissance **Château de Montal** which is beautifully furnished and definitely worth a visit. (*Open Easter to November, 9:30 am to noon and 2:30 to 6:00 pm, closed Saturdays, tel: 05.65.38.13.72.*)

From the Château de Montal it is a short distance farther on to the pretty market town of **Saint Céré** whose square comes alive and is particularly colorful when the commodity for sale is livestock. Worthy of a visit on the outskirts of Saint Céré in **Le Tours de Saint Laurent** is a tapestry museum, the **Atelier Musée Jean Lurçat**. (*Open mid-July to October, Telephone number for the tourist office in Saint Céré: 05.65.38.11.85.*)

From Saint Céré journey back along the D30, once again following the path of the Dordogne to the pretty village of **Carennac**, set just above the river. This idyllic little village is even more picturesque because of the river that weaves through it, in the shadow of the lovely old timbered homes and a handsome church sheltered behind an arched entry.

From Carennac, cross the river and travel north to **Turenne.** Turenne was the initial reason for my detour, it being the location of a charming country inn, **La Maison des Chanoines.** Before even investigating the inn, I was enamored of the village surrounded by a patchwork of farmland. Narrow, cobbled streets wind steeply up to a crowning church and castle. (*Open April to October, 10 am to noon and 2 to 6 pm, November and December open Sunday afternoons.*) Views from the top of the castle are very peaceful and pretty, and both the town and the inn offer a quiet setting for a night's repose.

From Turenne, according to the map, there is a road that appears to cross almost directly over to **Collonges la Rouge** (the D150 to connect with the D38, just 5 kilometers west of

Collonges) but it is extremely difficult to find—I never found how to access it from Turenne. It might prove easier, as I found, to detour north on the D8 to just north of Montplaisir and then turn east on the D38 and on to Collonges la Rouge, a lovely village favored by local artisans with cobbled streets winding through a maze of stone buildings all rich in a hue of burnt red. Probably the regional town most geared for tourists, it has a number of interesting craft shops to tempt you indoors. Collonges la Rouge is most beautiful on a clear day when the sun washes the stone in a rich, warm red against a backdrop of blue.

From Collonges la Rouge return west on the D38 in the direction of Brive and then just past Maranzat jog south on the D8 and then almost immediately west on the D158 to Noailles and the junction of N20. Traveling south on the N20, you rejoin the primary itinerary at Rocamadour.

From Rocamadour, travel a rocky valley (D673) west to Payrac (21 kilometers) where you join the N20 for the scenic 50-kilometer drive to Cahors and the Lot river valley.

Although it is a large city, you might want to venture into **Cahors**, a medieval city set on the bend of the River Lot, renowned for its wines. Cahors is also famous for its architectural richness, the dramatic Pont Valentré bridge built in the 14th century, the Arc de Diane that remains from a vast Gallo-Roman thermal establishment, the Saint Etienne Cathedral from the 11th and 12th centuries, the tower of Pope John XXII, and the Saint Barthelemy church. Not to be missed at the heart of the city is the old core with its houses, mansions, gates, and lanes. Just a few miles from Cahors, towering over the river is a magnificent château-hotel, the **Château de Mercuès**.

From the outskirts of Cahors turn left following signposts for Figeac along the north bank of the river. This portion of the **Lot Valley** can be driven in half a day on roads that wind along a riverbank that is narrower and quieter than that of the Dordogne. The River Lot winds along the curves of the wide, canyon, cutting into its chalky walls. At some stretches the route follows the level of the river and at others it straddles the cliff tops.

Vistas are dramatic at every turn although the restricting narrow roads will frustrate the eye of any photographer because there is rarely a place to stop.

Saint Cirq Lapopie

Cross the river at **Bouzies** and take a moment to look back across the bridge and see the medieval buildings constructed into the walls of the canyon above the small tunnel. Just outside Bouzies, the road (D40) climbs and winds precipitously to the top of the cliff and rounding a bend, you find **Saint Cirq Lapopie** clinging precipitously to the sheer canyon walls and cascading back down towards the river. Drive around the village to one of the car parks and walk back up the hill to explore. Many of the buildings have been restored and only a few of the houses are lived in. It's most enjoyable to wander the quiet streets without being overwhelmed by tourist shops. You can spend the night here at **Hôtel de la Pélissaria**, an engaging inn with idyllic views of the village and river below.

Travel down to the Lot and cross to its northernmost bank. As the river guides you farther, it presents a number of lovely towns and with each turn reveals another angle and view of the valley. **La Toulzanie** is a small, pretty village nestled into a bend of the river, interesting because of its houses built into the limestone cliffs. Calvignac is an ancient village clinging to the top of the cliff on the opposite bank. At Cajarc be careful to keep to the river road (D662). A short drive brings you to the village of **Montbrun**, a village that rises in tiers on jutting rock by steep cliffs. It looks down on the Lot, up at its ruined castle, and across the river to *Saut de la Mounine* (Jump of the Monkey). Legend recalls that to punish his daughter for falling in love with the son of a rival baron, a father ordered daughter to be thrown from the cliffs. A monkey was dressed in her clothes and thrown to its death instead. Father, regretting his harsh judgment, was overcome with joy when he discovered the substitution. Set on a plateau, the **Château de Larroque Toirac** is open to visitors and makes an impressive silhouette against the chalky cliffs and the village of **Saint Pierre Toirac**.

Less than 10 kilometers to the north of the Lot on the River Célé is the larger market town of **Figeac**. A wonderful example of 12th-century architecture, Figeac is an attractive river town and it is fun to explore the shops along its cobbled streets and alleyways.

Continue on to Conques, a bonus to this itinerary that requires that you journey farther along the winding Lot (on the N140 signposted Decazeville and then D963 and D42 signposted Entraygues). The route weaves through some beautiful farmland and attractive little villages. At La Vinzelle leave the Lot river valley and climb up the D901 to **Conques**, a tiny medieval town on a dramatic hillside site. Tucked a considerable distance off the beaten track, it is a delightful, unspoiled village that was once an important pilgrimage stop on the way to Santiago de Compostela in Spain. Conques' pride is its 11th-century **Abbaye Sainte Foy** whose simple rounded arches give it the look of a Gothic cathedral. The carving of the Last Judgment in a semi-circle over the central door shows 124 characters—the grimacing devils and tortured souls are far more amusing than the somber few who are selected to go to heaven. The abbey's treasure is the 10th-century Sainte Foy reliquary, a statue sheathed in gold leaf and decorated with precious stones.

Directly across from the abbey is the **Grand Hôtel Sainte Foy** and on a nearby cobblestoned street lies **Hostellerie de l'Abbaye**. Both hotels afford the opportunity of lingering in the town, when evening light plays on the wonderful old stone and cobbled streets. It is magical to hear the melodious bells as their sound echoes through the town.

Conques

Gorges du Tarn

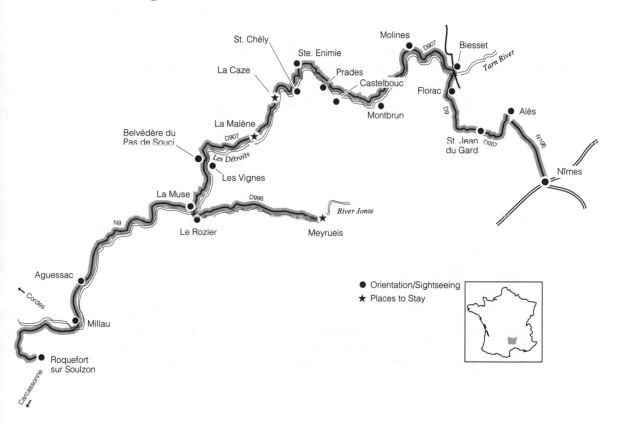

Molines

St. Chély

Biesset

D907

Ste. Enimie

Tarn River

La Caze

Prades

Castelbouc

Florac

Montbrun

La Malène

D9

Belvédère du
Pas de Souci

D907

Alès

Les Détroits

St. Jean
du Gard

D007

Les Vignes

N106

La Muse

D996

Nîmes

La Muse

River Jonte

Le Rozier

Meyrueis

● Orientation/Sightseeing
★ Places to Stay

N9

Aguessac

← Cordes

Millau

Roquefort
sur Soulzon

Carcassonne →

Gorges du Tarn

This itinerary follows the truly spectacular River Tarn as it winds back and forth along the Tarn Canyon or *Gorges du Tarn*. With each turn the drive becomes more beautiful, never monotonous. The road cuts through the canyon, hugging its walls, always in sight of the peaceful waters of the Tarn and its picturesque villages, clusters of warm stone buildings that nestle above its shore. Encased in deep limestone cliffs, the river canyon is at its most glorious in early autumn—a perfect time to visit. In the fall the traffic has subsided and nature's colors contrast beautifully with the canyon walls: grass carpets the mountains, making hillsides lush, all shades of green, and the trees blaze gold, red, and orange in the sunlight. But whatever time of year, the Gorges du Tarn is lovely.

Gorges du Tarn

Recommended Pacing: This itinerary covers approximately 220 kilometers and can be driven in about 4 hours. The stretch along the canyon from Florac to Millau, about 75 kilometers, is sometimes crowded, often narrows to two lanes, and there are no short cuts once you're following the river. If you plan to cover the distance in a day's journey, get an early start. We suggest that you overnight near the river and give yourself two full days to drive, walk, picnic, and even float your way through the Tarn Canyon.

With either **Avignon** or **Nîmes** on the western edge of Provence as a point of reference, travel northwest in the direction of Alès. Using a good map to plan the best route depending on your origin, travel southwest of Alès to the D907, going north in the direction of Saint Jean du Gard. **Saint Jean du Gard** is a very scenic village, located just before the **Corniche des Cevennes**. Just outside Saint Jean du Gard you are faced with the option of traveling the corniche along the canyon's south or north rim. This itinerary travels the D9 which follows the north rim and is the more scenic and better of the two roads. The drive is lovely, traveling through and above the forests of the region. At the northern tip of the corniche the road number changes from D9 to D983 and travels 6 kilometers to the junction of D907. Follow the D907 north just over 5 kilometers to **Florac** and then join the N106 continuing north in the direction of Mende, but at the tiny village of Biesset veer off and head west on the D907bis. It is here that your true journey of the Tarn Canyon begins.

To appreciate the region you need to simply travel it: each turn affords a lovely vista or breathtakingly beautiful portrait of a hillside village. Opportunities to stop along the roadside are limited and will frustrate most photographers, but drive it leisurely and stop when possible to explore the little hamlets. The following is an overview of the river and its path, and some of its most picturesque highlights. With a good map in hand, enjoy its scenic journey.

The **Ispagnac Basin**, located at the entrance to the canyon, is filled with fruit trees, vineyards, and strawberries. Here towns are scattered artistically about; châteaux and ruins appear often enough to add enchantment. A lovely wide bridge spans the river at

Ispagnac and farther along at **Molines**, set in the bend of the river, the canyon boasts a picturesque mill and castle. As the road hugs the hillside, the pretty town of **Montbrun** blends into the hillside on the opposite side of the river. The road then narrows and winds along the base of the canyon, looking up to rugged canyon walls and down to stretches of green along the river's edge. **Castelbouc**, on the other side of the river, is idyllically nestled on the hillside and is spectacular when illuminated on summer evenings. Just a short distance beyond Castelbouc the road carves a path to the north, providing a scenic overlook of the neighboring castle of **Prades**. One of the larger settlements in the region, **Sainte Énimie** is a charming village caught in the bend of the canyon where an old attractive bridge arches across the river and a church wedged into the mountainside piques the curiosity. From Sainte Énimie the road tunnels into the canyon walls colored in orange, gold, and green. **Saint Chély du Tarn** is nestled on the sides of the canyon wall and is illuminated in a spectacle of sound and light. A short distance south of Saint Chély, majestically positioned above the Tarn, is a fairy-tale castle offering accommodation, the **Château de la Caze**.

From the spectacular setting of La Caze, the road follows the river as it bends past the **Château Hauterives** and then passes through the lovely and probably most active village on the riverbank, **La Malène**. Many companies offer raft, kayak, and canoe trips departing from La Malène. From the river you have a better view of some of the old medieval towns and a section of the Tarn referred to as **Les Détroits**, the Straits, not visible from the road. Here the river is only a few meters wide, towered by canyon cliffs rising more than 300 meters straight above. From La Malène the road winds through the canyon rock and a cluster of buildings appears huddled on the other bank, just at the entrance to Les Détroits. Farther on, numerous buses stop at **Belvédère du Pas de Souci** and you can join the crowds to climb the steep metal stairway to views of the pools below (for an admission fee). From Pas de Souci, the river widens and the canyon walls turn to gentle slopes at the little village of **Les Vignes**. From Les Vignes it is worth a short detour following signs to **Point Sublime**. It is a steep climb up to one of the most impressive viewpoints of the canyon, 400 meters above the river.

Cross the river at La Muse to the village of **Le Rozier**, which enjoys a pretty setting at the junction of the Tarn and Jonte rivers. From Le Rozier you have a couple of options to extend your visit in this lovely region before continuing along the D907 the last 20 kilometers along the Tarn to Millau. You can venture east along the D996, a narrow, often roughly paved road following the dramatic **Gorges de la Jonte** to Meyrueis. Overpowered by the towering Jonte canyon walls, the picturesque village buildings of **Meyrueis** lie approximately 21 kilometers east of Le Rozier and huddle together along the banks of the Jonte. A farm-road's distance from this quaint village is the enchanting **Château d'Ayres**. Tucked away on its own expanse of rich grounds, this enchanting hotel offers a lovely peaceful escape. From Le Rozier you can also follow a narrow winding road 10 kilometers south to **Montpellier Le Vieux** where there is an admission charge for driving through this intriguing rock formation and then another twisting stretch of almost 20 kilometers on to Millau. **Millau** is a lovely city located at the junction of two rivers, the Tarn and the Dourbie, known for its leather goods, particularly gloves. Millau marks the end of the canyon.

However, from Millau we suggest that you journey southeast to Carcassonne stopping en route to visit Roquefort sur Solzon, Albi, and the hilltown of Cordes-sur-Ciel (a short detour). **Roquefort sur Solzon** is home to the distinctive Roquefort cheese: if this regional specialty appeals, you might enjoy a tour of one of the cheese cellars. **Albi**, a large city, is about a two-hour drive through farmland from Roquefort. With its cathedral dominating the entire city, Albi, mostly built of brick, is also referred to as "Albi the red." The **Musée Toulouse Lautrec** is one of its more interesting attractions. From Albi it is another half-hour drive to the medieval town of **Cordes-sur-Ciel**, also known as "Cordes in the Heavens," above the Cerou Valley. This is an enchanting hilltop village, a treasure that will prove a highlight of any itinerary. Known for its leather goods and hand-woven fabrics, Cordes-sur-Ciel offers many *ateliers* (craft shops) along its cobblestoned streets. At the heart of Cordes-sur-Ciel is the **Hôtel du Grand Écuyer**.

Retracing your path back to Albi, it is an undemanding drive south along the N112 and the D118 to Carcassonne. Europe's largest medieval fortress, **Carcassonne** is a highlight of any visit to France and a wonderful grand finale to this itinerary; Vieux Carcassonne rises above the vineyards at the foot of the Cevennes and Pyrenees. The massive protecting walls were first raised by the Romans in the 1st century B.C. Though never conquered in battle, the mighty city was lost to nature's weathering elements and has since been restored so that it looks as it did when constructed centuries ago. Stroll through the powerful gates along its winding cobbled streets and wander back into history. The walled city boasts numerous shops, delightful restaurants, and wonderful hotels. We recommend the **Hôtel de la Cité** and the **Hôtel Donjon** inside the city walls.

From Carcassonne you can take the autoroute back to Provence or northwest to Toulouse and on to connect up with the *Dordogne & Lot River Valleys* itinerary.

The Walled City of Carcassonne

Provence

Crillon le Brave ★

● Orientation/Sightseeing
★ Places to Stay

Paris

Pont du Gard
D981
Remoulins
N86
A9
Nîmes
A54

A9

Villeneuve
les Avignon ★
Avignon ★
Châteaurenard

L'Isle sur
la Sorgue
D938
Pernes les
Fontaines
Fontaine
de Vaucluse
Cavaillon

Venasque
D28
D177
D4
Senanque
Gordes ★ D2
Roussillon
D149
D4
N100
Apt

N570
D571
St. Rémy
de Provence
Les Antiques ★ ● Glanum
D17 D5 Les Baux
de Provence
Fontvieille
Abbaye de
Montmajour
Maussane
les Alpilles
N113
Aqueduct
Arles ★

A7

Bonnieux ★ D36
Loumarin
D943
Silvacane
D543

Salon
de Provence
A51
Lignane
N7
Meyrargues ★
Aix en
Provence
A7
A51
N8

Le Sambuc ★

A55

A52

Marseille ●

Provence

Provence, settled by the Romans around 120 B.C., is a region of contrasts and colors. This delightful region of the French *Midi* (the South) is associated with warm breezes, a mild climate, and rolling hillsides covered in the gray washes of olive trees and lavender. Its rich soil in the bath of the warm southern sun produces a bounty of produce that is incorporated into its regional cuisine. Some of the world's most popular wines are produced here and complement the delicious local dishes. The romance and beauty of Provence has inspired artists and writers for generations.

Pont du Gard

Recommended Pacing: This itinerary assumes the large port city of Marseille as a starting point, winds north to the beautiful university city of Aix en Provence, into the hilltowns of Haute Provence, and then circles back to the heart of the region and the lovely towns set in its valley. It is possible to see Provence in just a few days, but the countryside calls for you to linger, to settle and absorb the climate, the beauty, and the landscape. Our ideal would be a night in Aix en Provence, one to two nights in one of the hilltowns of Haute Provence, and at least three nights at the heart of Provence.

Marseille is the second-largest city in France. Settled as a Phoenician colony, this major Mediterranean port is where our Provence itinerary begins. Apart from the Roman docks and fortified church of Saint Victor, there are few monuments to its past within the city. However, you must see La Canebière, a major boulevard that captures the activity, gaiety, and pace of Marseille. The old port has a number of museums to draw your interest; the **Musée Grobet-Labadie** has a beautiful collection of tapestries, furniture, paintings, musical instruments, pottery, and sculpture. (*Open daily 10 am to 5 pm, Sundays noon to 7 pm.*)

From Marseille drive north following either the N8 or the Autoroute 51 to the southern periphery of **Aix en Provence**, an elegant city that deserves an overnight stay. Aix achieved fame when "Good King René," count of Provence, and his wife chose it as their preferred residence in the 1450s. Upon his death Aix fell under the rule of the French crown and was made the seat of parliament. The city flourished in the 17th and 18th centuries and became one of the most prosperous metropolises of the region. Much of Aix's elegant architecture is attributed to this period of affluence. Today it is predominantly a university town, home to some 40,000 students who represent almost a third of the city's population. Numerous fountains adorn the elegant tree-lined Cours Mirabeau, edged by aristocratic residences and numerous cafés. The Cours Mirabeau separates the Quartier Mazarin to the south from the Quartier Ancien on the north. The Quartier Mazarin attracted dignitaries and many lovely parliamentary homes still stand in this neighborhood. By contrast, the Quartier Ancien is the heart of the city, with a bustle of activity along its charming little back streets lined with numerous cafés and restaurants.

Aix is an enchanting city to explore. The beckoning cobblestoned streets of its **Old Quarter** are intriguing to wander along at night and the illuminated tree-lined Cours Mirabeau is enchanting—a bit reminiscent of Paris with its many sidewalk cafés. Nineteen 17th-century tapestries from Beauvois are on display in the **Museum of Tapestries**. Another fifteen Flemish tapestries can be found in the **Cathedral Saint Sauveur**. (*Closed noon to 2:00 pm and all day Tuesdays.*) Aix is also the birthplace of Paul Cézanne who was born here in 1839 but left to join his colleagues and the impressionistic fever that prevailed in Paris. He returned to his hometown in 1870 and settled here until his death in 1906. You can visit the studio he built, **Atelier Paul Cézanne**, set behind a little wooden gate just north of the old quarter. Paul Cézanne studied in Aix with Émile Zola and the distant Mont Saint Victoire, which inspired much of his work, can be seen from various vantage points in the city. (*Closed noon to 2 pm except in summer–noon to 2:30 pm, and all day Tuesdays.*)

Should you decide to use Aix en Provence as a base from which to explore Provence, or simply want to spend more than just an afternoon in a beautiful, aristocratic city, we recommend three hotels. At the heart of the old quarter is the **Hôtel des Quatre Dauphins**, while from the city fountain it is just a 15-minute walk to the attractive **Hôtel le Pigonnet,** and on the north side of town you find the elegant **Villa Gallici**.

From Aix en Provence travel north on country roads through groves of olive trees and acres of vineyards to the hilltowns of Haute Provence. Less traveled, the medieval hillside perched villages of this region are intriguing to explore.

From Aix follow the N7 northwest in the direction of Saint Cannat. Turn north 6 kilometers out of Aix at Lignane following the D543 north across the Chaîne de la Tréversse to Silvacane on the waters of the River Durance and the Canal de Marseille. Cross the river and the D543 becomes the D943, traveling first to Cadenet and then on to **Loumarin**, the capital of this region of Luberon. Loumarin is a small city surrounded by

Gordes

the bounty of the region: fruit trees, flowers, and produce. The château on the outskirts of town is a school for artists.

From Loumarin, the D943 enjoys the beautiful path of the Aigue Brun for 6 kilometers and then you take the D36 just a few kilometers farther west to the hillside village of Bonnieux. From Bonnieux you can wind a course northeast to the thriving city of **Apt**, known for its crystallized fruits and preserves, truffles, lavender perfume, and old Sainte Anne Cathedral which is still the site of an annual pilgrimage. From Apt follow the N100 west for 4½ kilometers to the D4 north to the turnoff west to Roussillon. Another option is to navigate a course directly north to Roussillon, an exploration along countryside roads.

Whichever the route, **Roussillon** is worth the effort to find. This lovely village is a maze of narrow streets, small shops, and restaurants that climb to the town's summit. In various shades of ochres, Roussillon is an enchanting village, especially on a clear day when the sun warms and intensifies the colors.

From Roussillon travel first north on the D105 and then west on the D2 to the neighboring village of **Gordes** perched at one end of the Vaucluse Plateau and dominating the Imergue Valley. Dressed in tones of gray, this is a wonderful place. Off its main square are some inviting cafés, restaurants, and shops selling Provence's wonderful bounties: lavender, olive oils, wines, regional dolls (*santons*), and garments in the charming local fabrics. At the heart of the village is a lovely hotel, **La Bastide de Gordes**, which opens up to glorious views of the surrounding countryside. Gordes is also known for the ancient village of 20 restored *bories,* or dry-stone huts, that lie in its shadow. Unusual in their round or rectangular shapes, these intriguing buildings (many of which accommodate 20th-century conveniences) are thought to date from the 17th century. **Hôtel les Bories**, a hotel that we recommend on the outskirts of Gordes, is actually named for the borie that houses its restaurant.

Restaurant, Les Bories

Just 4 kilometers to the north of Gordes lies the village of **Senanque** whose 12th-century Cistercian abbey stands at the edge of the mountainside surrounded by lavender and oak trees. Vacated by the monks in 1869, and accessible on foot, by a 2-kilometer path up from the car park, the abbey is now a religious cultural center and hosts concerts in the summer months.

From Senanque follow the small country road (D177) north to connect with the D4 and then travel west through the dense Forest of Vénasque to the beautiful and striking hilltop village of **Vénasque**. Charmingly untouched by civilization, this village is tucked in a dense forest cupped between two steep hills and is notable for its 6th-century **Église de Notre Dame** and the 17th-century **Chapelle Notre Dame de Vie**. The town comes to life during the early summer when it is the market center for the region's cherry crop.

From Vénasque weave a course south in the direction of the market town of **Cavaillon**. Known for its melon fields, Cavaillon is another village to include on your itinerary if your schedule permits. On the outskirts of Cavaillon, detour east to the amazing **Fontaine de Vaucluse,** fed by rainwater that seeps through the Vaucluse Plateau. In the late afternoon as the sun begins its descent, walk around this celebrated natural fountain: at certain times of the year the shooting water is so powerful that it becomes dangerous and the fountain is closed to observers. The most dramatic seasons to visit the spewing fountain are either winter or spring. Over a million tourists travel to Vaucluse each year to see the fountain, but few venture the 4 kilometers farther to the idyllic perched village of **Saumane de Vaucluse** whose hillside location affords magnificent views—an idyllic spot from which to watch the sun bathe the countryside in the soft hues so characteristic of Provence.

Retrace a path back in the direction of Cavaillon from Fontaine de Vaucluse and take the N100 23 kilometers south to Avignon. Considered a gateway to Provence, **Avignon** is one of France's most interesting and beautiful cities. Easy to navigate, its medieval encasement is encircled by one main boulevard and various gates allow entry into the walled city. The Porte de l'Oulle on the northwestern perimeter has parking just outside the wall and a small tourist booth with maps and information, and provides convenient access into the heart of the old city. The Porte de la Republique on the south side is opposite the train station and opens onto the Cour Jean Jaures, the location of the main tourist office. The Cour Jean Jaures becomes the Rue de la République and leads straight to the Place du Palais on the city's northern border. You might want to inquire at the tourist office about the miniature train that travels the city, highlighting the key points of interest, and the excellent guide service that conducts either full- or half-day walking tours of the city. Avignon is fun to explore—a wonderful selection of shops line its streets, a festive air prevails with numerous street performers, and the historical attractions are monumental.

Avignon was the papal residency from 1309 to 1377 and the **Palais des Papes** is a highlight of a visit to this lovely city—if only to stand on the main square and look up at the long, soft-yellow stone structure that dominates the city skyline, stretching the length of the square and towering against the blue skies of Provence. If time permits, enter the papal city through the Porte des Chapeaux into the Grande Cour. A little shop just off the

Avignon, Palais des Papes

entrance provides maps, information, and admission into the palace. Just off the entry, the impressive inner courtyard and beginning point for a palace tour is often a stage for the open-air theater performances of the popular summer festival. Allow approximately an hour to explore the palace effectively, noting the distinction between the old palace, built by Pope Benedict XII from 1334 to 1342, and the new palace commissioned by his successor, Pope Clement VI, and finished in 1348. The tour will take you down the Hall of the Consistory (*Aile du Consistoire*), hung with portraits of popes who resided in Avignon, to the upstairs banqueting hall (*Grand Tinel*), to the impressive Deer Room (*Chambre du Cerf*), whose walls display a beautifully painted fresco by Giovanetti depicting the decadent life of leisure led by the papal court in the 14th century, on to the Audience Hall (*Aile de Grande Audience*), elaborate with its star-studded ceiling, and the magnificent Saint Martial Chapel. *(Now open only on Sundays for church service, tel: 04.90.85.22.18.)*

Devote the majority of your time to visiting this feudal structure, but don't miss the two lovely churches, **Cathédral de Notre Dame des Doms** and the **L'Église Saint Didier**. Just off the Rue Joseph Vernet is the **Musée Calvet**, named for the doctor who bequeathed his personal collection of art and funds to launch it. The museum displays a rich collection of work from artists of the French and Avignon schools of painting and sculpture: Delacroix, Corot, and Manet are some of the impressive masters represented. (*Closed 1 pm to 2 pm and all day Tuesdays*.)

Although only four of its original twenty-two arches still stand, the **Pont Saint Bénezet** is an impressive sight. A small chapel still sits on one of its piers and shadows the waters of the encircling River Rhône. This is the bridge referred to in the song familiar to all French children, *"Sur le pont d'Avignon, on y dance, on y dance."* Even if all the arches still stood, passage would be difficult by modern-day transportation as the bridge was constructed at the end of the 12th century with pedestrians and horses in mind.

We recommend two elegant hotels within the city walls: the **Hôtel d'Europe**, easily located just off the Porte de l'Oulle facing the Place Crillon, and the truly luxurious **La Mirande** which backs onto the palace and once accommodated guests of the pope.

Villeneuve les Avignon is separated from Avignon by the Rhône. (Cross the river by following the N100 west of the city and then turn immediately on D900 in the direction of Villeneuve.) Villeneuve flourished when the pope held residence in Avignon and a number of cardinals chose it for their magnificent estates. Today it presents a lovely setting on the river, enjoys magnificent views of its neighbor, and yet benefits from a quieter setting and pace. A stronghold that once guarded the frontier of France when Avignon was allied to the Holy Roman Empire, it has towering on its skyline **Fort Saint André** whose vantage point commands a magnificent view across the Rhône to Avignon and the Popes' Palace. Another military structure still standing is the **Philippe le Bel Tower** and the curator is often on hand to provide all the historical facts. The Saturday morning antique and flea market is a popular attraction. Highly recommended as a place to stay in Villeneuve les Avignon is **Le Prieuré** which is housed in a 13th-century priory.

From Avignon it is a very pleasant drive south along a lazy, tree-lined road, the D571, to **Saint Rémy de Provence**, a pretty, sleepy town, nestled in the shade of its plane trees. On the outskirts of town is the **Château des Alpilles**, a lovely hotel offering a quiet setting and convenient base from which to explore the heart of Provence. Of interest in the town is a Romanesque church, Renaissance houses, and a busy public square.

On the outskirts of Saint Rémy, following the D5 south in the direction of Les Baux de Provence, you can visit the **Clinique de Saint Paul** where Van Gogh was nursed back to health after slicing off his earlobe; **Les Antiques**, an impressive arch and mausoleum commissioned by Augustus; and **Glanum**, a thriving point of commerce during the Gallo-Greek years that was virtually destroyed in the 3rd century.

From St. Rémy it is a beautiful drive along the D5 as it winds through the chalky gray hills referred to as *Les Alpilles* and then turns off to cover the short distance across the valley to the charming Provençal village of **Les Baux de Provence**. (The mineral bauxite was discovered here and derives its name from the town.)

The village appears to be a continuation of the rocky spur from which it rises. This site has been occupied for the past 5,000 years, and is now visited by more than a million visitors every year. A number of craft shops, inviting crêperies, and ice cream vendors are tucked away along the village streets. From Les Baux you not only have splendid views of the area, but also two marvelous hotels nestled in its shadow: **L'Auberge de la Benvengudo** and **Mas de l'Oulivie**.

En route to the lovely Roman city of Arles from Les Baux, the D17 travels first to the small roadside town of **Fontvieille**. Fontvieille is home to a wonderful hotel and restaurant, **La Régalido**, and is also worth a stop to visit the **Moulin de Daudet**, an abandoned mill set on the hillside above town, reputedly where Daudet wrote *Letters*

Les Baux de Provence

from My Windmill. Continuing on the back road from Fontvieille, the D33, as it travels beyond the mill, passes the ruins of an old **Roman Aqueduct** that stand unceremoniously in a field just off the road at the intersection of the D82. Head west from the aqueduct along the D82 to connect with the D17 and travel once again in the direction of Arles. On the approach to the city, surrounded by fields, stand the ruins of **Abbaye de Montmajour**, which was built in the 10th century by Benedictine monks.

The skyline of **Arles** can be seen as you approach the city. Abounding in character, this is a truly lovely city whose growth is governed by the banks and curves of the Rhône river. It has fierce ties to its Roman past when it thrived as a strong port city and gateway. Arles is glorified because of its magnificent Gallo-Roman arenas and theaters in the heart of the old city. This is a city to explore on foot: it is fun to wander through the narrow maze of winding streets that weave through the old section. Bullfights and festivals are still staged in the magnificent **Amphithéâtre**, or arena, able to accommodate in its prime more than 20,000 spectators. (*Open June to September all day, October to May.*) The **Théâtre Antique**, although apparently a ruin by day, becomes a lovely stage on summer nights under the soft lights of the Festival d'Arles. (Same hours as the Amphithéâtre.) The Place du Forum is bordered by cafés and is a social spot to settle in the afternoons and into the balmy evenings of Provence. Just a block from the Place du Forum, the **Muséon Arlaten** was conceived and funded by the town's poet, Frédéric Mistral, from the moneys he received for winning the Nobel Prize in literature, to honor all that is Provençal. The museum is rich in its portrayal of the culture and fierce traditions of Provence. (*Closed noon to 2 pm and all day Mondays in winter.*) A new museum has just opened in Arles, the **Musée de l'Arles Antique**, just south of the Nouveau Pont, which you can reach by walking along the ramparts on the edge of the Rhone. Large and open, the museum houses a dramatic display of sarcophagi, mosaics, statuary, models, and replicas depicting the dramatic arenas and theaters as well as jewelry, tools, and pottery that lend a glimpse of life in ancient Arles. It is built on a site overlooking the ruins of the Roman hippodrome and from the rooftop of the museum you can see the outline of the track which in time they hope to restore to its original dimensions. (*Open April to October 9 am to 7 pm daily, October to April 10 am to 6 pm, closed Tuesdays*.)

At the gateway to the Camargue and nestled at the heart of Provence, Arles is a wonderful base from which to experience the region. The **Hôtel d'Arlatan** and the **Grand Hôtel Nord-Pinus** are in the old quarter, while the more elegant **Hôtel Jules César** is found on a main road that bounds the ramparts.

Nîmes lies approximately 35 kilometers west of Arles. A Gaelic capital, it was also popular with the Romans who built its monuments. Without fail see the **Amphithéâtre** that once held 21,000 spectators, the **Arénas**, **Maison Carrée**, the best preserved Roman temple in the world, and the magnificent **fountain gardens**.

As a final destination, journey just another 20 kilometers or so north of Nîmes (N86 Remoulins, D981) to the spectacular **Pont du Gard**, an aqueduct that impressively bridges the River Gard. Still intact, three tiers of stone arches tower more than 36 meters across the valley. Built by Roman engineers about 20 B.C. as part of a 50-kilometer-long system bringing water from Uzès to Nîmes, the aqueduct remains one of the world's marvels. Park in the car park amidst the tourist stalls and food stands and walk a pedestrian road to the span of river that thankfully lies uncluttered, dominated only by the impact and shadow of the towering structure.

From Pont du Gard you can easily return to Nîmes or complete the circle back to Avignon.

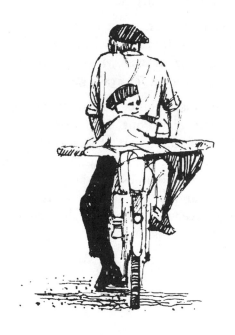

Provence

Gorges du Verdon

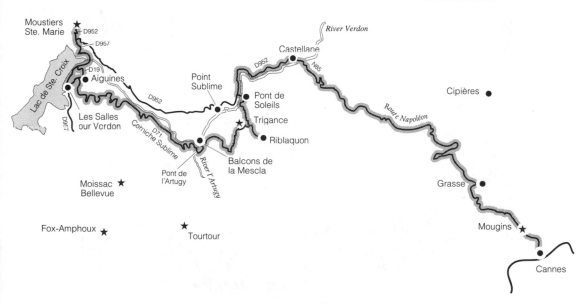

● Orientation/Sightseeing
★ Places to Stay

Moustiers
Ste. Marie ★ D952
D957
D19
● Aiguines
Lac de Ste. Croix
D957
Les Salles
sur Verdon
D952
Corniche Sublime
D71
Pont de
l'Artugy
River l'Artugy
Point
Sublime
● Pont de
Soleils
Trigance ★
Balcons de
la Mescla
● Riblaquon
River Verdon
Castellane ●
D952
N85
Route Napoléon
Cipières ●
Grasse ●
Moissac ★
Bellevue
Fox-Amphoux ★
★ Tourtour
Mougins ★
Cannes ●

Gorges du Verdon

The Gorges du Verdon is the French equivalent of the Grand Canyon. The striking blue-green water of the Verdon is dramatic in its intensity as it carves through and contrasts with the magnificent limestone plateau. The river then plunges into the spectacular trench-like Gorges du Verdon and is enclosed within its steep jagged walls. When you are traveling between the Riviera and central Provence, the Gorges du Verdon makes for a wonderful detour, and a few days spent in this region will prove memorable.

Gorges du Verdon

Recommended Pacing: This itinerary extends from Castellane to the delightful village of Moustiers Sainte Marie just to the north of Lac de Sainte Croix. The total distance covered is only about 40 kilometers, including the dramatic 20-kilometer span of the canyon from the Pont de Soleils to the town of Aiguines. The most logical access from the Riviera is to follow the N85, a lovely forested road that winds from Grasse northwest along the Route Napoléon to Castellane, a town set on the banks of the Verdon. You can include a visit to the canyon and cover the distance between the Riviera and Provence in one day, but it would require a very early start and make for an exceptionally long day. We recommend an overnight on the edge of the canyon at the Château de Trigance in the small hillside village of Trigance. Breaking the journey here gives you time to enjoy an unhurried drive along the dramatic canyon rim and then a leisurely next day to explore Moustiers Sainte Marie. We would also recommend including an overnight in Moustiers Sainte Marie—as we are certain the town and its setting will captivate you as it has us, before continuing your journey on to Provence.

Castellane is a natural starting point for an exploration of the canyon. It enjoys a lovely setting on the banks of the River Verdon and is famous for its crowning rock that towers above the town, crested by the **Nôtre Dame du Roc Chapel**. Traveling the D952 west following the path of the Verdon, at Pont de Soleils you can either choose to follow the south bank or the north bank of the canyon. (If time and enthusiasm allow, it is also possible to make one grand circle journey traveling both sides of the canyon.) For the purposes of this itinerary, the suggested routing follows the south bank, the *Corniche Sublime*, as it affords spectacular vistas of the canyon and also conveniently passes the enchanting medieval village of Trigance whose thick stone walls guard a wonderful hotel and restaurant, the Château de Trigance. To reach Trigance from Pont de Soleils, travel first south 16 kilometers on the D955 and just before the village of Riblaquon cross over the Jabron river to Trigance on the opposite hillside. **Trigance** is a sleepy little town whose population seems to double with the occupancy of its château-hotel, the **Château de Trigance**.

Following the road round the back of Trigance, the D90 travels a short distance (6 kilometers) before it ends at the D71. Turn north on the D71 and you will soon be rewarded with a spectacular vista of the dramatic Verdon at the **Balcons de la Mescla**. You can pull off here, and there are terraced points from which you can look down at the dramatic loop in the path of the river some 760 meters below. (There is also a small café where you can purchase snacks and postcards.) From Mescla the road winds through sparse vegetation of boxwood and then crosses over a dramatic span, the **Pont de l'Artugy**, a concrete, one-arch bridge that rises precariously high above the waters below. From the bridge, the drive is constantly spectacular in its drama and scenery. It rises and falls above the canyon walls, winding in and out of tunnels impressively cut into its rock face. From Artuby the road climbs on the fringe of the ravine to the **Fayet Pass**. Here a tunnel carves through the rock and square openings through the thick tunnel walls create windows that afford glimpses of the river's dramatic passage. Every second of the drive following the jagged mouth of the Verdon Canyon is spectacular. The canyon is almost overpowering: the river forges a path through narrow stretches where the canyon sides plunge down to depths far below, and then slows and calms in wider sections, pausing to create glistening, dark-green pools.

The road periodically veers away from the edge of the canyon and rolls past beautiful green meadows dotted by a few mountain cabins and hamlets. In spring wildflowers bloom everywhere. As the ruggedness and fierceness of the canyon wanes, the road gradually returns to the valley, opening up to vistas of the brilliant blue waters of **Lac de Sainte Croix** where you see **Aiguines**, a rosy-hued village of a rosy hue silhouetted against the backdrop of the lake. The numerous docks hint at what a paradise the lake is for sportsmen in summer months. At the water's edge, the road, now numbered D957, travels in the direction of Moustiers Sainte Marie, crossing over the Verdon as it flows into the lake. Be sure to take a moment and park just before the bridge as it is a beautiful sight looking back up the narrow canyon and if you are fortunate, you might see kayakers at the conclusion of their journey.

Moustiers Sainte Marie is a grand finale to this itinerary. Famous for its pottery, it is a wonderful village whose cluster of buildings with their patchwork of red-tiled roofs hugs the hillside and crawls back into the protection of a sheltered mountain alcove. Monks came here in 433, took shelter in caves dug into the mountainside, and founded the monastery **Nôtre Dame de Beauvoir** which towers over the village. The church was rebuilt during the 12th century and enlarged in the 16th. You can reach the sanctuary by a winding footpath paved with round stones leading up from the heart of the village.

This is a beautiful Provençal hilltown whose narrow, winding streets offer a wealth of stores displaying the famous Moustiers pottery. As early as 1678, the first master potter created a pattern that originated the style associated with the village. Today, some 15 master potters offer high-quality handmade and hand-decorated products, and pottery is the principal industry in the area. You can actually come to Moustiers and commission a personalized pattern with one of the workshops. Considering the size of the village and its seemingly remote location, it is hard to believe that the workshops of Moustiers Sainte Marie fulfill requests from all over the world for their hand-painted *faience*.

Located at the heart of the village overlooking the river is one of France's most charming restaurants, **Les Santons de Moustiers** (*Place de l'Église, tel: 04.92.74.66.48, closed Tuesdays*). I was drawn to the restaurant because of its bountiful array of windowboxes hung heavy with overflowing red geraniums. Inside, beautiful antiques decorate a number of individual dining rooms, each intimate and cozy in size. Michelin has awarded this restaurant, named for the regional dolls that you will see throughout the region, a coveted star.

Moustiers Sainte Marie

We recommend two places to stay in Moustiers, giving you the opportunity to linger in this lovely spot and time, perhaps, to contemplate that special purchase or order. Opposite the bridge is a simple country hotel, **Le Relais,** and on the outskirts, looking back to the village, is the more elegant **La Bastide de Moustiers**, whose owner and chef, Alain Ducasse, is world-renowned.

From Moustiers Sainte Marie it is a 1½-hour drive to Aix en Provence where you can join our *Provence* itinerary.

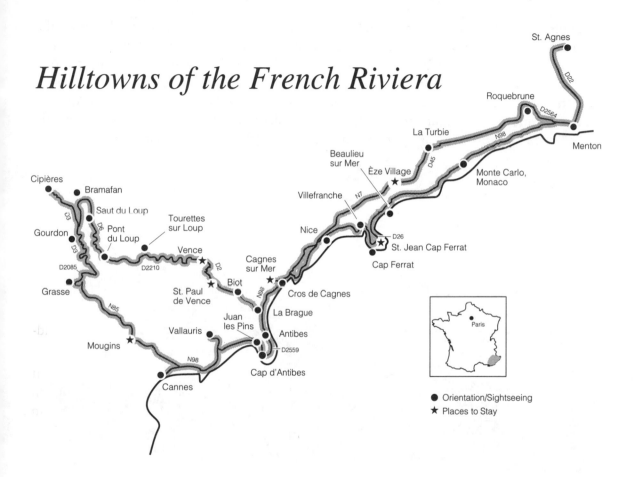

Hilltowns of the French Riviera

St. Agnes

D22

Roquebrune

D256A

La Turbie

N98

Menton

Beaulieu
sur Mer

Èze Village ★

Monte Carlo,
Monaco

D45

Villefranche

N7

Cipières

Bramafan

Nice

Saut du Loup

D3

Tourettes
sur Loup

D6

Pont
du Loup

D3

Gourdon

D26

St. Jean Cap Ferrat ★

Vence

Cap Ferrat

D2085

D2210

D2

Cagnes
sur Mer

Grasse

Biot ★

St. Paul
de Vence

N98

Cros de Cagnes

N85

La Brague

Juan
les Pins

Vallauris

Antibes

Mougins ★

N98

D2559

Cannes

Cap d'Antibes

Paris

● Orientation/Sightseeing
★ Places to Stay

85

Hilltowns of the French Riviera

People in the hundreds of thousands flock to the Riviera for its sun and dazzling blue waters. When planning your trip, be aware that most of these sun-worshipers congregate during the spring and summer with the coastal towns as their base and during this time the coastside is a constant hub of activity and excitement. The Riviera attracts an international group, jet-setters here to see and be seen. In the mountains overlooking the Mediterranean are a number of smaller, "hillside-perched" towns, removed from the continuous activity of the Riviera and offering a beautiful setting and escape.

View from Èze Village

Recommended Pacing: We suggest at least three full days to explore the coastal and hilltowns of the French Riviera. Assuming your time is going to be devoted to the Riviera, this itinerary traces a routing that both begins and ends in Nice. Keep in perspective that distances between destinations are short (Nice and Menton are just 23 kilometers apart), and although you can make a circle trip staying at one or two places, it would also be feasible to select one hotel as a base from which to explore the entire region. Remember that during peak summer months the Riviera is crowded with tourists—it is difficult to find places to stay and dine, negotiate the roads, find parking, and visit museums, so you must incorporate more time into your itinerary to do so. Our suggestion would be to avoid summer on the Riviera and, if nothing else, escape up into the hills above the coastal towns.

The French Riviera, or the Côte d'Azur, is the area between Menton and Nice. Its inhabitants are a breed apart: even the French themselves say the *Niçoise* are not typically French—warmed and subdued by the climate, they are more gentle and agreeable. We recommend that you begin your explorations in the region's capital, Nice, "Queen of the Riviera." France's wonderful express trains service the Nice train station and convenient connections can be made from many cities within Europe into the Nice airport (the second busiest in France). Equally appealing, both the train station and airport are small and easy to get around, and car rental agencies are represented at both.

Nice is a large city whose population of 400,000 has carpeted the land with apartments and condominiums bounded only by the ocean and the surrounding hills. Along the waterfront, the **Promenade des Anglais** takes a grand sweep from the city's western edge along the Baie des Anges and the new city to the edge of the picturesque old quarter. The new district of Nice is a mecca for tourists with the promenade along the seashore lined with elegant hotels and casinos. Lighted at night, the promenade is a romantic place for strolling. Just off this majestic promenade is the **Musée International d'Art Naïf** (Avenue Val Marie) which boasts an inventory of over 6,000 paintings from all over the world. (*Open daily noon to 2 pm and all day Tuesdays, tel: 04.93.71.78.33.*) The **Musée Chérit des Beaux Arts** (33, Avenue des Baumettes) focuses on a wealth of paintings from the 19th century. (*Closed November, daily noon to 2 pm except in summer and all day Mondays, tel: 04.92.15.28.28.*) A landmark of the promenade is the stately **Hôtel Negresco** whose terrace is a wonderful place to settle and enjoy a café or ice cream, a tradition to be equated with tea at Harrods. Just a little farther on, the Jardin Albert 1 is dressed with fountains and a bandstand that hosts numerous rock concerts. From the Jardin a mini-train departs every 20 minutes to tour the old town, the flower market, and castle gardens. The lovely Place Masséna stands proud on the promenade with its dramatic fountains and fronts the area's principal shopping district along the Avenue Jean Médecin. Also stemming off the Place Masséna, the Rue Masséna and the Rue de France are charmingly restricted to pedestrian traffic, banked by cafés, boutiques, and restaurants.

On the other side of the River Paillon is the old quarter of Nice, **La Vieille Ville**, full of character and ambiance. Narrow alleys wind through this district of cobbled streets shaded by towering buildings. The district is colored with flowerboxes and upward glimpses of sky are crisscrossed by banners of laundry. The flower market is very picturesque—a display of color all day and every day on the Cours Saleya, except on Mondays when a flea market of antiques and collectibles invades its space. A bountiful fish market is set out every morning (except Mondays) on the Place Saint François. From the Cours Saleya it is possible to climb the hill, known as the Château (by stairs, a lift, or by strolling up the Rue Ségurane), to some spectacular views of the Baie des Anges. "Château" refers to the château that last stood between the harbor and the old town some 300 years ago. The harbor with its colorful melange of fishing boats and neighboring yachts is fun to explore.

The territory mapped out and referred to as **Cimiez** is where the Romans constructed Cemenelum, a town to rival the then existing Greek town of Nikaia (Nice) in the 1st century B.C. The renovated Roman amphitheater hosts a famous jazz festival that takes place every July. Cimiez also flourishes in March during the *Festival des Cougourdons*, and in May, Sundays are an offering of dances, picnics, and folklore presentations during the *Fêtes des Mais*. Cimiez is also worth the journey to visit the **Musée d'Archéologie**, 160 Avenue des Arènes (*closed noon to 2 pm, Sunday mornings, and all day Mondays, tel: 04.93.81.59.57*), the **Musée Chagall** at the corner of Boulevard de Cimiez and Avenue Dr Ménard (*open 10 am to 5 pm, tel: 04.93.53.87.20*), and the **Musée Matisse** in the Villa des Arènes (*Open 10 am to 5 pm except Tuesdays, tel: 04.93.81.08.08*). The Musée Chagall houses the largest single collection of the master's work, while the Musée Matisse honors its namesake, who made Nice his home for 20 years, through the artist's paintings, drawings, and figurines.

Leaving Nice in the direction of Menton, you have a choice of three roads which all run somewhat parallel to each other following the contours of the coast. The **Grande Corniche** or "high" road was built by Napoleon and passes through picturesque *villages perchés*. The **Moyenne Corniche** or "middle" road is a lovely, wide, modern road. The **Corniche Inférieure** or "low" road was built in the 18th century by the Prince of Monaco and enables you to visit the wealthy coastal communities and the principality of Monaco. Each road offers a uniquely appealing route. A suggestion would be to loop in one direction on the Corniche Inférieure to enjoy the water and the coastal towns (this is the busiest road during the summer months), and return via a combination of both the Grande and Moyenne Corniches.

La Voile d'Or Overlooking the Port of Saint Jean Cap Ferrat

From Nice the Corniche Inférieure, the N98, hugs the contours of the coast and the lovely inlet of **Villefranche sur Mer** whose gentle waters are home to numerous yachts and fishing boats. Round the bay from Villefranche and follow the D26 through the exclusive residential district and peninsula of **Cap Ferrat**. Sometimes only glimpses are possible of the million-dollar mansions, home to many celebrities, which stand proud behind towering hedges and security gates along this 10-kilometer drive. It is possible to visit the former residence of the Baroness Ephrussi de Rothschild, who commissioned the Italian-style palace to house her personal art collection. It is now owned by the state and open to the public as a museum—the gardens and setting alone merit a visit. Traveling along the peninsula, climb the steps of the lighthouse for a wonderful view. Farther out on the tip is a tower which housed prisoners in the 18th century.

Saint Jean Cap Ferrat is nestled on the other side of the peninsula from Villefranche, enjoying a picturesque setting and a quiet ambiance, with just a few homes, restaurants, and hotels tucked into the hillside. It has lovely views across the towering masts of yachts that grace its waters. **La Voile d'Or**, a lovely, elegant hotel overlooking the water, is a wonderful choice for overnighting in Saint Jean Cap Ferrat.

Continuing on from Saint Jean Cap Ferrat, the road winds back to the N98 through another wealthy enclave of homes and luxurious hotels enjoying the protected climate of the neighboring town of **Beaulieu sur Mer**.

As the N98 leaves Beaulieu sur Mer, the road hugs the mountain and tunnels through the cliff face just above the Mediterranean, through Cap d'Ail, and into the principality of **Monaco**. First-class hotels and excellent restaurants are numerous in **Monte Carlo**, catering to the millions of annual visitors who come to play in its casino and hope to catch a glimpse of the royal family or resident international celebrities. Monaco is independent of French rule, and an exclusive tax haven for a privileged few. If you have time, step inside the **Palais du Casino**, fronted by beautifully manicured gardens. To really experience gambling fever, in the afternoon step inside the private salons where high stakes are an everyday agenda.

Beyond Monaco the N98 merges with the N7 and continues on to the graceful city of **Menton**, on the Italian border. Menton boasts streets shaded by fruit trees and stretches of sandy beach in addition to a colorful harbor, casino, and an endless array of shops. At the heart of the old town, Rue Saint Michel is a charming shopping street restricted to foot traffic. The nearby Place aux Herbes and Place du Marché are picturesque with their covered stalls and flower displays. Menton is also known for its gardens, the most famous being the **Jardin des Colombières** (Rue Ferdinand Bac) located on the hill above the town, enjoying lovely views through pines and cypress trees to the waters of the Mediterranean.

From Menton, a 10-kilometer detour into the hills brings you to the picturesque walled town of **Sainte Agnes**. The D22, often just a single lane, winds precariously up into the hills to this attractive mountain village of cobbled streets, a few restaurants, shops, and unsurpassed views of the coastline. (Although the hillside town of **Gorbio** is often recommended in connection with Sainte Agnes, the drive is even more demanding, and the time and energy expended is not worth the journey—Sainte Agnes is a little larger and very similar, with better views.)

Returning in the direction of Nice with Menton and the Italian border at your back, follow signs to Roquebrune Cap Martin and you find yourself traveling on the D2564 and the Grande Corniche. **Roquebrune** is divided into two districts: the new town on the water and a medieval village on the hillside dating from the dynasty of Charlemagne. Very picturesque on the approach, the medieval Roquebrune is well worth a detour and some time for exploration. Park on the main square and follow its maze of narrow, cobbled streets to the 13th-century keep, protected at the core of the medieval village.

From Roquebrune the Grande Corniche continues along a very scenic stretch affording beautiful views of the principality of Monaco stretched out below. Just past the charming hillside town of **La Turbie**, watch for the D45, a short connector to the Moyenne Corniche and the idyllic village of Èze.

Like Roquebrune, there are two divisions of Èze, **Èze Village**, the medieval village perched on the hillside above the Riviera, and **Èze Bord de la Mer**, a modern town on the water's edge. Of all the perched villages along the Riviera, Èze Village, a quaint medieval enclave with cobblestoned streets overlooking the sea, remains a favorite: park your car below the village and explore it on foot. If you decide to use Èze as a base, you will discover two fabulous hotels protected within its walls: the **Château de la Chèvre d'Or** and the **Château Eza**, residences that for more than a thousand years have soaked up the sun and looked down upon the beautiful blue water associated with the magnificent Côte d'Azur.

Èze Village

From Èze the Moyenne Corniche follows a beautiful route, the N7, that winds back into Nice. Once in Nice you can either follow the Promenade des Anglais along its waterfront, the N98, in the direction of Cannes, or circumvent the city and traffic by taking the Autoroute A8, exiting at Cagnes Est and following signs to Haut de Cagnes. (If you opt for the N98, take the D18 at Cros de Cagnes and follow signs away from the coast in the direction of Haut de Cagnes.) **Cagnes sur Mer** is on the waterfront, a port town struggling to resemble the other coastal centers. **Haut de Cagnes**, however, is an old section located on the hill, with an abundance of charm and character. Follow narrow, steep, cobbled streets to the heart of the old village. Opt for the underground parking just on the approach to the village crest—you might find space on the street, but it takes a brave soul to negotiate a spot, and unless you find a generous section, the streets are so narrow, it's never certain that there is enough room left for passing vehicles. The most visited site in Haut de Cagnes, the **Château Grimaldi** was originally built as a fortress in 1309, commissioned by Raynier Grimaldi, Lord of Monaco and Admiral of France. A citadel was built a year later and then, in the 17th century, Henri Grimaldi had the citadel refurbished into very spacious accommodations. His descendent, Gaspard Grimaldi, was forced to abandon the castle at the time of the French Revolution. During the reign of the Grimaldis, the residents within the walls of this medieval enclave prospered by cultivating wheat, wine, and olives. (*Open all year, closed 12:30 pm to 1:30 pm, and all day Tuesdays.*) Mules were used to haul the bounty of produce from the neighboring hillsides and a wealth of seafood from the coast to the village. **Le Cagnard**, a marvelous hotel-restaurant, is tucked away in the old village.

On the other side of Cagnes Sur Mer from Haut de Cagnes and definitely worth the hassle of its congested streets is the absolutely wonderful **Musée de Renoir**. Advised to move to a warmer climate because of ill health, Renoir relocated to the coast and lived his last years in this sun-washed villa above the town. Surrounded by a sprawling, peaceful garden graced with olive trees, rhododendrons, iris, geraniums, and stretches of lawn, you can almost sense the peace and quiet that he must have experienced and the environment that inspired him to paint—artists today frequent the gardens seeking their own inspiration. The town of Cagnes purchased the home which displays many of Renoir's works, photos, and personal and family memoirs. Especially moving is the sentimental staging in his studio: Renoir's wheelchair is parked in front of the easel, dried flowers rest on the easel's side, and a day bed which enabled Renoir to rest between his efforts is set up nearby. When you study the photo of Renoir during his later years, he appears so old and yet determined to give the world his last ounce of creativity. (*Closed October 20 to November 9, noon to 2 pm except summer months—12:30 pm to 1:30 pm and all day Tuesdays.*)

Return to the water from Haut de Cagnes and follow the N7 or the N98 along the Baie des Anges in the direction of Antibes. At La Brague detour just a few kilometers off the coastal road following the D4 to the hillside village of **Biot**. Biot, where glassware has been made for just under three decades, has won high acclaim. A visit to a glass factory to see the assortment of styles and types of glassware available is very interesting. Bottles vary from the usual types to the Provençal *calères* or *ponons-bouteilles* that have two long necks and are used for drinking. This medieval village of small narrow streets, lovely little squares, and a maze of galleries and shops is a gem.

After retracing your path back to the coastside, continue to **Antibes**—allow at least half a day for exploring this waterfront fortress. **Fort Carré**, not to be confused with the Château de Grimaldi, is closed to the public and located on the south entrance of town. The fort guards the waters of Antibes which is home to thousands of yachts berthed in the modern Port Vauban Yacht Harbor. The rectangular towers and battlements of the **Château de Grimaldi** can be seen beyond the fort, within the ramparts of the medieval village. At the heart of the village the château commands some of the town's best views and now houses some of Picasso's work in the **Musée Picasso**. Picasso resided at the château just after the war in 1946 and, in appreciation of his stay, left much of his work to the town. Spacious and uncluttered, open bright rooms in the château admirably display his work and photographs of the master when he resided here in addition to contemporary works by Léger, Magnelli, and Max Ernst. Entry to the museum also gives you some of Antibes' most beautiful views of the Mediterranean framed through the thick medieval walls. (*Closed Mondays and noon to 2 pm in winter months.*) The town itself is charming and its cobbled streets are fun for wandering.

From Antibes a scenic drive follows the D2559 around the peninsula to its point, **Cap d'Antibes**, another exclusive residential community which boasts gorgeous homes, exclusive hotels, and lovely sandy beaches. The dramatic **Hôtel du Cap** enjoys acres of lawn stretching down to the water which afford privacy for a long list of celebrities who sequester away here.

On the other side of the peninsula from Antibes is the pretty resort town of **Juan les Pins** which is popular for its lovely stretch of white-sand beach and whose sparkling harbor shelters many attractive boats.

As the N98 hugs the bay of Golfe Juan and before it stretches to **Pointe de la Croissette** in Cannes, you can detour into the hills just up from the town of Golfe Juan to **Vallauris**. Picasso settled in Vallauris after his time in Antibes and tested his skill at the potter's wheel, producing thousands of pieces of pottery using the Madoura pottery shop as his *atelier*. He restored the craft and brought fame to the village and in gratitude the town made him an honorary citizen. He, in turn, showed his appreciation by crafting a life-size bronze statue which stands on Place Paul Isnard outside the church. A museum, **Musée de Vallauris,** displaying Picasso's work is housed in the château, originally a 13th-century priory rebuilt in the 16th century. Now considered the ceramic capital of France, there are numerous workshops in Vallauris—the **Galerie Madoura** remains one of the best, and stores sell a vast assortment of styles and qualities. (*Closed November, Saturday and Sunday, and 12:30 pm to 2:30 pm, tel: 04.93.64.66.39.*) Over 200 craftsmen reside in Vallauris, creating original designs and copying patterns made famous by Picasso.

From Vallauris, return to the coast and continue on to the cosmopolitan city of Cannes. Located on the Golfe de Napoule, **Cannes** is the center for many festivals, the most famous being the Cannes Film Festival held annually in May. The **Boulevard de la Croissette** is a wide street bordered by palm trees separating the beach from the elaborate grand hotels and apartment buildings. La Croissette is congested with stop-and-go traffic in the summer, and the lovely beaches that it borders are dotted with parasols and covered with tanning bodies. The **old port** (*Vieux Port*) is a melange of fishing boats and sleek luxury craft. You find the flower market, Forville, along the Allées de la Liberté and the bounty displayed at the covered market is set up every morning except Mondays. The picturesque pedestrian street of Rue Meynadier is worth seeking out for delicious picnic supplies such as cheeses, bread, and paté. Rising above the port at the western end of the popular Boulevard de la Croissette is **Le Suquet**, the old quarter of Cannes which has a superior view of the colorful port.

It is easy to escape the bustle of the cosmopolitan fever of Cannes by traveling just a few short miles directly north out of the city along the N85 to the hilltown village of **Mougins**. This charming village achieved gastronomic fame when Roger Vergé converted a 16th-century olive mill into an internationally famous restaurant. Other notable chefs have been attracted to the village and Michelin has awarded the village and its restaurants in total four gourmet stars. **Les Muscadins**, located at the entrance to the old village, is a delightful inn that we recommend and we feel deserving of one of those coveted stars. The fortified town of Mougins is characteristic of many of the medieval towns that are accessible only to pedestrian traffic, which luckily preserves the atmosphere that horns and traffic congestion all too often obliterate. Located in the center of Mougins is a small courtyard decorated with a fountain and flowers and shaded by trees. Here you will discover a few small cafés where locals meet to gossip about society, life, and politics.

Continuing into the coastal hills, you come to a region of lavender, roses, carnations, violets, jasmine, olives, and oranges. Approximately 12 kilometers north of Mougins in the heart of this region is **Grasse**. Grasse's initial industry was the tanning of imported sheepskins from Provence and Italy. It was Catherine de Médici who introduced the concept of perfume when she commissioned scented gloves from the town in a trade agreement with Tuscany. When gloves fell out of fashion and their sales dwindled, the town refocused on the perfume industry. The town is constantly growing, but the old section is fun to wander through. Interesting tours of perfume factories are given in English by **Fragonard** (at 20 Boulevard Fragonard and at Les 4 Chemins), **Molinard** (60 Boulevard Victor-Hugo), and **Gallimard** (73 Route de Cannes).

Leave Grasse to the northeast on the D2085 and travel for 6 kilometers to the D3 which travels north and winds back and forth along a steep ascent to the beautiful village of Gourdon. Endeared as one of France's most beautiful villages, **Gourdon** is an unspoiled gem that commands an absolutely spectacular setting as it hugs and clings to the walls of the steep hillside. Vistas from the village look north down the Loup Canyon or southeast

Cipières

over the countryside dotted with villages of sun-washed stucco and tiled roofs to the glistening water of the distant Riviera. On clear days you can see from Nice to the Italian border. The village's cobbled streets are lined with delightful, untouristy shops and a handful of restaurants. **Le Nid d'Aigle** on the Place Victoria is a restaurant whose terraces step daringly down the hillside.

From Gourdon the D3 hugs the hillside and affords glimpses of the twisting River Loup far below. As the road winds down to a lower altitude, you can either drive north on the D603 to the medieval village **Cipières** and cross the river at a more northerly point or continue on the D3 and cross the Loup on the Pont de Bramafan. After crossing the river, just before Bramafan, follow the D8 south in the direction of Pont du Loup. This 6-kilometer stretch of road winds through the **Gorges du Loup**. The canyon's beauty and its high granite walls beckon you into the ever-narrowing gorge. The River Loup flows far below, only visible to the passenger who might chance a peek over the edge.

The road passes through some jaggedly carved tunnels—pathways blasted through sheer rock that open to glorious vistas of the canyon, trees, and rock. Pull off the road at **Saut du Loup**. The stop requires no more than 15 minutes and for an entrance fee of 1,50F you can walk down a short, steep flight of steps to a terrace overlooking magnificent waterfalls and pools. The small riverside village of **Pont du Loup** is situated at the mouth of the canyon, on a bend in the river shadowed by the ruins of a towering bridge. It is a pretty town and a lovely end to the Loup Canyon.

Beyond Pont du Loup, traveling east along the D2210 in the direction of Vence, you pass through a few more towns, each consisting of a cluster of medieval buildings and winding, narrow streets that, without exception, encircle a towering church and its steeple. **Tourrettes sur Loup** is an especially lovely town whose medieval core of clustered rosy-golden-stone houses enjoys a backdrop of the three small towers that give the town its name. Every March the hillsides of Tourrettes sur Loup are a mass of violets and the village is dressed with fragrant bouquets for the *Fête de Violettes*. After World War II the town revived its long-abandoned textile production and is one of the world's top *tissage à main* (hand weaving) centers. The workshops are open to the public.

The D2210 continues from Tourrettes sur Loup and approaches the wonderful old town of **Vence** from the west. Located just 10 kilometers above the coast and Riviera, the hillsides surrounding Vence afford a lovely coastal panorama and are dotted with palatial homes and villas. Entering through the gates into the old village, you find dozens of tiny streets with interesting shops and little cafés where you can enjoy scrumptious pastries. The Place du Peyra was once the Roman forum and it's now the colorful town marketplace. In 1941 Matisse moved here and, in gratitude for being nursed back to health by the Dominican Sisters, he constructed and decorated the simple **Chapelle du Rosaire**. (Follow the Avenue des Poilus to the Route de Saint Jeannet La Gaude.) (*Open 10 to 11:30 am and 2:30 to 5:30 pm Tuesdays and Thursdays, tel: 04.93.58.03.26.*) Vence makes a wonderful base from which to explore the coast and the hilltowns. A favorite, simple inn and wonderful country restaurant, **L'Auberge des Seigneurs et du Lion d'Or**, sits off one of the old town squares. We also recommend the very luxurious

Château Saint Martin on the outskirts of Vence with spectacular distant views across the hills to the blue waters of the Riviera.

A few kilometers beyond Vence (D2 in the direction of Cagnes sur Mer) is the picturesque mountain stronghold of **Saint Paul de Vence** which once guarded the ancient Var Frontier. Cars are forbidden inside the walls of the old town whose cobbled streets are lined with galleries and tourist shops. From the encircling ramparts you get panoramic views of the hilltowns of the Riviera. Located outside the walled town in the woods along the Cagnes road, the **Foundation Maeght**, a private museum that sponsors and hosts numerous collections of works of some of the world's finest contemporary artists, is one of the principal attractions of Saint Paul de Vence. (*Open October to June 10 am to 12:30 pm and 2:30 to 6 pm; in summer 10 am to 7 pm.*) Saint Paul de Vence is also a convenient base from which to explore the Riviera, and for places to stay, we recommend **Hôtel la Colombe d'Or** and **Hôtel le Saint-Paul** within its fortified walls, and **Hôtel le Hameau** and **La Grande Bastide** on its outskirts. From Saint Paul de Vence it is a short drive back to Nice.

From Nice you can join our *Provence* itinerary by taking the scenic autoroute through the mountains, bridging the distance with our *Gorges du Verdon* itinerary. Or you can follow the coastline, referred to as the Corniche d'Or, between La Napoule (just outside Cannes) and Saint Raphaël which offers spectacular views: fire-red mountains contrasting dramatically with the dark-blue sea. Saint Raphaël is a small commercial port with a pleasant, tourist-thronged beach. Continuing on, Saint Tropez is easily the most enchanting of the dozens of small ports and beaches that you'll pass. If you choose to continue along the coastal road, take the Corniche des Maures which hugs the waterfront at the base of the Massif des Maures. At Hyères the scenery wanes, and we suggest you take the A50 to the A8-E80 which travels west to Aix en Provence.

Wine Country–Burgundy

Orientation/Sightseeing
Places to Stay

Paris

D 965

Auxerre

Chablis

Noyers

D 49

Avallon

Vallée du Cousin

St. Père
sous Vézelay

Vézelay

A 6

Pont de Pany

A 38

Dijon

Curtil-Vergy

Gevrey
Chambertin

N 74

A 31

Chambolle
Musigny

Morey St Denis

Vougeot

A 31

D 122

Savigny-les-
Beaune

Nuits St. Georges

St. Romain

Aloxe Corton

Orches

Levernois

N 73

N 5

La Rochepot

Beaune

Autun

Meursault

N 81

A 31

Chalon sur Saône

N 73

Wine Country–Burgundy

Burgundy lies in the heart of France, and we introduce you to its charms at Vézelay, an idyllic medieval village sitting high atop a hill. We briefly explore Chablis and then travel the backbone of its wine district, the Côte d'Or, which is divided into Côte de Nuits from Dijon to beyond Nuits Saint Georges, and Côte de Beaune which continues south from Aloxe Corton to Chagny. Exploring the area is like traveling through a wine list, for the region supports half the famous names in French wine.

Vézelay

Recommended Pacing: It would be a shame not to spend time in or around Vézelay because it is such a lovely region. While it is possible to cover all that we propose using Vézelay as a base, we recommend two nights in Vézelay and two nights at a hotel in or around Beaune.

Leave Paris to the southeast and take the A6 autoroute for the 1½-hour drive to the *Auxerre Sud* exit where you take the D965 for the 12-kilometer drive into **Chablis**, a busy little town synonymous with the dry white wine of Burgundy. Chablis wine roads extend like spokes of a wheel into the surrounding hills, with the finest vineyards being found just northeast of the town. Cross the River Serein and turn left on the D91, a small road that leads you to the region's seven grand crus which lie side by side: Bougros, Les Preuses, Vaudésir, Les Clos, Grenouilles, Valmur, and Blanchot. Returning to Chablis, follow the Serein upstream to **Noyers**, a charming little walled town of timbered houses.

Crossing the A6 just beyond Nitry, a 30-kilometer drive brings you into **Vézelay** sitting high on its hilltop above the surrounding countryside and for many people the highlight of a visit to Burgundy. This little town is full of narrow streets lined with old houses with sculptured doorways and mullioned windows leading up to the 12th-century **Basilica Sainte Madeleine**, the enormous building that sits above the village. This extraordinarily long church is beautiful in its simplicity with its soaring columns and paved floor and when religious pilgrimages were the fashion, it was an important stop on the pilgrimage route to Santiago de Compostela in Spain. Amongst the winding streets you find the charming **Résidence Hôtel le Pontot.** The Pontot is its own tranquil oasis protected behind the walls of the village. A gorgeous garden, magnificent vistas of the surrounding countryside, and elegant accommodation are for the lucky few who are able to secure a reservation. Nestled at the foot of Vézelay is the tiny village of **Saint Père sous Vézelay** where you find Marc Meneau's famous restaurant, L'Espérance, a modern-day pilgrimage site for gourmands.

Continue on to Pontaubert, cross the river, and turn immediately right, signposted **Vallée du Cousin**, on a country road that follows the picturesque narrow wooded valley of the rushing River Cousin and up the hill into the narrow cobbled streets of **Avallon**, a larger town with cozy old houses at its center. On the outskirts of Avallon is a marvelous hotel, the **Château de Vault de Lugny**. From Avallon follow signposts for the autoroute A6 which you take to the A38 towards Dijon.

If you like bustling cities, follow the A38 all the way to **Dijon** where sprawling suburbs hide a historic core. Rue des Forges is the most outstanding of the old streets. Even if you are not a museum lover, you will enjoy the **Musée des Beaux Arts** in the palace of Charles de Valois. It is one of France's most popular museums, with some wonderful old wood carvings and paintings. (*Open all year 10 am to 6 pm except Tuesdays, tel: 03.80.74.52.70.*) The aperitif Kir (cassis and white wine) was named after Canon Kir, the city's mayor and wartime resistance leader. On a food note: There are plenty of opportunities to purchase Dijon mustard and if you visit in November, you can attend the superb gastronomic fair.

For a greater dose of the countryside, leave the autoroute after Sombernon at the village of Pont de Pany, pass the large hotel on your right, cross the canal, and turn right on the D35, signposted Urcy and Nuits Saint Georges. This scenic little country road winds steeply up a rocky limestone escarpment past the Château Montclust and through rolling farmland to **Urcy**, a tight cluster of cottages set around a church. After passing through Quemigny Poisot, turn left for Chamboef and left again in the village for Gevrey Chambertin. Down the limestone escarpment you go through a rocky tunnel around a couple of precipitous bends and you're in the vineyards.

Turn right and follow the D122 into Gevrey Chambertin where you join the great wine route, **Route des Grands Crus**, a tourist route which winds you through the villages that produce the premier Burgundian wines. As you drive around, look for the Flemish-style colored tiles, arranged in patterns, that decorate the roofs of the region—a reminder of the time when the Dukes of Burgundy's duchy stretched into the Low Countries. There are very few large estates in this region, most of the land belonging to small farmers who live and make wine in the villages and go out to work amongst their vines. Fields are called *climats* and every *climat* has a name. Some *climats* produce better wines which are identified by their own name; others are identified by the name of the village. This is fine for the larger centers such as Beaune and Pommard, but the little villages—searching for an identity—have incorporated the name of their best-known vineyard into the village name. Thus Gevrey became Gevrey Chambertin, Saint Georges became Nuits Saint Georges, and Vougeot became Clos de Vougeot. **Gevrey Chambertin** is one of the region's most delightful villages, with narrow streets lined with gray-stone houses and numerous vintners' signs inviting you in to sample their wares.

Village on the Burgundy Wine Road

Arriving at **Morey Saint Denis**, park in the large car park before the village and walk along its narrow streets.

The vineyards of **Chambolle Musigny** produce some spectacular wines and you can learn about them at the wine museum housed in the cellars of the **Château-Hôtel André Ziltener** (also a hotel). This informative tour (given in English, French, or German) includes a tasting of the four grades of wine produced in the area.

The hillsides of **Clos de Vougeot** were first planted by Cistercian monks in the 14th century and a stone wall was built to encircle the vineyards and protect them from raiders in the One Hundred Years' War. An organization called **Chevaliers du Tastevin**, now recognized worldwide, chose the 16th-century **Château de Vougeot** in 1944 as a base from which to publicize Burgundy wines. You can see the courtyard, the great pillared hall where banquets take place, and the impressive cellars and 12th-century wine presses of Beaune. If you want to stay nearby, you can cross back over the N74 and drive up over one arm of the moat to **Château de Gilly**, a lovely hotel.

Nuits Saint Georges is somewhat larger than the other towns along the route. A great deal of wine is blended here under the town's name. After Nuits Saint Georges the Route des Grands Crus continues along the N74 to end at Corgoloin. The Côte de Beaune begins virtually where the Côte de Nuits ends.

After the Route des Grands Crus the first great commune is **Aloxe Corton** whose vineyards were once owned by Charlemagne. Legend states that Aloxe Corton is known for both its red and white wines because during the time that Charlemagne owned the vineyards, his wife claimed that red wine stained his white beard and so he ordered the production of white wine too. He is commemorated by the white wine Corton-Charlemagne.

Arriving in **Beaune**, do not follow signs for *Centre Ville* but stay on the ring-road that circles the city's walls in a counter-clockwise direction. Park in one of the car parks adjacent to the ring-road and walk into the narrow old streets of the wine capital of Burgundy. Today the most important landowner in the region is the Hospices de Beaune,

Hôtel Dieu, Beaune

a charitable organization which over the years has had valuable plots of land donated to it. Every year they hold a wine auction at the Hôtel Dieu—it is one of the wine trade's most important events. Built as a hospital, the **Hôtel Dieu** is so elegantly decorated that it seems more like a palace. You will want to take a guided tour of this lovely building. (*Open March to November 9 am to 6:30 pm, Closed December to March 11:30 am to 2 pm, tel: 03.80.24.45.00.*) You can also visit the **Musée du Vin de Bourgogne** in the Hôtel des Ducs de Bourgogne. (*Open 9:30 am to 6 pm, Closed Tuesdays December to April, tel: 03.80.22.08.19.*) There are delightful shops, restaurants, and cafés aplenty and wine lovers may want to visit one of the *négotiant-éleveurs* who buy wines of the same *appellation* from growers and blend and nurture them to produce an "elevated" superior wine. At the heart of the wine region, Beaune serves as a wonderful base. We recommend three hotels in Beaune from which to chose.

Leave Beaune on the A74 in the direction of Chagny. After a short distance take the D973 to **Pommard** where tasting is offered at the château on the outskirts as well as at vintners in the crowded confines of the village. Detour into **Meursault**, a larger village that offers tasting at small vintners as well as the larger Domaine du Château de Meursault. Tucked off the village streets is a charming hotel, **Les Magnolias**.

The D973 brings you into Auxley Duresses. At the far end of the village turn right following the brown signs indicating **Haute Côte de Beaune**. This wine route takes you on a narrow country lane up through the steeply sloping village of **Saint Romain**, high above the vineyards and back down to vineyards in **Orches**, a village clinging to the limestone cliffs, through **Baubigny** and into the wine center of **La Rochepot**. A short drive brings you to the N74 which will quickly bring you back to Beaune.

From Beaune a 250-kilometer drive (three hours) on the autoroute will bring you to Alsace where you can join another of our wine country itineraries, or a 330-kilometer drive (four hours) on the autoroute will bring you to Reims where you can join the Champagne wine route.

Wine Country–Burgundy

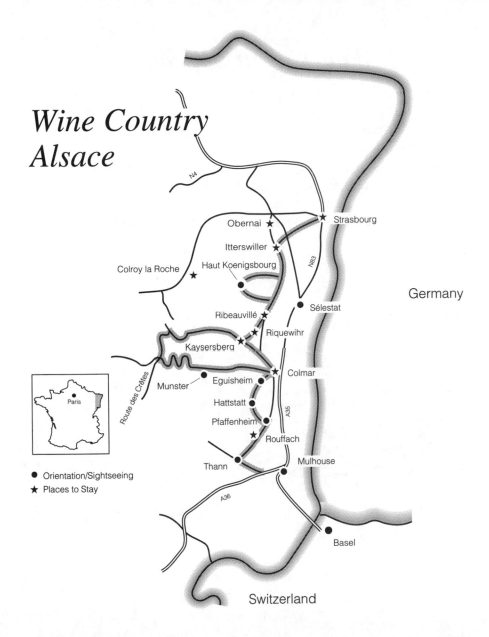

Wine Country
Alsace

Strasbourg ★

Germany

Obernai ★

Itterswiller ★

N83

Colroy la Roche ★

Haut Koenigsbourg ●

Ribeauvillé ★

Sélestat ●

Riquewihr ★

Kaysersberg ★

Colmar ★

Paris

Route des Crêtes

Munster ●

Eguisheim ●

Hattstatt

A35

Pfaffenheim ●

Rouffach ★

● Orientation/Sightseeing

★ Places to Stay

Thann ●

Mulhouse ●

A36

Basel ●

Switzerland

Wine Country–Alsace

Alsace borders Germany—in fact, from the Franco-Prussian war to the end of World War I Alsace was part of Germany. After World War II the district began to market its white wines sold in distinctive long, thin, green or brown bottles. The vineyards are at the foot of the Vosges mountains on east-facing hills set back from the broad Rhine river valley. The hills are never particularly steep or spectacular but are laced by narrow roads that wind amongst the vines from one picturesque village to the next. Villages such as Riquewihr and Kaysersberg are picture-book perfect with their painted eaves and gables, narrow cobbled streets, archways, and windowboxes brimming with colorful geraniums.

Riquewihr

Recommended Pacing: Select a hotel in the wine region and use it as a base for your explorations of the area—two nights minimum. Finish your tour with a night or more in Strasbourg, a beautiful city.

In Alsace the wines are known by the names of the vineyards or villages and are identified by the type of grape from which they are made: Riesling, Gewürtztraminer, Muscat, or Pinot Gris, and sometimes by the phrase *Réserve Exceptionelle* which indicates a higher price and premier wine. The grapes are similar to those used for German wines but the majority are used to make dry wines, not dessert wines.

Just before Mulhouse, a sprawling industrial city, leave the autoroute (exit 6) and take the N83, following signposts for Thann, around the outskirts of Cernay (signposted Colmar) to **Pfaffenheim**, a tiny wine village just to the north of the larger wine town of **Rouffach** where the **Château d'Isenbourg** sits above the town amidst the vineyards.

At Pfaffenheim you leave the busy N83 to weave through the narrow village streets and into the vineyards to join the **Route du Vin**, a signposted routing that follows a winding itinerary through the vineyards. You soon arrive at **Gueberschiwiler**, a cluster of gaily painted houses where, as you reach the village square, intricate painted signs advertise wine tasting in cobbled courtyards.

From the square turn right and drive 2 kilometers to Hattstat, and on to Obermorschwir where the narrow road climbs steeply to **Husseren les Châteaux**, a cluster of homes with its castle perched high above the village.

Plan on spending some time in **Eguisheim**, a trim little town with lovely old timbered houses, shops, and restaurants set along narrow cobbled lanes. From Eguisheim the road drops down to the busy N83 which quickly brings you into Colmar.

Colmar is the largest town along the wine road and an important center for wine trade. Beyond the suburbs lies a pedestrian zone—an interesting mix of French and German culture and architecture. Short streets wind round old buildings between the plazas and lead you to the town's old quarter with its intricately carved and leaning houses known as **Petite Venise** because a shallow canal weaves its way through the narrow streets. The Dominican monastery is now the **Unterlinden Museum** with an excellent collection of portraits and an exhibition of crafts and customs. One room is a re-created Alsatian vintner's cellar complete with wine presses. (*Closed Tuesdays November to March, and noon to 2 pm, tel: 03.89.20.15.58.*) With a very pretty and convenient location right on the canal, we recommend the **Hostellerie le Maréchal**.

From Colmar make a detour off the Route du Vin up the D417. As the vineyards wane, the valley narrows and pine trees decorate the heights as you drive the 15 kilometers to **Munster**, situated at the foot of the Vosges. Munster is famous for being the home of the celebrated cheese, rather than for its picturesque streets.

From Munster the D417 climbs and twists through green Alpine fields dotted with farms. Climbing higher, you enter a vast pine and oak forest to emerge at the summit, **Col de la Schlucht**, which offers spectacular views across the wild slopes of the Vosges mountains. Turn right on **Route des Crêtes** (D61), a skyline road constructed by the French during World War I to ensure communications between the different valleys. Now the route winds a scenic trip and signposts several beauty spots that you can walk to before coming to **Col de Calvair**, a tiny ski resort. At Col du Bonhomme join the D415 that travels down the ever-widening valley to Kaysersberg.

Kaysersberg rivals its neighbors as being one of the most appealing towns in Alsace. Vineyards tumble down to the town from its ancient keep and 16th-century houses line narrow roads along the rushing River Weiss. **Albert Schweitzer** was born here and his house is open as a small museum. (*Open May to October, closed noon to 2 pm.*)

Leave Kaysersberg on the narrow D28 in the direction of Ribeauvillé and pass **Kinzheim**, a picture-perfect little village encircled by a high wall and surrounded by vineyards. Riquewihr, the finest walled town and a gem of Alsace, lies just a few kilometers north.

Riquewihr is completely enclosed by tall protective walls and encircled by vineyards. This picture-book village is a pedestrian area, its narrow streets lined with half-timbered houses. Signs beckon you into cobbled courtyards to sample the vintners' produce, and cafés and restaurants spill onto the streets. It is easy to understand why this picturesque spot is a magnet for visitors. If you opt to use Riquewihr as your base of explorations, we recommend the **Hôtel l'Oriel,** which is as charming as the village. The local museum is housed in the tall square stone-and-timber tower **Dolder Gate** and **Tour des Voleurs** (Thieves' Tower) which exhibits grisly instruments of torture. (*Open July and August, closed October to Easter, open weekends rest of year, closed noon to 2 pm, tel: 03.89.49.08.40.*)

Nearby **Hunawihr** boasts a much-photographed fortified church sitting on a little hill amongst the vineyards beside the village and the **Center for the Reintroduction of Storks**. Just a few years ago the roofs of the picture-book villages of Alsace were topped with shaggy storks' nests. Alas, in recent years fewer and fewer storks have returned from their winter migration to Africa and the center is dedicated to their reintroduction into the area. (*Closed November 11 to April and noon to 2 pm, tel: 03.89.73.72.62.*)

Rising behind the attractive town of **Ribeauvillé** are the three castles of Ribeaupierre, a much-photographed landmark of the region, with cars continually climbing the main street. The shady side streets with their beamed houses are quieter and contain some lovely buildings. Ribeauvillé is an ideal base from which to explore the region, and we recommend one hotel on the hillside set in the vineyards, **Le Clos Saint Vincent** and at the heart of the village and one of the finest inns in the region, the **Hostellerie des Seigneurs de Ribeaupierre**.

Continuing on the Route de Vin just a few kilometers to the north is the charming town of **Bergheim.** Protected by its walls, Bergheim lies just off the main road and is a much quieter village than many along the wine route.

Haut Koenigsbourg

Wine Country–Alsace

Continuing north from Bergheim, make a sharp left on the D1 bis at the medieval village of **Saint Hippolyte** and climb steeply up from the vineyards to **Haut Koenigsbourg**, the mighty fortress which sits high above the town. This massive castle was rather over-zealously restored by Kaiser Wilhelm II in the early part of this century to reflect his concept of what a medieval fortress should look like, complete with massive walls, towering gates, a drawbridge, a keep, a bear pit, towers, a baronial great hall, and an armory. From the walls the view of vineyards tumbling to a sky-wide patchwork of fields that stretches to the Rhine river valley is superb. On especially clear days you can see the very distant outline of the Black Forest. (*Closed in January and noon to 1pm except in summer.*)

Leave the castle in the direction of Kintzheim and turn left on the D35 for **Chatenois**. Take the narrow entry into the town square and continue straight across the busy N59 on the D35 through **Schwiler**, dominated by the ruined castles of Ortenbourg and Ramstein high on the hill above, through the vineyards to **Dieffenthal** and **Dambach la Ville** where a bear clutching a flagon of wine between its paws decorates the fountain in front of the Renaissance town hall. **Itterswiller** has its attractive houses strung along the ridge facing south to the vineyards. Here you find the **Hôtel Arnold** and the Arnold family's other enterprises including a most attractive gift shop and restaurant.

From Itterswiller the Route du Vin wanes and you may prefer to follow the well-signposted route to Strasbourg rather than continuing to the larger towns of Molsheim and Obernai before taking the A352 into Strasbourg.

Strasbourg, on the border with Germany, is one of France's largest cities and also one of its most beautiful. Set on the banks of the River Rhine where it meets the Ill, the city center is full of charm. Around its lacy pink-sandstone **Nôtre Dame Cathedral** the old quarter is filled with interesting little streets of shops, restaurants, and hotels and leads to the footbridges which span the River Ill. The nearby **Petite France** quarter, where craftsmen plied their trades in the 16th and 17th centuries, is full of old timbered houses, most notably the fine **Maison des Tanneurs** with its intricate wooden galleries. Many of the craftsmen's old workshops are now delightful restaurants. We recommend two wonderful hotels in Strasbourg, both in walking distance to the heart of the city. The **Hôtel des Rohan** is just around the corner, and the **Romantik Hôtel Beaucour** is just across the River Ill, from the cathedral.

From Strasbourg you can cross into Germany's Black Forest, journey on into Switzerland, or travel a 350-kilometer drive (four hours) on the autoroute to Reims where you can join the Champagne wine route. It is also approximately a 300-kilometer drive (three and a half hours) from Strasbourg to the heart of the Burgundy region and its capital city, Beaune.

The Heart of Old Strasbourg, Petite France

Wine Country–Alsace

Wine Country–Champagne

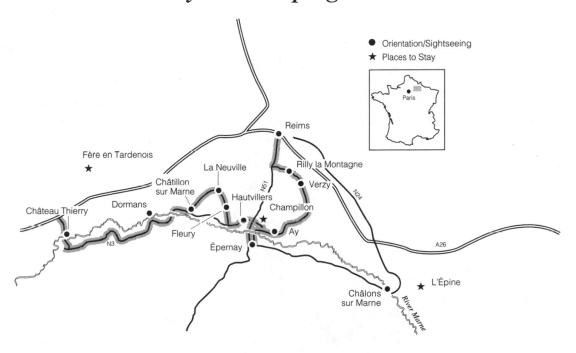

Orientation/Sightseeing
Places to Stay

Paris

Reims

Fère en Tardenois

La Neuville

Rilly la Montagne

Châtillon
sur Marne

Verzy

Hautvillers

Champillon

Château Thierry

Dormans

Fleury

Ay

Épernay

N3

N51

N24

A26

Châlons
sur Marne

L'Épine

River Marne

Wine Country–Champagne

Champagne is a small wine district dedicated to the production of the effervescent liquid that we associate with happy occasions and celebrations. The name "champagne" can be used only for the wines produced by this region's vineyards. Its capital is Reims, a not-very-attractive city due to being almost razed in World War I, but many of its buildings and its fine old Gothic cathedral have been restored. Below the city is a honeycomb of champagne cellars. Nearby lies the most important town for champagne, Épernay, where the mighty mansions of the producers alternate with their *maisons* (the term for their offices, warehouses, cellars, and factories). The vineyards are south of Reims, along the valley of the Marne. It is not particularly beautiful countryside, just gentle slopes facing towards the sun, interspersed with workaday villages that offer opportunities for sampling, but few tourist facilities such as cafés, restaurants, or shops.

Épernay, Mercier Champagne Cellar

Recommended Pacing: Our Champagne itinerary covers a very small geographic area. Two or three nights at one location should afford all the time you need for exploring this region and sampling its bounty.

Unlike Burgundy, the quality of champagne is not derived solely from the area but also from the manufacturing process. It is the dose of sugar or "bead" that makes the bubbles, and the smaller the bead, the better the champagne. The essence of champagne is the blending of several different grapes; a branded wine, it is known by the maker and not by the vineyard. There are three distinct zones in the 55,000 acres in Champagne: the *Montagne de Reims*, the *Vallée de la Marne*, and *Côte des Blancs*. This itinerary visits the champagne houses in Reims and Épernay and drives round the Mountain of Reims and along the Valley of the Marne before returning you to Paris.

This journey begins in **Reims**, once the capital of France (4th to 9th centuries) and now one of the capitals of the Champagne district. The **Nôtre Dame Cathedral** dates from the 12th century and is where the kings of France used to be crowned (follow signs for *Centre Ville*). Begun in 1211, it is one of the oldest examples of Gothic architecture in France, and while it suffered heavy damage in World War I, it was beautifully restored in 1938. Traffic around the cathedral is terribly congested.

You may want to save your cellar tours until Épernay, but if you like to visit a house in each city, several invite you to come by without appointment. While the basic procedures and methods used to produce champagne are similar, the grand names for champagne all have their own history and interesting stories to tell. Tours are available in English and take about an hour. Except in July and August the houses are usually closed between 11:30 am and 2 pm.

Mumm, 34 Rue de Champ de Mar, offers a film, guided tour of the cellars, and tasting. (*Closed 11 am to 2 pm and weekends in winter, tel: 03.26.49.59.70, fax: 03.26.40.46.13.*)

At **Piper-Hiedsieck**, 51 Blvd. Henry Vasnier, visitors tour the galleries in six-passenger cars that take you on a Disney-like tour of the cellars with giant dioramas of grapes and interesting explanations on the production of champagne from harvest to disgorging.

(*Closed Tuesdays and Wednesdays in winter, tel: 03.26.84.43.00, fax: 03.26.84.43.49.*)

Pommery, 5 Place du Général Gourard, offers a film, guided tour of the cellars, and tasting. (*Open all year, closed weekends in winter, tel: 03.26.61.62.63, fax: 03.26.61.63.98.*)

Tattinger, 9 Place Saint-Nicaise, offers a film, guided tour of the cellars, and tasting. (*Open all year, closed weekends in winter, tel: 03.26.85.45.35, fax: 03.26.85.17.46.*)

Leave Reims in the direction of Épernay (N51). After leaving the suburbs and light industrial areas behind, when you're amongst the fields and vineyards take the first left turn signposted **Route du Champagne** which charts a very pleasant horseshoe-shaped drive around the **Montagne de Reims** to Épernay. Above, the vineyards end in woodlands and below, they cascade to the vast plain, the scene of so much fighting during World War I.

Faux de Verzy

The first small village you come to on the D26 is **Villers Allerand**, which leads you to **Rilly la Montagne**, a larger village which offers the opportunity for a stroll and a drink in a café as well as the chance to sip champagne. As you drive along, look for the peculiar-looking tractors with their high bodies and wheels set at a width that enables them to pass through the rows of vines and meander down the little lanes.

As the route nears **Mailly Champagne** and **Verzy**, you pass some of the most superior vineyards for the production of champagne grapes. The picturesque windmill, found between the two villages, was used as an observation post during World War I.

The wine route rounds the mountain at Verzy where a short detour up into the woodlands brings you to **Faux de Verzy**, an unusual forest of gnarled, stunted, and twisted beech trees hundreds of years old. Return to Verzy and continue along the D26, turning south through **Villers Marmery**, **Trépail**, and **Ambonnay** to **Bouzy**, a community famous not only for its champagne grapes but also for its red wine. At Bouzy the wine route splits and our route follows signposts into nearby Épernay.

Traffic is much less of a problem in **Épernay** than Reims. While much of the damage has been repaired, there are still several scars from the severe bombing that Épernay suffered in World War I. Follow signposts for *Centre Ville* and particularly *Office de Tourisme,* which brings you to your destination in this sprawling town, the Rue de Champagne, a long street lined with the *maisons* (offices, warehouses, factories, cellars) and mansions of the premier champagne producers Möet et Chandon, Perrier Jouët, Charbaut, De Venoge Pol Roger, and Mercier.

Try to allow time to take both the Möet et Chandon and Mercier cellar tours. **Möet et Chandon**, founded in 1743, is across the street from the tourist office. They offer a very sophisticated tour of their visitors' center (where Napoleon's hat is displayed), a walk through one of the largest champagne cellars in the world, and an excellent explanation on how champagne is made. (*Open all year, tel: 03.26.51.20.00, fax: 03.26.54.84.23.*)

Just as the Rue de Champagne leaves behind its grand mansions, you come to **Mercier's** modern visitors' center where the world's largest wine cask sits center stage. Holding the equivalent of 200,000 bottles of champagne, it was made to advertise Mercier at the World Trade Fair in Paris in 1889 and proved as great an attraction as the Eiffel Tower. Houses that interrupted its progress to Paris had to be razed. Mercier's tour gives you an upbeat movie history of Mercier champagne, then whisks you down to the galleries in a glass-sided elevator past a diorama of the founders ballooning over their estate. An electric train weaves you through the vast cellars past some interesting carvings and boundless bottles of bubbly. (*Open all year, closed Tuesdays and Wednesdays, December to March, tel: 03.26.51.22.22, fax: 03.26.55.12.63.*)

Set in the imposing 19th-century Château Perrier behind tall wrought-iron gates, **Musée du Champagne et de la Préhistoire**, 13 Rue de Champagne, has interesting exhibits of maps, tools, wine labels, and bottles. (*Closed December to March, and Tuesdays, tel: 03.26.51.90.31.*)

Leaving Épernay, follow signposts for Reims until you see the Route de Champagne signpost to both the left and right. Turn left to **Ay** and follow the route along the Vallée de la Marne to **Hautvillers**, the prettiest of Champagne's villages with its spic-and-span homes and broad swatch of cobbles decorating the center of its streets. It was in the village basilica that Dom Perignon performed his miracle and discovered how to make still wine sparkling by the *méthode champenoise*. He also introduced the use of cork stoppers (tied down to stop them from popping out as pressure built up in the bottles) and blended different wines from around the region to form a wine with a superior character than that produced by a single vineyard. The abbey is now owned by Möet et Chandon and contains a private museum. However, you can enjoy the lovely view of the valley from the abbey terrace.

From Hautvillers descend through the vineyards to **Cumièrs**, a workaday village known for its red wine, and on to **Damery** with its pretty 12th- and 16th-century church. Climbing through vineyards, you have lovely views across the River Marne to the villages and vineyards strung along the opposite bank.

Hautvillers

Pass through **Venteul** and **Arty** and on to the more attractive village of **Fleury** which offers tasting in the large building decorated with murals. As you climb through pretty countryside to **Belval**, vineyards give way to fields. Passing through woodland, you come to **La Neuville aux Larris** with its enormous champagne bottle sitting next to the church, and return to the River Marne at **Châtillon-sur-Marne**. A huge statue overlooking the river proclaims this village as the birthplace of Pope Urban II.

At **Verneuil** cross the river and continue on the N3 into **Dormans** which saw fierce fighting in World War I and was badly damaged. Set in a large green park, the **Chapelle de la Reconnaissance** (Chapel of Gratitude) commemorates those killed in the battles of the Marne in 1914 and 1918 and offers splendid views over the valley. You can quickly return to Épernay on the N3 or continue to Paris via **Château Thierry** set on the River Marne against a lovely wooded backdrop. The English claimed the town as theirs in 1421, then Joan of Arc recaptured it for France. The gates through which she entered the city still stand—**Porte Saint Pierre**. Napoleon defended the city against Russian and Prussian troops in 1814.

Wine Country–Champagne

Traveling the
Countryside by Train

★ Suggested overnight stops
○ Train connections
● Sightseeing
⌂ Châteaux
Rail route
Side trips
Access by car or bike

Giverny
Vernon
PARIS
Strasbourg
Colmar
Besançon
Saumur
Tours
Blois
Amboise
Beaune
Périgueux
Les Eyzies
Lyon
Agen
Avignon
Arles
Nice
Carcassonne

Traveling the Countryside by Train

Traveling by train is an attraction in its own right—I love the anticipation when a train pulls away from a station, departing for a new adventure. Train travel provides the opportunity to sit back in comfort, relax without the hassle and burden of traffic or map-reading, and enjoy a continually changing panorama of passing scenery. This itinerary, designed for those who want to experience the French countryside but are hesitant to venture out on their own by car, covers a wide sweep of France, with Paris as a point of origin. It starts with a side trip to Giverny, then travels first to the Loire Valley, on to the Dordogne, includes a stop in the magical walled town of Carcassonne, continues on to the heart of Provence, suggests a side excursion to the Riviera, follows the passage of the Rhone north to Burgundy, and then moves on to the German border and the region of Alsace, with the option of circling back to Paris.

Carcassonne

In choosing destinations for this itinerary, I took into account not only the appeal of the town itself, but also, since it was to be used as a base for exploration with limited transportation options, how representative it was of a given region, the convenience of train schedules and connections, and the proximity of the train station to sightseeing and recommended accommodations. I selected destinations that are truly in the country, not just the easily accessible large towns and cities: anyone who travels in France, regardless of means of transportation, deserves to know her lovely countryside.

This sojourn by train was designed to provide an enjoyable and anxiety-free experience, easing the burden and hassle of travel without making you feel as if going by train limited or compromised the "countryside experience." For those traveling with children, the luxury of space and the ability to move around, dining cars, observation cars, even some "playroom" cars, offer more appealing conditions than being confined to seat belts in a car.

Not being a seasoned rail traveler, I felt it important to travel this itinerary myself, so that I could better convey to you the experience. I traveled alone, on a first-class Eurailpass ticket, always by day, and felt completely comfortable and safe in the stations, on the trains, and getting to and from my selected hotel or sightseeing. I honestly felt safer than when I travel alone by car—I was never alone, never lost by my own misdirection, or fearful of being stranded on a country road. I opted not to travel at night on my own, but night travel might appeal to some as it eliminates the need for overnight accommodation, allowing you to cover miles as you sleep and effectively adding to your sightseeing hours. If traveling at night, however, you would need to be concerned for the security of your belongings while you sleep. If you are uncomfortable with neighboring companions, the conductor will always assist you in relocating, space being available. On the other hand, if the train is full, there is reassurance and safety in numbers. I found travel by train extremely efficient, being able to turn hours normally spent behind the wheel into an opportunity to work on my computer, catch up on needed sleep, relax, and simply enjoy what seemed a continually changing canvas.

GENERAL INFORMATION ON TRAIN TRAVEL IN FRANCE

In preparation for your train trip in France, following are some basic practical information, tips based on my own experiences.

TRAINS, TICKETS, AND RESERVATIONS

The French Railway system has three main categories of trains: *Trains à Grande Vitesse,* colloquially and very proudly referred to as the T.G.V., intercity trains, referred to as *express* or *rapide* trains, and local trains, the *autotrains*.

You can obtain information and purchase tickets for point-to-point travel in the United States from either your travel agent or Rail Europe, and in France at agencies that display the S.N.C.F. (French Railway Network) logo in their windows or at train stations—ticket offices in most towns' stations are open from 5:30 am to midnight and 24 hours in some cities such as Paris. You might also consider purchasing the S.N.C.F. *Ville à Ville* timetable (available at most newsstands and stations in France) which details many of the main-line and important international services, or my bible, the *Thomas Cook European Timetable* (available in bookstores), which provides train schedules both in France and throughout Europe. The Thomas Cook guide is invaluable for working out your many options for connections, routings, and schedules. I found it extremely important to **always** double-check published times as schedules do change, however slightly. Note: Train schedules are published and referenced using a 24-hour clock: for example, 1620 is the equivalent of 4:20 pm.

Tickets are available for either first or second class and on a one-way or round-trip basis. First-class travel costs approximately 50% more than second class, and you usually pay a premium for faster, more direct trains. During the prime summer months, fewer people will travel first class and so the minimized hassle of finding a seat might well be worth the additional cost.

It is always advantageous to pre-purchase a round-trip ticket to avoid standing in line for a ticket on the return, but know that there are no cost savings until the trip exceeds 1,000 kilometers. A point-to-point ticket does not restrict you to a specific date or time of travel: as long as you are traveling between two points you can get off and on the train, even over a period of a few days, provided you continue on to the final destination on the same route.

Point-to-point travel is expensive, so if you are going to travel much at all by train you might want to consider a rail pass as opposed to individually purchased tickets. The France Rail'n Drive Pass affords three days of unlimited train travel and two days' use of an Avis car within a one-month period. The cost per person (based on an economy car) is offered in either first class or second class, with an option available to purchase six additional rail days and additional car days (based on an economy car). Note: The France Rail 'n Drive Pass might prove the ideal package for anyone following this itinerary as a car from any of the recommended destinations would afford the opportunity for a personal venture deeper into the countryside. France is also one of 17 countries that recognizes the Eurailpass. Available only for first-class travel, passes may be purchased for unlimited travel for periods of 15 days, 21 days, one month, two months, and three months. If you are not traveling alone, look into the savings available with a Saverpass that is priced per person and is valid for 15, 21, 30, 60, and 90 days when you are traveling with at least one other person—children ages 4 to 11 travel for half the adult fare and children under 4 travel free. Flexipasses allow you to travel for any 10 or 15 days within a two-month period. If you are going to spend any time in Paris we also recommend the Paris Visite card which affords unlimited travel for 2, 3 or 5 consecutive days anywhere in Paris (bus and metro) in the greater Paris region (RER and SNCF), including the Paris airports and bonuses such as museum and Seine cruise discounts. These passes are not available in Europe and must be purchased in the United States through your travel agent or Rail Europe. (*Rail Europe: tel: 800-438-7245 or 888-382-7245; from Canada, tel: 800-361-7245. Website: www.raileurope.com.*)

Neither a pass nor a regular ticket guarantees a seat reservation. Whether or not to secure seat reservations in advance poses the same question we address concerning hotel reservations—do you want to be tied to a specific train and departure time and date or do you want to be footloose and travel on a whim? If you are traveling during the peak summer months or during holiday periods, it would be prudent to make reservations in advance for all your travel or you might find yourself perched on a suitcase between compartments. There is a charge for making seat reservations—approximately $11 per seat if purchased in the United States and less if purchased in Europe closer to travel time. Seat reservations for a train can be made only 60 days prior to the travel date, up to 8 pm if the departure is between midnight and 5 pm or up to noon for trains leaving that same day between 5 pm and midnight. Rail Europe can best advise you if reservations are recommended for various routes or periods of travel. It is important to note that reservations are obligatory on some trains in France, specifically the T.G.V. (*Trains à Grande Vitesse*), France's high-speed trains, and the T.E.E. (*Trans Europa Express*).

Reservations are also necessary for overnight sleeping accommodations in *couchettes* or *voiture-lits*. A *couchette* provides an open bunk equipped with sheet, blanket, and pillow in a compartment of four (first class) to six (second class) bunks (top bunks without the restriction of arm rests are a bit more commodious). True luxury is a *voiture-lit,* or sleeping car, which offers more privacy, available in both single and double occupancy, with self-contained washing facilities and the attention of one conductor per coach or train car. You pay a supplemental charge to any rail pass for sleeping cars and couchettes and, assuming availability, can make reservations up to two hours before departure.

LUGGAGE

It is imperative to travel with minimal luggage to minimize both the physical burden and the chore of storing and looking after it. My recommendation is, ideally, to take one manageable suitcase per person and to use the luggage on wheels or luggage carriers. For safety reasons, smaller quantities are easier to keep track of and with you at all times, and it is also convenient having your luggage at hand when you need that extra sweater or toiletries when you want to freshen up.

By traveling light, walking the kilometer or so to your hotel won't seem unbearable and will allow you to save on cab or bus fare.

If you are simply sightseeing at a given destination and continuing on elsewhere by train that same day, you might want to consider storing your luggage at the station. One option is to check luggage with an attendant at a depot (these facilities are usually open from 5 am to midnight), the other is to store left luggage in self-serve lockers that allow you to retrieve it at any time.

AT THE STATION

Train departure and arrival schedules are posted in the main lobby of stations on elevated boards, referencing each train by its assigned number (sometimes by name in the case of Trans-European trains), its platform (*quai*), and the time of arrival or departure. Announcements over the loudspeaker are clear but often only in French unless you are in the largest of cities such as Paris or Marseilles, although more and more stations, both in towns and cities, are installing computerized multi-lingual information units.

If you are not traveling on a pass, you definitely want to purchase your ticket before boarding as otherwise a substantial surcharge will be levied by the ticket inspector on board. Tickets can be purchased by cash or most major credit cards (Visa, MasterCard, and American Express). As there are no longer inspectors on the platforms for validating tickets, you are entrusted and required to validate your ticket yourself at an orange machine, *consignés automatiques* (the main ticket as well as the reservation voucher) before boarding. You are liable to pay a fine to the conductor on the train if your ticket is not validated in advance. Rail passes cannot be validated by the machine, so you are required to have the pass validated at a ticket counter at the station before you use it for the first trip, then with any flexi-pass, each time you use a day of travel, before boarding the train, write the date in one of the boxes in sequential order and in the European fashion, for example, 11-05-00 to indicate May 11, 2000. However, you must validate any supplemental fare tickets or reservations in conjunction with the rail pass vouchers at the automatic machine. All issued tickets are valid for two months but once they are validated the journey must be commenced within 24 hours of validation. Point-to-point tickets and seat reservations bought in the USA **do not** need to be validated before boarding the train.

When you reach your platform, reconfirm that you are on the correct one by checking the posted sign announcing the next train. For the more regularly scheduled trains there will often be a chart showing where the train's cars will be positioned once it has come to a stop—this is particularly helpful if you have reservations and are assigned to a specific car but only have a few minutes to board, so that you can be waiting at the appropriate spot—it is easier to negotiate luggage down the length of the platform than through moving cars on the train. One note of caution: At all times be careful to stand behind the yellow line on the platform as it is not unusual for a high-speed train, not scheduled for a stop, to careen through the station.

ON THE TRAIN

If you haven't reserved a specific seat, simply select a car (smoking or non-smoking) with your final destination posted on the outside (various cars are added or dropped during the course of a journey) and settle into an unreserved seat. An assigned seat will be tagged as reserved, *reservé*, or with the span of passage that it has been reserved for, for example, *Beaune–Lyon*.

Except for late night to early morning, some trains will have a dining car and most will have a buffet-bar. Published timetables as well as the station directory will detail the type of meal service or bar service available. The dining car serves full-course meals while light snacks, hot and cold sandwiches, candies, juices, sodas, and alcoholic beverages can be purchased in the buffet car. There are also carts stocked with coffee, sodas, snacks, etc. which are rolled periodically through the train. If a dining car is not available on a T.G.V., you can order meals in advance to be served to you at your seat by a steward during traditional mealtimes or, if extra meals are available, you can arrange with the steward to purchase a meal on board. Although on a train, you are traveling in France and meals, although not necessarily good value, are definitely gourmet. Note: Advance meal reservations can be made through Rail Europe, but are paid for on board.

Another option when a dining car is not available or if you are economizing would be to pack a picnic meal. A croissant, brioche, loaf of French bread, cheese, pâté, and fruit are French staples and readily available—they can often even be purchased at the kiosk or bar in the station. Since drinking water is not available from the train's water supply, you might want to purchase some bottled water or beverages before boarding the train. Picnicking on board is fun and quite common.

EXCURSION: PARIS TO VERNON (GIVERNY)

Before you embark on this itinerary's first leg to the Loire Valley, I suggest you take a day trip to **Vernon** in Normandy to visit **Monet's** magnificent home and gardens at **Giverny**. I would recommend an early departure from Paris for Vernon in order to have a leisurely visit of Giverny and return to the city before nightfall. (Note that you will be departing from and returning to the Gare Saint Lazare, one of Paris's six train stations.)

dep: Paris (Gare Saint Lazare) 0816, 1043 or 1200
arr: Vernon (Eure) 0902, 1122 or 1245

Upon arrival in Vernon you can either take a taxi, bus, or bike to travel the approximately 3 kilometers from the station to Monet's home, Giverny. Walking is a bit difficult and dangerous as the roads are not well marked and have no sidewalks. There are usually numerous cabs sitting in front of the station—if you take a cab to Giverny, ask for a phone contact so that you can call them for the return to Vernon. There is also a bus that travels the distance in about ten minutes on the following schedule:

Vernon to Giverny, Tuesday through Saturday: departs 0915, 1315, 1520, 1640
  Sunday: departs 1053, 1135, 1445

Giverny to Vernon: Tuesday through Saturday: departs 1212, 1412, 1517, 1600
  Sunday: departs 1470, 1715

The more energetic can rent a bike at the station. Rentals are available from concession window 6 at a cost of 55 francs per day, and a security deposit of 1000 francs. There are only a dozen or so bikes available and in the season they are in great demand so it is advisable to reserve one in advance by calling the Vernon train station, tel: 02.32.51.01.72.

Monet's home is open from the beginning of April to the end of October. Another more recent attraction to Giverny and opened just 200 meters from Monet's home is the **Musée d'Art Américan** featuring work of American artists influenced by the Impressionist period. For more information refer to the Normandy itinerary, pages 17 and 18.

New to this additition is a wonderful inn tucked in the orchards literally in the hills above Monet's home. **La Réserve** is spectacular and wonderfully adds a new dimention to your options. One can truly walk or bike the few kilometers up the hill (turn at the Charcuterie) and settle in at La Réserve before returning to Paris and the continuation of this itinerary. See the hotel description section for more information.

When you decide to return to Paris in the early to late afternoon, you might want to consider the following schedules:

dep: Vernon 1453, 1536, 1734, or 1914

arr: Paris (Gare Saint Lazare) 1542, 1651, 1827, or 2009

PARIS TO TOURS

From Paris there are two options for traveling to Tours and the heart of the Loire Valley. If you want to travel on the ultimate, fast train, the T.G.V., you leave from Gare de Montparnasse and arrive in Tours' relatively new station, Saint Pierre des Corps. You then have to take a connecting train the short distance on to Tours' old station. Alternatively, you can travel on a traditional train from the Gare d'Austerlitz directly to Tours without changing at Saint Pierre. The following are some suggested timetables:

Traveling by T.G.V. from the Montparnasse station (reservations obligatory):

dep: Paris 0900 (T.G.V.), 1215 (T.G.V.), or 1525 (T.G.V.)

arr: Saint Pierre des Corps 0955, 1316, or 1621

arr: (by connecting train) Tours 1005, 1326, or 1641

Traveling by regular train from the Austerlitz station:

dep: Paris 1108, 1339, or 1600

arr: Tours 1353, 1622, or 1810

Tours, the capital of the Loire Valley, is almost overwhelming when approached by car since it is large and industrial on its outskirts and parking at the center is difficult. However, when you arrive by train at its heart, it appears to be a lovely old town, easily explored on foot and quite safe. The station is especially lovely and has beautiful murals depicting regional attractions. Here you find a welcome and exchange bureau, a large display map for locating hotels, and a bike rental office. A large expanse of park fronts the station and to the right as you exit, on the other side of Boulevard Heurteloup, is the tourist office.

Prepare yourself with a map from the tourist office and chart a course through the winding cobbled streets of the old district, along the river front, to the lovely old **Cathédral Saint Gatien**, the **Musée de Beaux Arts**, and the unique **Trade Guild Museum** which has on exhibit archives and historical masterpieces of the trades of the *Compagnons du Tour de France*. It is the only museum of its kind in the world. The medieval streets at the heart of the old town are wonderfully shadowed by timbered buildings and open to inviting plazas set with sidewalk cafés. There are over 90 restaurants in the old town and menu prices seem very reasonable compared with Paris.

You could not be more central for exploring the **Loire Valley** than with Tours as a base. However, although hotels in Tours are numerous, I found nothing exceptional. For the purposes of this itinerary, I recommend the **Hôtel du Manoir**, a nice small hotel within walking distance of the station as well as old Tours.

Another option which requires just a bit more travel is to journey by train northwest from Tours to **Amboise** (20 minutes). Amboise hugs the river's edge and is a charming town with lots of shops and a wonderful château in whose shadow sits a recently opened hotel, **Le Manoir les Minimes**, once a beautiful home. This would serve as an ideal and convenient base from which to explore the region.

You could also take advantage of the train/car packages through Rail Europe and rent a car in Tours for a few days to explore the châteaux at your own pace and select from one of the numerous inns or bed and breakfasts recommended in the region.

With Tours as a base, you can readily make a few excursions by train. It is an easy journey from Tours to **Saumur** (40 minutes) with its impressive château dominating this riverside city at the junction of the Thouet and the Loire. The train station is located on the opposite side of the river from the heart of town, but you can either walk the few kilometers or catch a local bus. From Saumur you can then continue the journey on to **Angers** (another 25 minutes on from Saumur). Although this is a large modern city, the capital of the ancient province of Anjou, the train station is within walking distance of its remarkably untouched medieval core, its magnificent 13th-century fortress, and the splendid **Cathédral Saint Maurice**. Regal **Blois,** full of history and intrigue, located one hour away to the northwest, is a city not to be missed.

Tours itself is manageable on foot but you also might want to consider exploring the nearby vicinity and neighboring châteaux by bike. Daily rentals are available at the train station or inquire at the tourist office for the few other independent operations in town. The tourist office also publishes a suggested routing along countryside roads that weaves a journey to various châteaux.

Another option for leisurely exploring the châteaux would be to take a bus tour. Departures by large coach leave from just in front of the train station and by mini-van in front of the tourist office. Information on the various companies and their offerings is available from the tourist office, as is almost any other information you might desire on the region. (*Tours Tourist Office—Accueil de France, 78 Rue Bernard-Palissy, B.P. 4201, 37042 Tours Cedex, tel: 02.47.70.37.37, fax: 02.47.61.14.22, open all year except a few holidays, hours vary according to the season.*) For more detailed information on the various châteaux refer to the Châteaux Country itinerary, beginning on page 35.

TOURS TO LES EYZIES

Approximately four hours to the south and parallel to the Loire Valley is one of my favorite regions in France, the **Dordogne**. This area is beautiful, with a rich and varied landscape studded with numerous chateaux and cut by the wide sweeping path of the River Dordogne. With a fertile soil that produces the incomparable truffle and farms that raise geese and market the culinary gold, *foie gras*, this is a region not limited to its beauty or its gourmet delights—it is also considered the prehistoric capital of the world. As with the Loire Valley, you might opt to take advantage of the car/rail package with Rail Europe to explore the region in great depth (refer  to *Dordogne & Lot River Valleys*, beginning on page 45) or let this itinerary simply deliver you to the heart of the prehistoric capital, Les Eyzies de Tayac.

To reach Les Eyzies from Tours, you can travel either via Vierzon or via Perigueux.

Option 1:

dep: Tours 0843, 1203, or 1547
arr: Vierzon 0950, 1315, or 1656
dep: Vierzon 1046, 1440, or 1737
arr: Les Eyzies 1434, 1638, or 1925

Option 2:

Take the connecting shuttle: Tours to Saint Pierre des Corps (dep: 0921)
dep: Saint Pierre des Corps 1038
arr: Angouleme 1159
dep: Angouleme: 1222
arr: Coutras 1308
dep: Coutras 1421
arr: Perigueux 1515
dep: Perigueux 1721 or 1855
arr: Les Eyzies 1756 or 1925

Traveling the Countryside by Train

The one-platform train station on the edge of **Les Eyzies** is more of a depot and literally just steps away from a lovely, family-run, country hotel, the **Cro-Magnon**. With the Cro-Magnon as a base you can visit the prehistoric museum whose statue of Cro-Magnon man stands guard over this small but bustling town, then walk to the opposite edge of town to visit some of the world's most famous caves. **Font de Gaum** and **Les Combarelles**, with their prehistoric drawings and etchings, are some of the few last remaining caves still open to the public and the daily number of visitors is limited to protect and preserve the ancient artwork. Reservations can be made by contacting the tourist office in Les Eyzies, tel: 05.53.06.90.80. (For more information refer to page 49, the Dordogne & Lot itinerary.)

LES EYZIES TO CARCASSONNE

This is a lovely train journey that sweeps across the southern part of France to the dramatic medieval fortress of **Carcassonne**. Rising high above the vineyards at the foot of the Cevennes and the Pyrenees, Europe's largest fortress is visible in the distance as the train slows down on the approach to the station and town in the shadow of the ramparts. (See p. 64 for more description.)

dep: Les Eyzies 1435 or 1756
arr: Agen 1614 or 1937
dep: Agen 1738 or 1944
arr: Carcassonne 1941 or 2152

Although it is just 3 kilometers from the station to the walled town, even the most adventurous must consider that it is also a steep climb, especially when burdened by luggage. A taxi will deliver you to the wall's entrance, and from there it is necessary to continue on foot. If you decide to stay at the elegant **Hôtel de la Cité**, or the more reasonably priced, **Hôtel Donjon**, either hotel will send a van, usually parked just inside the entrance, that will transport you and your luggage to their doorstep. If contacted in advance, they will arrange to meet your train on your arrival. The vans run periodically back and forth from the plaza to the hotel. If you have minimal luggage and do not want to wait for the van, it is just a short, five-minute walk to the hotel—walk straight through to the other side of the village to the outer ramparts where the hotel is located next to the cathedral. When it is time for your return trip, arrangements can be made for a van to take you directly to the station. A taxi fare cost me approximately 40 francs one way.

CARCASSONNE TO ARLES

It is an easy train ride direct to Arles continuing through the southern countryside of France. The architecture in this region is greatly influenced by its southern neighbor, with buildings of sun-washed tile and terra cotta very reminiscent of the Mediterranean. You will know when you have reached Arles, without needing to read the signs, as the station walls display an impressive mural of black on stucco—a lovely artistic introduction to the tradition and character of the Camargue with the portrayal of bullfighters and the festival of which Arlesians are fiercely proud.

dep: Carcassonne 0955, 1055, or 1219
arr: Narbonne 1018, 1205, or 1246
dep: Narbonne 1020 or 1249
arr: Arles 1210 or 1450

Arles is one of Provence's beauties and a wonderful monument to the days of old Rome. In a peaceful riverside setting, the town with its arenas, theaters, and museums within the walls is intimate in size and quite easy to explore on foot. The train station of Arles is just minutes from Porte de la Cavalerie, one of the entrances to the old walled town. If you are staying at the **Hôtel d'Arlatan** or the **Grand Hôtel Nord-Pinus**, it is just a five- to ten-minute walk to either along cobbled streets, and the hotels are well signposted from the moment you pass through the gate. If you are staying at the **Jules César**, the distance again is not very far—maybe five minutes more—but you might want to opt for a taxi as it is located on the periphery of the old town and a busier road. A note of

Traveling the Countryside by Train

caution about the uneven, cobbled streets: You definitely want to avoid high-heeled shoes and should have luggage with sturdy wheels and, as stressed previously, very little of it. The tourist office has an office right at the station that is open every day except Sundays. For more information on Arles, refer to the Provence itinerary, page 65.

ARLES TO AVIGNON

There are trains that travel frequently back and forth between Arles and **Avignon**, cities that, although both rich in Roman history, enjoy their own character and style. In the morning or early evening you will be in the company of businessmen or children commuting to and from jobs or school. The Avignon station is, like that in Arles, conveniently just outside the entrance to the walled citadel. Avignon is, however, a larger city, evidenced by the size of the station and the loiterers.

If you like to settle at one hotel for several nights, you could use either Arles or Avignon as a base from which to explore either town since it is just about a 20-minute rail journey between the two. Below are train schedules for both Arles to Avignon and the return, in case you choose to travel back and forth between the two in the course of the day.

dep: Arles 0932, 1324, or 1507
arr: Avignon 0949, 1343, or 1524

dep: Avignon 1051, 1443, or 1630
arr: Arles 1110, 1236, or 1725

If you decide to base yourself in Avignon, with minimal luggage, it is feasible to walk to either the **Hôtel d'Europe** or **La Mirande** from the station in no more than 15 minutes. Directions are to cross over from the station and enter through the Porte de la République and go right up through town on the Rue de la République. Turn left on Rue Saint Agricole and then right on Rue J. Vernet to the Place de Crillon for the **Hôtel d'Europe**, or continue on through the central Place de l'Horloge and on to the Palace of the Popes. The cobbled street that winds around behind the Palace to its right-hand side takes you to the doorstep of **La Mirande**. If you have lots of luggage, you can also journey by taxi. For more information refer to the Provence itinerary, pages 65–78.

SIDE TRIP TO THE RIVIERA: AVIGNON TO NICE

Being just a few hours away by train from the legendary **French Riviera**, I did not want to continue our journey north along the Rhone Valley to Burgundy without mentioning the possibility of a side trip to **Nice**. If you decide to visit the Riviera, I would recommend renting a car in conjunction with your train travel in order to venture beyond the cosmopolitan city and explore the coastal villages and wonderful medieval *villages perchés*. Refer to *Hilltowns of the French Riviera*, beginning on page 85, for more sightseeing suggestions.

Depending on your schedule, if you need to conclude your trip on the Riviera, you can easily journey directly back to Paris from Nice (the T.G.V. conveniently travels this route), or you can depart from the international airport for home or other destinations within Europe. I have included suggested timetables for traveling to Nice from Avignon, and then from Nice back to Lyon, should you wish to rejoin the continuation of this itinerary, or on to Paris if this is the conclusion of your travels.

Journey from Avignon to Nice to spend time on the Riviera:

dep: Avignon 1051, 1157, 1403, or 1502
arr: Nice 1436, 1533, 1750, or 1845

Journey from Nice back to Avignon to explore Provence:

dep: Nice 0925 (TGV) or 1842
arr: Avignon 1254 or 2242

When ready, journey from the Riviera back to Paris via Lyon:

dep: Nice 0952 (T.G.V.) or 1256 (TGV)
arr: Paris, Gare de Lyon 1624 or 1922

AVIGNON TO LYON

Elegant and grand, Lyon seems almost as large as Paris: if driving, you must be armed with maps studied well in advance and have a patient and forgiving companion and navigator, so it is particularly relaxing to arrive by train.

dep: Avignon 0731 (T.G.V.), 1014, or 1426
arr: Lyon Part Dieu 0908, 1215, or 1603

Lyon has two stations, Lyon Perrache and Lyon Part Dieu, both servicing the T.G.V. and both situated almost 4 kilometers from the wonderful hotels we recommend at the heart of Vieux Lyon, the **Cour des Loges** and the **La Villa Florentine**. Either hotel will send someone to meet you when provided in advance with the number of your train car (*voiture*) and arrival time. The luxury of assistance right where you disembark from your

train is most welcome in a station that is almost a city in its own right with shops, banks, restaurants, etc. Taxis are also readily available outside the stations (it costs approximately 55 francs to Vieux Lyon from either one). However, the pedestrian streets of Vieux Lyon are a bit hard to negotiate and might frustrate even the most aggressive cab driver—you might find yourself dropped a few blocks from the hotel.

LYON TO BEAUNE

There do not seem to be many trains that travel directly between Lyon and Beaune. Besides the few suggested trains below, other connection options are to travel to Chalons sur Saône and then connect to Beaune or overshoot Beaune to the more frequently serviced Dijon and then take one of the many connecting trains back.

dep: Lyon Part Dieu 1357, 1744, or 2150
arr: Beaune 1536, 1905, or 2326

Beaune continues to be one of my favorite towns. The station, although off the town's Michelin map in the red guide, is just outside the city walls on the east side and it took me just ten minutes to walk to the town's center. Catering to the many visitors that journey to this beautiful capital of Burgundy, there are many signs for the city center and streets are easy to travel, most with good sidewalks. We recommend two hotels in Beaune, the **Hôtel le Cep** and the **Hôtel de la Poste** both on the southern perimeter beyond the city center (approximately 15 to 20 minutes on foot). Should you decide not to walk, cabs are also readily available at the station, at a cost of around 30 francs.

Beaune, a wonderful town to settle in for a while, has fine old buildings, sophisticated shops, cobbled streets, and delightful squares, with the prosperity it has enjoyed as a wine-making center over many centuries reflected in its beautiful homes and the richness of its architecture. Even if you never venture beyond the walls of the town, once home to the Dukes of Burgundy, with its gorgeous **Hôtel Dieu**, **Église Notre Dame**, and the

Musée du Vin de Bourgogne housed in the Hôtel des Ducs de Bourgogne, you will leave with a true feeling for Burgundy.

There are also many local vineyards represented in Beaune offering samples of their wine. If the tastings serve to tease rather than satisfy the palate, know there are lots of options should you decide to venture into the countryside to travel the scenic **wine routes**. Monsieur Epailly, tour company owner, conducts small groups in vans to surrounding regions. Tours depart every day (May through October) from outside the Hôtel Dieu (tourist office at city center) or with prior arrangements he will gladly pick you up from any hotel in Beaune. I was told that just a few days' notice were sufficient to reserve a spot on a tour during season. Tours are also available November through April, but by reservation only. Tours offered are Number 1: the north Côte de Beaune; Number 2: the south Côte de Beaune and Haute Côte de Beaune; or Number 3: the Côte de Nuits and Haute Côte de Nuits. The owner's personal favorite is Number 2—a  wonderful blend of wine towns, old villages, and wine. Monsieur Epailly, Safari Tours, can be contacted in France, tel: 03.80.24.79.12, 03.80.24.09.20 or fax: 03.80.22.49.49, or through H.S.A. Voyages in the United States, tel: (800) 927-4765, fax: (817) 483-7000.

Another memorable adventure is to travel the vineyards by horse-drawn carriage. The man in charge of the operation is Monsieur Barbeillon of Dili Voyage, who can be contacted for reservations and information through the Agence de Tourisme, 10 Ave. de la Republique, 21200 Beaune, tel: 03.80.24.24.82, fax: 03.80.24.24.94. Monsieur Barbeillon offers three circuits during the day, leisurely traveled by carriage, and you can either pack a picnic or dine at a restaurant of your choice when he stops in the little towns. His carriages depart for a half-day excursion (0930 to 1800), with a group of at least six persons, from the Square des Lions and travel either the Circuit Hautes Côtes on Tuesdays, the Circuit Corton on Fridays, or the Circuit Meursault on Sundays. Each journey covers

25 to 30 kilometers. Afternoon and morning excursions (1400 to 1800) are offered on Tuesdays, Wednesdays, Saturdays, and Sundays traveling the Circuit Pommard. For the more athletic, Dili Voyage also offers guided tours by bike.

BEAUNE TO COLMAR

I found the following, easy daily connection, Beaune to Colmar, changing trains just once in Besançon that was a local schedule and not published in Thomas Cook:

dep: Beaune 0940 (weekdays)

arr: Besançon-Viotte 1121 (weekdays)

dep: Besançon-Viotte 1153 (weekdays)

arr: Colmar 1357

(Note: It is possible to continue on to Strasbourg, arriving at 1426.)

Most routings, however, add one more leg to the journey, requiring that you travel first to Dijon and then on to Besançon and Colmar, for example:

dep: Beaune 1046 or 1255

arr: Dijon-Ville 1106 or 1334

dep: Dijon-Ville 1224 1406 (T.G.V.), or 1609

arr: Besançon-Viotte 1327, 1459, or 1710

dep: Besançon-Viotte 1514 (weekends) or 1732

arr: Colmar 1719 or 1949

(or continue on to Strasbourg, arriving at 1753 or 2026)

As you approach **Colmar** by train, you can see towns in the distance dotting the landscape and the wonderful **Alsatian Wine Route,** or Route du Vin that weaves in between. Lovely with its old timbered buildings, intersected by the river and cobbled streets, Colmar is a delight. The train station is pleasingly small and manageable and you can easily walk to the heart of town. It took me no more than 20 minutes by heading a few blocks on Avenue R. Poincaré which leads directly out from the station, past a park, turning left on Rue des Américans which took me to the doorstep of the charming **Hostellerie le Maréchal** and on into the heart of town. If you are just going to spend the day in Colmar, leave your luggage at the station and walk but do not forget your camera as the city is very picturesque.

COLMAR TO STRASBOURG

It is just an approximately 40-minute rail journey between Colmar and Strasbourg and trains depart almost on the hour between the two. The relationship between the two cities is very similar to Arles and Avignon, with business people and students commuting back and forth. Either city could be used as a base from which to explore the other.

Sample train schedules between Colmar and Strasbourg:

dep: Colmar 0921, 1319, or 1645
arr: Strasbourg 0955, 1350, or 1716
dep: Strasbourg 1152, 1454, or 1629
arr: Colmar 1222, 1533, or 1707

Strasbourg is a beautiful, large city but the train station, although much grander in scale than Colmar, is definitely easy to get around. It would be possible to walk the 2 to 3 kilometers from Strasbourg station to the heart of town and the recommended **Hôtel des Rohan** and the **Romantik Hôtel Beaucour**, but I would advise taking a cab (approximately 35 francs) as streets are busy with fast-moving traffic, and if you opt to travel streets open only to pedestrian traffic, your walk becomes even longer. Another, more reasonable option is to travel to the heart of town by the fast and convenient city tram that departs every 10 to 15 minutes from the station. To locate the tram, exit the train station and then descend two levels by escalator to the underground lines. There is just one tram in Strasbourg, traveling in the direction of Illkirch (heading toward town) or in the direction of Hautepierre (returning to the station). You will want to disembark at Homme de Fer at the Place Kleber or Grand Rue next to the cathedral. (Note: Grand

Rue would be the stop for Hôtel Rohan, the Porte de l'Hopital on Rue de la Première Armeé for the Hôtel Beaucour.) The tram fare is 7 francs and tickets can be obtained from the automatic dispenser (select "Unipass," one way). Please refer to the Alsace Itinerary, page 109, for sightseeing suggestions.

STRASBOURG TO PARIS

For the home stretch of this itinerary, back to Paris, there are numerous schedules to select from, all direct to the capital city. The following are samples:

dep: Strasbourg 0755, 1220, 1312, 1440, or 1820
arr: Paris, Gare de l'Est 1155, 1623, 1755, 1833, or 2222

As a final note to this itinerary, I would like to stress that **all train schedules are offered as a guideline only**. Schedules do change, particularly from season to season, and it is important to reconfirm timetables with Rail Europe or at the stations rather than assume that the times published in this itinerary are accurate.

Traveling the Countryside by Train

Paris
Hotel Descriptions

Map Key

SIGHTS & LANDMARKS

A Trocadéro
B Palais de Chaillot
C Arc de Triomphe
D Grand Palais
E Petit Palais
F Place de la Concorde
G Sainte Marie Madeleine
H Gare Saint Lazare
I Opéra
J Place Vendôme
K Jardin des Tuileries
L Palais du Louvre
M Palais Royal
N Forum
O Centre George Pompidou
P Hôtel de Ville
Q Île de la Cité— Nôtre Dame
R Île Saint Louis
S Musée Picasso
T Gare du Nord
U Gare de l'Est
V Place des Vosges
W Gare de Lyon
X Gare d'Austerlitz
Y Panthéon
Z Palais du Luxembourg
AA Musée d'Orsay
BB Hôtel des Invalides
CC École Militaire
DD Tour Eiffel

HOTELS

First Arrondissement
1 Le Relais du Louvre
2 Hôtel de Vendôme
Third Arrondissement
3 Pavillon de la Reine
Fourth Arrondissement
4 Hôtel de la Bretonnerie
5 Hôtel Caron de Beaumarchais
6 Hôtel Saint Merry
7 Hôtel du Jeu de Paume
Fifth Arrondissement
8 Familia Hôtel
9 Hôtel de Nôtre Dame
10 Hôtel Résidence Henri IV
11 Les Rives de Nôtre Dame
Sixth Arrondissement
12 Hôtel Aubusson
13 Relais Christine
14 Prince de Conti
15 Saint Germain Left Bank Hôtel
16 Relais Saint Germain
17 Au Manoir Saint Germain des Prés
Seventh Arrondissement
18 Hôtel Duc de St. Simon
Eighth Arrondissement
19 Hôtel Beau Manoir
20 Hôtel Lido
21 Hôtel San Regis
22 Hôtel de Vigny
Sixteenth Arrondissement
23 St James Paris

Paris

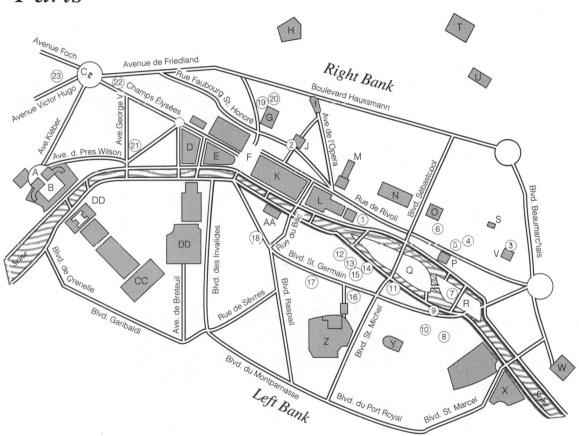

Right Bank

Left Bank

Avenue Foch

Avenue de Friedland

Avenue Victor Hugo

Ave. Kléber

Ave. George V

Ave. d. Pres. Wilson

Champs Élysées

Rue Faubourg St. Honoré

Boulevard Haussmann

Ave. de l'Opera

Rue de Rivoli

Blvd. Sébastcool

Blvd. Beaumarchais

Seine

Blvd. de Grenelle

Blvd. Garibaldi

Ave. de Breteuil

Blvd. des Invalides

Rue de Sèvres

Rue du Bac

Blvd. St. Germain

Blvd. Raspail

Blvd. St. Michel

Blvd. du Montparnasse

Blvd. du Port Royal

Blvd. St. Marcel

Seine

Paris

Paris, beautiful and sophisticated, lives up to her reputation. Sectioned off by *arrondissements*, there is not just one interesting area to visit, but many. Each arrondissement has its own character, flavor, and style. It is almost as if "Paris" were a name given to a group of clustering villages. Depending on the reason for your trip or the number of times you've been to Paris, each arrondissement will have its own appeal and attraction. We include descriptions of selected arrondissements and a few small hotels found within each. The arrondissements chosen are especially interesting and have some charming hotels to offer. Avoid disappointment and make hotel reservations as far in advance as possible.

Paris Hotel Descriptions

First Arrondissement

The First Arrondissement is an ideal location for "first-timers" in Paris. At the heart of the city, many of the major tourist attractions are situated here: the Place de la Concorde, Rue de Rivoli, the Madeleine, elegant and expensive shops along the well known Rue du Faubourg Saint Honoré, the Tuileries, and the Louvre. Find a hotel here and you will never have to deal with the Métro or taxi drivers. You can take romantic walks along the Seine or in the Tuileries Gardens. Excitement was born on the Champs Élysées, a wide boulevard that runs from the Place de la Concorde to the Arc de Triomphe at the Place de l'Étoile, officially known as the Place Charles de Gaulle.

Le Relais du Louvre	First Arrondissement	Paris Map #1

Tucked on a small side street practically in the shadow of the Louvre and close enough to enjoy the sounds of Nôtre Dame, the Relais du Louvre is a lovely hotel, reasonably priced for its location and comfort. Set under old beams, rooms are pretty with their pastel-washed walls and floral fabrics. Guestrooms that open on to the central courtyard enjoy the quiet, and those that overlook streets enjoy views out over the Louvre at the front or Nôtre Dame at the back. Rooms tend to be small, and some of the suites are simply elongated rooms with a sitting area—not very practical for the money. The apartment on the sixth floor offers a large bedroom, full bath, and large dining room with fireplace. Breakfast is served only in the rooms. I was impressed by this little hotel and with the warmth and graciousness of the reception.

LE RELAIS DU LOUVRE
Owner: Mr. Roger Thiery, Directrice: Sophie Aulnette
19, Rue des Prêtres-Saint-Germain-l'Auxerrois, 75001 Paris, France
Tel: 01.40.41.96.42, Fax: 01.40.41.96.44, E-mail: au-relais-du-louvre@dial.oleane.com
www.karenbrown.com/franceinns/lerelaisdulouvre.html, Open all year, Credit cards: all major
Non-smoking rooms, 21 rooms, Double: 850F–2200F, Breakfast: 50F per person
No restaurant, Garage: 70F, Located behind the Louvre, Métro: Louvre

The Hôtel de Vendôme stands proudly on a corner of the distinguished Place Vendôme in the heart of Paris and the Rue du Faubourg St. Honoré, known for its haute couture. This was once the site of the ancient mansion of the Vendôme family, now its small, elegant, marbled lobby is made welcoming by a young and friendly staff. Very recently, extensively, and beautifully remodeled, the hotel offers every amenity one could want, including round-the-clock room service, coupled with the latest in technologies: sound-proofed windows, in-room faxes, voice mail, two phone lines, and video-cam security for screening visitors outside your door. Each high-ceilinged room is individually decorated with original antique and period furniture, upholstered by the best French craftsmen, and the bathrooms are compositions in imported marble. This jewel of a small hotel, with its pink and white geraniums draping every balcony, conveys warmth and sophisticated elegance with the feeling of a beautiful private home.

HÔTEL DE VENDÔME **New**
Directeur: Mme Lina El Bawab, 1, Place Vendôme, 75001 Paris, France
Tel: 01.55.04.55.00, Fax: 01.49.27.97.89, E-mail: reservations@hoteldevendome.com
Open all year, Credit cards: all major, 29 rooms, Double: 2800F–3200F, Breakfast: 165F per person
2 restaurants, Garage: none, Located on the Place Vendôme, Métro: Tuilerys

Third & Fourth Arrondissements

The highlight of the Third Arrondissement is the picturesque Place des Vosges and the focus of the Fourth Arrondissement is Paris's two quaint and charming islands, the Île Saint Louis and the Île de la Cité. The Place des Vosges is a tranquil park, shaded by trees and echoing with the sound of children at play. The Île Saint Louis is a charming island with many enticing antique and craft shops and neighborhood restaurants. The larger Île de la Cité is home to Paris's *grande dame*—the spectacular Nôtre Dame and the intricate and delicate Sainte Chapelle with its stunning display of stained glass.

Crossing bridges in either direction, it is a short walk along the *quai* to the Latin Quarter or a pleasant stroll to the Louvre.

Pavillon de la Reine   Third Arrondissement   Paris Map #3

This charming hotel offers visitors to Paris a wonderful location on the beautiful square and park, the Place des Vosges. Trademarks of the Pavillon de la Reine are tasteful furnishings and, most importantly, pride and excellence of service. Set back off the Place, fronted by its own flowered courtyard, the Pavillon de la Reine was built on the site of an old pavilion. With every modern convenience, the hotel offers luxurious comfort and a warm decor of beamed ceilings, antiques, handsome reproductions, and beautiful art and paintings. Accommodations are offered as standard double rooms, two-level duplexes, and two-bedroom suites. The hotel has a lovely salon, and breakfast is served under the vaulted ceilings of the old cellar.

PAVILLON DE LA REINE
Hôtelier: Veronique Ellinger, 28, Place des Vosges, 75003 Paris, France
Tel: 01.40.29.19.19, Fax: 01.40.29.19.20, E-mail: pavillon@club-internet.fr, Open all year
Credit cards: all major, 55 rooms, Double: 1950F–3300F, Breakfast: 115F per person
No restaurant, Garage: no charge, Located on the Place des Vosges, Métro: Saint Paul

Hôtel de la Bretonnerie   Fourth Arrondissement   Paris Map #4

This is a lovingly cared-for hotel whose owners believe in offering good value and quality in terms of accommodation and price. Walk the streets of Paris looking at other hotels and you will realize that the Sagots offer an excellent buy and charming accommodation. In the basement under vaulted beams, heavy wooden tables are matched with high-backed chairs and stage a medieval atmosphere for breakfast. The reception is on the first floor and sits opposite an inviting sitting area. The rooms are found tucked along a maze of corridors, all attractive in their furnishings, with lovely modern bathrooms. Many of the rooms are set under heavy wooden beams, some cozy under low ceilings—ours was quite spacious, with 13-foot-high ceilings at the back. Madame Sagot has done a lovely job selecting complementary fabrics, drapes, and furnishings for each room. A few rooms are two-level and offer a loft bedroom and sitting room below. The hotel has a great location within walking distance of the Place des Vosges, the Picasso Museum, the Pompidou Center, and Les Halles. The hotel is set on a quiet street and offers a comfortable and quiet night's sleep.

HÔTEL DE LA BRETONNERIE
Hôtelier: Valerie Sagot, 22, Rue Sainte-Croix-de-la-Bretonnerie, 75004 Paris, France
Tel: 01.48.87.77.63, Fax: 01.42.77.26.78, www.karenbrown.com/franceinns/hoteldelabretonnerie.html
Closed August, Credit cards: MC, VS, 30 rooms, Double: 660F–1030F, Breakfast: 60F per person
No restaurant, No garage, Located across the river from Nôtre Dame, Métro: Hôtel de Ville

Hôtel Caron de Beaumarchais   Fourth Arrondissement   Paris Map #5

Set just off the Rue de Rivoli where it changes to the Rue Saint Antoine, the Hôtel Caron de Beaumarchais is in a lively area just a few blocks up from the Seine and the Île Saint Louis, convenient to the Picasso Museum, Pompidou Center, Les Halles, the Hôtel de Ville, and Place des Vosges. The Caron, with its attractive blue façade, is a cute little hotel with small rooms, recently renovated to three-star standard, on each of the six floors. The front two rooms on three floors enjoy balconies set with two chairs and a small table—the back room of each level overlooks the quiet corridor. Rooms without balconies benefit from a little extra space. The 18th-century-style decor includes attractively framed original documentation from the Paris Theater. All the rooms are air conditioned, and enjoy pocket-sized but modern bathrooms with lovely hand-painted tiles. Fresh flowers abound in the lovely front reception with its stone floor, fabric-covered walls, and centrally planted courtyard. The Bigeard father-and-son team offers a warm welcome.

HÔTEL CARON DE BEAUMARCHAIS
Hôteliers: Etienne & Alain Bigeard, 12, Rue Vieille du Temple, 75004 Paris, France
Tel: 01.42.72.34.12, Fax: 01.42.72.34.63, Open all year, Credit cards: all major
19 rooms, Double: 730F–810F, Breakfast: 54F per person
No restaurant, No garage, Located in the Marais District, Métro: Hôtel de Ville

Hôtel du Jeu de Paume   Fourth Arrondissement   Paris Map #7

To find the Hôtel du Jeu de Paume it is easier to locate the imposing deep-blue door than the small identifying brass plaque. Behind the large door, a long outdoor corridor with stone-tiled floor and heavy wooden timbers buffers the hotel from any street noise. Inside, the Jeu de Paume is an architectural wonder whose walls and vaulted ceilings are striped with beams. Dramatic in its furnishing, the decor is an artistic blend of tapestries, chrome, glass, and leather set against a backdrop of wood and plaster. The core of the hotel, converted from a 17th-century Jeu de Paume, is one large room divided up into a series of rooms: the entry, the living room warmed by a lovely fire, and the dining room whose tables are overpowered by the stunning end beams and soaring rafters. A few guestrooms open onto the central room, while the majority of rooms are located in a side annex and open onto a courtyard and garden. The Jeu de Paume closed its doors recently in order to refurbish all the guestrooms and include the addition of a lovely Junior Suite with the luxury of two bathrooms and a private terrace.

HÔTEL DU JEU DE PAUME
Hôtelier: Elyane Prache, 54, Rue Saint -Louis-en-l'Île, 75004 Paris, France
Tel: 01.43.26.14.18, Fax: 01.40.46.02.76, www.karenbrown.com/franceinns/hoteldujeudepaume.html
Open all year, Credit cards: all major, 31 rooms, Double: 1250F–2625F, Breakfast: 80F per person
No restaurant, No garage, Located on the Île Saint Louis, Métro: Pont-Marie

A beautiful wooden façade trimming the doorway, a flowerbox overhanging with geraniums, and what I could glimpse looking up through the arched windows of the second floor beckoned me into the Hôtel Saint Merry. A lovely stairway of old wood trimmed in brass winds up within thick stone walls to the various levels, illuminated by a faux stained-glassed window. The first level is manned by Monsieur Crabbe with his reception desk facing a small sitting room and fronting a little kitchen equipped to prepare breakfast. I was able to see only his most expensive rooms, which were dramatic with their Gothic decor, handsome woods, wrought-iron fixtures, and exposed beamed ceilings, all enriched by handsome fabrics and Oriental rugs. Room 9 has its bed set remarkably under the arch of two protruding buttresses—not recommended for anyone who sleepwalks. Ten guestrooms have private bathrooms, while two have private showers and shared toilet—none has TV. At the heart of the Marais, a wonderful old section of Paris, the Hôtel Saint Merry is set on the corner of two cobbled streets (a designated pedestrian district), a tree-lined passage of one block off the Rue de Rivoli, backing on to the Saint Merry Church of which it served as the presbytery in the 17th century. Convenient for guests, an underground public parking garage is located just in front of the hotel. Note: It is possible and recommended to reserve parking in advance.

HÔTEL SAINT MERRY
Hôtelier: Christian Crabbe, 78, Rue de la Verrerie, 75004 Paris, France
Tel: 01.42.78.14.15, Fax: 01.40.29.06.82, www.karenbrown.com/franceinns/hotelsaintmerry.html
Open all year, Credit cards: all major, 11 rooms, Double: 480F–1800F, Breakfast: 55F per person
No restaurant, No garage, Located near Les Halles, Métro: Hôtel de Ville or Chatellet

Fifth, Sixth, & Seventh Arrondissements

The Fifth, Sixth, and Seventh Arrondissements together comprise the ever-popular Latin Quarter. Here you will find activity and companionship abounding. There are crêperies, sidewalk cafés, food stands, the Sorbonne and its students, antique shops and art galleries, and so many restaurants—all promising "favorites" to be discovered. At night many of the small streets are blocked off and the Latin Quarter takes on a very special ambiance. The Left Bank of the Latin Quarter is separated from the Right Bank by the Seine and the Île de la Cité. The grandeur of Nôtre Dame is overpowering when illuminated at night. Along the *quai* are many secondhand-book stalls. The Musée d'Orsay in the grand old train station houses an exhibition of Paris's greatest collection of Impressionist art. With the Left Bank as a base, you can also conveniently tour the Luxembourg Gardens and Les Invalides, and view Paris from the Eiffel Tower. The Left Bank and Latin Quarter offer an endless wave of activity and several charming hotels.

Familia Hôtel	Fifth Arrondissement	Paris Map #8

Eric Gaucheron, a third generation hôtelier, aims to offer charming, affordable, welcoming accommodations and certainly seems to succeed. He and his parents, Bernard and Colette, along with wife, Sylvie, see to it that each guest is looked after like family. Eric is proud to carry on this tradition in the Familia with its red-geranium-covered balconies in the colorful Latin Quarter. The walls of the hotel's lobby are decorated with custom murals of street scenes from the neighborhood and the small sitting room and halls are adorned with tapestries over original stone walls and Oriental carpets. Small, clean rooms have modern marble-tiled baths, TVs, phones, small refrigerators, and double-paned windows, and some have tiny balconies overlooking the street (the highest floor has a view of the towers of Nôtre Dame). Some of the rooms also have sepia-colored murals of Paris scenes or landmarks. Bedspreads are of nice quality. All in all, a welcoming family hotel at a very affordable cost. This hotel has many American guests who rave in the comment books about the warm and caring service from a hôtelier who believes that small details make the difference.

FAMILIA HÔTEL **New**
Hôteliers: Eric Gaucheron & Family, 11, Rue des Écoles, 75005 Paris, France
Tel: 01.43.54.55.27, Fax: 01.43.29.61.77, Open all year, Credit cards: all major
30 rooms, Double: 380F–580F, Breakfast: 30F or 35F per person in the room
No restaurant, No garage, Located between the Panthéon & Nôtre Dame, Métro: Cardinal Lemoine

Hôtel de Nôtre Dame   Fifth Arrondissement   Paris Map #9

The Left Bank offers some of Paris's most reasonable hotels, but they are not always clean or convenient. The Hôtel de Nôtre Dame is simple in terms of accommodation, but I was impressed by its location just a few blocks off the Seine on a bend of a quiet side street. With a handsome façade painted maroon and topped by large letters that boast its name, the hotel is inviting. The entry is basic but sweet with a few chairs set against the heavy stone walls. Beyond the entry a few tables serve as a breakfast room or resident bar. Upstairs, guestrooms are simple; the only old-world adornment being the few old exposed beams, but fabrics selected are attractive, and furnishings, although modern, are functional. The price is right and the location is excellent.

HÔTEL DE NÔTRE DAME
Hôtelier: Monsieur Fouhety, 19, Rue Maître Albert, 75005 Paris, France
Tel: 01.43.26.79.00, Fax: 01.46.33.50.11, Open all year, Credit cards: all major
34 rooms, Double: 750F–850F, Breakfast 40F per person, No restaurant, bar
Located near the Seine & Quai Tournelle, Métro: Maubert-Mutalité & St. Michel

Quiet and peaceful, the classic Haussman-style 19th-century building that houses the Hôtel Résidence Henri IV stands in the shadow of the large trees of the Paul Langevin Square gardens. This location at the end of a small street off the Rue des Écoles, next to the École Polytechnique of the Sorbonne, offers luxury and refined serenity. You are welcomed into the pretty and tasteful lobby by a sweet, helpful, and multilingual receptionist, Jenny Delchir. To your right is a small sitting room and beyond the lobby an iron-balustrade staircase rises up the height of the building. Each small but pleasantly decorated guestroom is equipped with cable TV, phone, safe box, and a compact kitchenette behind a sliding louver door that amazingly has a cooktop, sink, microwave, and refrigerator, as well as flatware and dishes. Baths are roomy and bright, with shower-in-tub, warming towel bars, and hair dryers. Because of the hotel's shady location, only the two rooms on its top floor are air-conditioned. Suites have a small sitting room with marble mantel, desk, sofa and several chairs. It is indeed a peaceful location in the midst of a colorful, bustling district.

HÔTEL RÉSIDENCE HENRI IV   **New**
Directrice: Marie Jose Gernigon, 50, Rue des Bernardins, 75005 Paris, France
Tel: 01.44.41.31.81, Fax: 01.46.33.93.22, E-mail: henri4@hotellerie.net
Open all year, Credit cards: all major, 14 rooms, Double: 900F–1200F
Breakfast: 40F per person, No restaurant, No garage
Located between the Panthéon and Nôtre Dame, off Rue des Écoles, Métro: Maubert-Mutualité

There is something very intimate about this enchanting riverfront hotel set off the street behind a handsome dark-green door. The tiled entry is informal, with a single desk and keys gathered in a country basket. The song and chatter of birds tempt you a few steps past the reception to a sitting room dramatic under a vaulted ceiling of exposed heavy beams and glass. An elevator takes you up to the guestrooms, all set behind handsome arched wooden doorways. With just ten guestrooms, the owners were able to focus on

the luxury of decor and appointments, which are in warm and inviting Tuscany- and Provence-inspired colors. Standard rooms are uncluttered and functional, with a bed, sitting area, table, and chairs. Room 6, in colors of blue and salmon, has a queen bed, sofa, and views over the Seine. The top floors accommodate a large apartment and the one suite. Set right on the edge of the Seine across the bridge from the Île de la Cité, this hotel could be one's imaginary *pied à terre à Paris*.

LES RIVES DE NÔTRE DAME
Hôteliers: Philippe & Annie Degravi, Directrice: Grace Dos Santos
15, Quai Saint-Michel, 75005 Paris, France
Tel: 01.43.54.81.16, Fax: 01.43.26.27.09
10 rooms, Double: 1100F–2500F, Breakfast: 65F per person
Non-smoking rooms, Open all year, Credit cards: all major
No restaurant, but room service from neighboring brasserie
Located across from Nôtre Dame, Métro: Saint Michel-Nôtre Dame

Hôtel Aubusson	Sixth Arrondissement	Paris Map#12

Large brass letters contrast with the dramatic, heavy, deep-blue doors that enclose the entrance of the Hôtel Aubusson. The ambiance of the Aubusson is handsome rather than cozy or charming—almost spartan, the entry has just a few chairs placed against the cream stone walls. Through a glass partition in the hotel reception you can glimpse clusters of mahogany tables and chairs that accommodate guests in the bar, which is attractive and also uncluttered in its decor. Venture just round the corner from the bar, however, to the room that I was drawn to. Dramatic with its high-beamed ceilings and full-length windows draped in heavy tapestry fabric, the guest lounge is warm and inviting, with seating round a large open fire—one would almost wish for a cold day to justify an afternoon before the crackling logs. On warm days breakfast and drinks are offered in the pleasant courtyard. Authenticating the name of the hotel, a beautiful Aubusson covers the stone wall above the buffet in the breakfast room. Guestrooms circle the central corridor. The rooms in the back are in the original part of the hotel dating from the 17th century. They enjoy high-beamed ceilings and the quiet of the back corridor. Rooms at the front are in a newly constructed section that circles round to create the inner corridor. Although traditional in materials and decor, these rooms enjoy more modern amenities and ceiling heights more practical for this century.

HÔTEL AUBUSSON
Directeur: (Gérant) M. Pascal Gimel, 33, Rue Dauphine, 75006 Paris, France
Tel: 01.43.29.43.43, Fax: 01.43.29.12.62, 50 rooms, Double: 1200F–2200F, Breakfast 110F per person
Non-smoking rooms, Open all year, Credit cards: all major, No restaurant, Private car park 100F
Located just a few blocks up from the Pont Neuf, Metro: Odéon

Au Manoir St. Germain des Prés   Sixth Arrondissement   Paris Map #17

The Teil Family is responsible for yet another gem in Paris. Handsome woods specially crafted in the Auvergne cover the walls and beautiful fabrics dress walls, beds, chairs, and windows. Much attention has been paid to the comfort of the guest, with excellent lighting, plumbing, and fixtures (all baths have Jacuzzi jets), comfortable mattresses, and plush towels. Rooms at the back enjoy the quiet of the courtyard, and double-paned windows block the noise from rooms overlooking the boulevard. Sixth-floor guestrooms are tucked under beams—ask for our favorite, which also enjoys its own terrace. Rooms vary by color scheme: rich creams enhanced with Provençal blue, soft pink, a striking amber, and rich red. A few bedrooms are equipped with a futon to accommodate a third person. A Continental breakfast is graciously served in the privacy of your room, or you can enjoy a more lavish self-service buffet (cereals, breads, cakes, cheeses, yogurt, juice, and fruit) at intimate tables set in a charming room or garden courtyard off the entry.

AU MANOIR SAINT GERMAIN DES PRÉS
Hôteliers: Teil Family, 153 Boulevard Saint Germain, 75006 Paris, France
Tel: 01.42.22.21.65, Fax: 01.45.48.22.25, E-mail: msg@paris-hotels-charm.com
www.karenbrown.com/franceinns/aumanoirsaintgermaindespres.html
32 rooms, Double: 980F–1500 F, Breakfast: included, Open all year, Credit cards: all major
No restaurant, Located across from the cathedral of St. Germain des Prés, Métro: St. Germain des Prés

The entry of this lovely hotel is set back off a quiet street behind heavy wooden doors. Public areas include a lovely sitting area and a charming lounge adorned with English prints and an inviting nook set with breakfast tables—both at the bottom of the winding stair. Housed within thick stone walls of an 18th-century mansion, guestrooms are quiet and equipped with modern conveniences of air conditioning, direct-line phone, mini bar, hair dryer, television, and double glazing. Many rooms open onto the patio, where tables provide a lovely spot on a warm morning for breakfast or a refreshing afternoon drink. The decor is more English than French, with flower-patterned chintzes, English prints, and mahogany furnishings. With a very loyal, returning clientele, the Prince de Conti is often booked. If it is unavailable, you might want to consider its sister hotel, the Prince de Conde, located just around the corner on the Rue de Seine. The rooms are similar in decor to those at the Conti, but the public areas are minimal.

PRINCE DE CONTI
Directeur: Philippe Roye, 8, Rue Guénégaud, 75006 Paris, France
Tel: 01.44.07.30.40, Fax: 01.44.07.36.34
26 rooms, Double: 1083F–1214F, Breakfast: 79F per person
Open all year, Credit cards: all major, No restaurant, Non-smoking and handicap rooms
Located just a few blocks from the Seine & the Pont Neuf, Métro: Odéon

Saint Germain Left Bank Hôtel   Sixth Arrondissement   Paris Map #15

The Saint Germain Left Bank Hôtel has a great location on a quiet street just off the Boulevard Saint Germain within comfortable walking distance of the Île de la Cité and the heart of the district with its narrow cobbled streets, many restaurants, and shops. The Saint Germain Left Bank also offers charming accommodation and very professional service. The entry is inviting with its handsome wood paneling, tapestries, paintings, and attractive furnishings. Set with tables, a small room tucked off the entry serves as an appealing spot for a breakfast of croissants, rolls, juice, and coffee which can also be enjoyed in the privacy of your room. A small elevator conveniently accesses the thirty-one rooms evenly distributed on six levels. Windows of rooms at the back open up to views of distant Nôtre Dame and the panorama improves with each floor. Attractive in their decor, often set under exposed beams, the air-conditioned rooms are small but comfortable, with writing desks, built-in armoires, direct-dial phones, and modern bathrooms.

SAINT GERMAIN LEFT BANK HÔTEL
Hôteliers: Teil Family, Directrice: Veronique Dumont
9, Rue de l'Ancienne Comédie, 75006 Paris, France, Tel: 01.43.54.01.70, Fax: 01.43.26.17.14,
www.karenbrown.com/franceinns/stgermainleftbankhotel.html, E-mail: lb@paris-hotels-charm.com
Open all year, Credit cards: all major, 31 rooms, Double: 980F–1600F, Breakfast: included
Handicap room, No restaurant, No garage, Located off the Boulevard Saint Germain, Métro: Odéon

Relais Christine   Sixth Arrondissement   Paris Map #13

The Relais Christine achieves an elegant countryside ambiance at the heart of Paris's Latin Quarter. A large, flowering courtyard buffers the hotel from any noise and a beautiful wood-paneled lobby ornamented with antiques, Oriental rugs, and distinguished portraits is your introduction to this delightful hotel. A converted monastery, the hotel underwent complete restoration and modernization in 1990. Fully air-conditioned, there are 35 double rooms whose beds easily convert to twin beds. There are two-level and single-level accommodations, all individual in their decor—ranging from attractive contemporary to a dramatic Louis XIII. A few of the bedrooms overlook a small back street, but the majority open onto the garden or front courtyard. The Relais also has sixteen beautiful suites, of which four on the ground floor open directly onto a sheltered garden. The Relais Christine is an outstanding hotel. I hesitate to publish it as one of our favorites as it is already so difficult to secure a reservation—but it *is* exceptional and distinguished by its exceptional personalized service and elegant comfort. Once you experience the Relais Christine, you, too, will become one of their devoted clientele and one of many returning guests. For those who arrive in Paris by car, also note that it is the only property on the Left Bank to offer secure, underground parking.

RELAIS CHRISTINE
Hôtelier: Yves Monnin, 3, Rue Christine, 75006 Paris, France
Tel: 01.40.51.60.80, Fax: 01.40.51.60.81, E-mail: relaisch@club-internet.fr
Open all year, Credit cards: all major, 51 rooms, Double: 1800F–3500F, Breakfast: 110F per person
Non-smoking rooms, No restaurant, Garage: no charge, Located near Pont Neuf, Métro: Odéon

Relais Saint Germain   Sixth Arrondissement   Paris Map #16

Look for the rich-green door standing proud under windows hung with geraniums and you will discover an enchanting Left-Bank hotel. This was once three separate buildings but the walls between them were knocked down to accommodate a lift, shared hallways, and elegant guestrooms. Originally, the hotel had just ten guestrooms with two rooms sharing the landing of each floor, all facing onto the Carrefour de l'Odéon, a quiet plaza. The original ten rooms are narrow, intimate, and set under heavy beams. Recently there has been an addition of twelve more rooms, four of which are large studios with private kitchens, and three deluxe and spacious doubles. Regardless of room, the decor is lavish. The prints chosen for the furnishings, spreads, and drapes coordinate beautifully and are individual to each room. Accommodations, although not always spacious, are extremely comfortable, with excellent lighting, modern bathroom, direct-dial phone, mini bar, and cable television. Prices are at the top end but then so are the style and accommodation. Also new to the property is a charming little bistro-wine bar called the Comptoir du Relais, decorated in a 1930s art-deco style and offering a menu of salads, quiches, pastries, and wine by the glass.

RELAIS SAINT GERMAIN
Hôtelier: Gilbert Laipsker, 9, Carrefour de l'Odéon, 75006 Paris, France
Tel: 01.43.29.12.05, Fax: 01.46.33.45.30, www.karenbrown.com/franceinns/relaissaintgermain.html
Open all year, Credit cards: all major, 22 rooms, Double: 1600F–2050F, Breakfast: included
Bistro-bar, No garage, Located off the Boulevard Saint Germain, Métro: Odéon

Hôtel Duc de Saint-Simon   Seventh Arrondissement   Paris Map #18

On a small, quiet side street of the same name, the Hôel Duc de Saint-Simon is just steps from the Boulevard Saint Germain and the pulse of the Left Bank. Guarded by handsome gates and buffered from the street by its own shaded courtyard, this charming hotel offers a very peaceful retreat. The decor throughout is sumptuous and elegant in its use of furnishings, fabrics, paintings and fixtures. Lavish flower arrangements are the perfect complement to the refined ambiance. Guestrooms are each individual in decor and vary from comfortable standard rooms to more spacious two-room suites. If you are fortunate to enjoy repeated trips to Paris, you, as do so many of its loyal clientele, will soon establish your personal favorite. In the basement, against the exposed rough stone of the old coal and wine cellar, is a breakfast room as well as an intimate bar where you can enjoy a beverage or light snack.

HÔTEL DUC DE SAINT-SIMON
Hôtelier: M. Lindquist, Directrice: Mme Lalisse, 14, Rue de Saint-Simon, 75007 Paris, France
Tel: 01.44.39.20.20, Fax: 01.45.48.68.25, E-mail: duc.de.saint.simon@wanadoo.fr
34 rooms, Double: 1200–1950F, Breakfast: 75F per person, Open all year, Credit cards: all major
Wine cellar, No garage, Located off the Blvd St. Germain, just up from the Seine, Métro: Rue du Bac

Eighth Arrondissement

The Eighth Arrondissement, crowned by the Arc de Triomphe and graced by the Champs Élysées, is a bustle of activity. There are shops, sidewalk cafés, nightclubs, cinemas, and opportunities for endless people-watching. It makes for a wonderful evening's enjoyment to stroll the wide boulevard: people are always about and it is safe and well lit. It is also a lovely walk down the "Champs" to the Louvre.

Hôtel Beau Manoir	Eighth Arrondissement	Paris Map #19

Just around the corner from its sister hotel, the Hôtel Lido, the Hôtel Beau Manoir is found on a side street off the Place de Madeleine. The Hôtel Beau Manoir resembles the decor in the Teils' other hotels, with beautiful rich woods from the Auvergne enhancing the walls, rough-hewn beams, exposed stone walls, handsome tapestries, and rich, Provençal fabrics used to decorate the rooms—all ingredients married together to achieve a cozy and intimate atmosphere. Guestrooms are comfortable in size and appointments: all with marbled bath, air conditioning, cable TV, mini bar, and direct-dial phone. Three top floor suites are tucked under the eaves and each has an intimate sitting room and views out through dormer windows. A buffet breakfast is included.

HÔTEL BEAU MANOIR
Hôteliers: Teil Family, Directrice: Lucie Duhommet, 6, Rue de l'Arcade, 75008 Paris, France
Tel: 01.42.66.03.07, Fax: 01.42.68.03.00, E-mail: bm@paris-hotels-charm.com
www.karenbrown.com/franceinns/hotelbeaumanoir.html, Open all year, Credit cards: all major
32 rooms, Double: 1200F–1700F, Breakfast: included, Handicap rooms, No restaurant, No garage
Located on the Place de Madeleine, Métro: Madeleine

Bright, overflowing windowboxes hung heavy with red geraniums caught my eye and tempted me down a small side street just off the Place de Madeleine to the Hôtel Lido. My small detour was greatly rewarded—the Lido is a gem. Tapestries warm heavy stone walls and Oriental rugs adorn tile floors. Copper pieces are set about and wooden antiques dominate the furnishings in the entry lobby, an intimate sitting area, and cozy bar. Downstairs, breakfast is served under the cellar's stone arches. Comfortable but not large, the air-conditioned bedrooms, set under heavy beams, are charmingly decorated with reproduction antiques and handsome fabrics. A bountiful breakfast buffet is served in the hotel's vaulted cellar. This hotel is an excellent value for Paris and a quiet location.

HÔTEL LIDO
Hôteliers: Teil Family, Directrice: Catherine Padel, 4, Passage de la Madeleine, 75008 Paris, France
Tel: 01.42.66.27.37, Fax: 01.42.66.61.23, E-mail: lido@paris-hotels-charm.com
www.karenbrown.com/franceinns/hotellido.html, Open all year, Credit cards: all major
32 rooms, Double: 980F–1100F, Breakfast: included
No restaurant, No garage, Located off the Place de Madeleine, Métro: Madeleine

Small, traditional, and intimate, the San Regis was once a fashionable townhouse. With exclusive boutiques and embassies as its sophisticated neighbors, the hotel maintains an air of simple yet authentic elegance. It is easy to pass this marvelous hotel by: a small sign is the only thing that advertises its presence. Beyond the small foyer you find a comfortable, ornately decorated lounge area and small dining room where you can enjoy a quiet drink and/or lunch and dinner. The bedrooms are large and handsomely furnished, and the bathrooms are very modern and thoughtfully stocked. Huge double doors buffer sounds from other rooms. The rooms that front the Rue Jean-Goujon are favored with a view across to the tip of the imposing Eiffel Tower, but courtyard rooms are sheltered from street noise.

HÔTEL SAN REGIS
Hôtelier: Maurice Georges, 12, Rue Jean-Goujon, 75008 Paris, France
Tel: 01.44.95.16.16, Fax: 01.45.61.05.48, E-mail: message@hotel-sanregis.fr
www.karenbrown.com/franceinns/hotelsanregis.html, Open all year, Credit cards: all major
44 rooms, Double: 2400F–3900F, Breakfast: 120F per person
Restaurant, No garage, Located between the Seine & Champs Élysées, Métro: Franklin Roosevelt

Hôtel de Vigny	Eighth Arrondissement	Paris Map #22

For those who appreciate discreetly elegant small hotels, the Hôtel de Vigny is very appealing. The lounge has the understated, yet expensive look of a private club with comfortable chairs, the finest fabrics, paneled walls, handsome oil paintings, and a fireplace. A small writing desk where guests register is the only subtle indication that this is not a private home. Not just the decor, but the location is also excellent: just a couple of blocks north of the Champs Élysées.

HÔTEL DE VIGNY
Hôtelier: Christian Falcucci, 9–11 Rue Balzac, 75008 Paris, France, E-mail: vigny@relaischateaux.fr
Tel: 01.42.99.80.80, Fax: 01.42.99.80.40, www.karenbrown.com/franceinns/hoteldevigny.html
Open all year, Credit cards: all major, 37 rooms, Double: 2300F–4500F, Breakfast: 100F per person
Non-smoking rooms, Restaurant, Garage: 100F, Located near Champs Élysées, Métro: George V/Étoile

Sixteenth Arrondissement

The Sixteenth Arrondissement is Paris's elite residential district. It is a quiet area, characterized by stately, elegant apartment buildings, lovely shopping streets, and exclusive corner markets. The Rue de la Pompe and the Avenue Victor Hugo are two well-known avenues lined with beautiful and expensive shops. The Sixteenth Arrondissement is bordered on one side by the expanse of the Bois de Boulogne, a scenic park where people walk, exercise their dogs, cycle, run, play soccer and escape the frenzy of the city.

The Saint James Paris is an elegant property, with the richness of decor and ambiance of a sophisticated club, under the direction of the company that offers the elegant Relais Christine and Pavillon de la Reine. Although it previously catered more to members than hotel guests, and while it still has a few membership ties, the principal focus has changed from a club to a hotel. An elegant stone manor, the Saint James was built in 1892 as a memorial to the President of the French Republic. It housed the Adolphe Thiers foundation and was a residence for France's most outstanding students. It was first converted to a gentleman's club by a British businessman in 1986. An imposing arched entry frames the manor, which is set back behind a lovely large fountain and circular drive. The interior is quite grand in its spaciousness and furnishings, with a fresh, clean, albeit somewhat modern, decor, with a gorgeous selection of coordinating fabrics and handsome furnishings. The bedrooms are equipped with every imaginable comfort, from exterior blinds that open and close at the touch of a switch within reach of the bed to a coffee table that rises to accommodate a morning breakfast tray. The traditional roof of this mansion has been replace with a glass dome to benefit the four top suites. A wide central corridor is a maze of ivy-covered lattice work that sections off individual garden patios for each suite. Appropriate to its British ties, the hotel has a richly decorated library bar, and the basement sports a Jacuzzi, sauna, and exercise room. The dining room is elegant and private, being available only to members and resident guests.

SAINT JAMES PARIS
Directeur: Tim Goddard, 43, Avenue Bugeaud, 75116 Paris, France
Tel: 01.44.05.81.81, Fax: 01.44.05.81.82, E-mail: stjames@club-internet.fr
48 rooms, Double: 2300F–4200F, Breakfast: 120F (Continental) or 145F (buffet) per person
Open all year, Credit cards: all major, Restaurant (closed weekends and holidays), Courtyard parking
Non-smoking rooms, Located a few blocks from the Place Victor Hugo, Métro: Victor Hugo

Countryside
Hotel Descriptions

Aix is an intriguing city to explore. The cobbled streets of the old quarter are lovely to wander around and at night the illuminated tree-lined Cours Mirabeau is enchanting—reminiscent of Paris with its many sidewalk cafés. It is just a 15-minute walk from the old quarter to the attractive Hôtel le Pigonnet, run very professionally by the Swellen family. A tree-lined road leads you away from the noise and traffic of the city center to this hotel. Set in its own 2½-acre garden, the Hôtel le Pigonnet is surrounded by an abundance of flowers and towering ancient chestnut trees. It was from this garden that Paul Cézanne painted the Mountain of Sainte Victoire. The hotel also has a lovely large pool, most inviting on a hot summer day in Provence. Inside are cozy sitting rooms and a large airy restaurant whose tables are set on the back patio on balmy evenings to overlook the lush expanse of garden. The hotel's bedrooms, all with private bathroom, vary dramatically from elegant suites to attractive, but standard hotel rooms. Le Pigonnet is not a country inn, but a lovely hotel with first-class accommodation and service that maintains a country ambiance and setting within the city of Aix en Provence. *Directions:* Take the Pont de l'Arc exit off the autoroute and turn north in the direction of the center of town. At the third light turn left. Le Pigonnet is 50 meters on the left.

HÔTEL LE PIGONNET
Hôteliers: Swellen Family
5, Avenue du Pigonnet
13090 Aix en Provence, France
Tel: 04.42.59.02.77, Fax: 04.42.59.47.77
E-mail: reservation@hotelpigonnet.com
52 rooms, Double: 900F–2200F
Breakfast: 80F–130F per person
Open all year, Credit cards: all major
Restaurant, courtyard parking, pool
Region: Provence, Michelin Maps 245, 246
www.karenbrown.com/franceinns/hotellepigonnet.html

This lovely little hotel is a gem at the heart of the old quarter of Aix, on the south side of Cours Mirabeau. Monsieur Juster has tastefully decorated the one little entry salon, stairway, and the 13 small but comfortable guestrooms with the warm flavor and style of Provence. Walls are painted in a wash of warm colors, fabrics are reminiscent of Pierre Deux, simple furnishings are attractive with their hand-painted motifs, and there are lovely accents such as handsome prints and a wonderful terra-cotta pot filled with dried flowers. An old stairwell with a skylight casting a wealth of light in the hotel winds up from the reception to the various floors—be forewarned that the hotel does not have an elevator. The top-floor rooms are worth the climb as they are set under the old beams which lend a bit more character. All guestrooms have en-suite bathrooms. These rooms are definitely intimate in size—if you have lots of luggage or prefer spacious accommodation, while the price is definitely tempting, this hotel might not fit your needs. Parking is always difficult in Aix. If you are fortunate enough to find a place on one of the side streets, grab it and then the hotel can direct you to one of the long-term parking areas nearby. Be sure to lock your car and secure belongings where they are not visible. *Directions*: Follow signs to city center, then travel along the Cours Mirabeau, turn right on Rue du 4 Septembre to Rue Roux Alphéran.

HÔTEL DES QUATRE DAUPHINS
Hôtelier: Jean-Louis Juster
54, Rue Roux Alphéran
13100 Aix en Provence, France
Tel: 04.42.38.16.39, Fax: 04.42.38.60.19
13 rooms, Double: 343F–428F
Breakfast: 42F per person
Open all year, Credit cards: MC, VS
No restaurant
Region: Provence, Michelin Maps 245, 246
www.karenbrown.com/franceinns/hoteldesquatredauphins.html

This lovely property set on a hillside shaded by a clustering of trees is imbued with the air of an elegant home rather than a commercial hotel. The numerous staff are a "family" and all are eager to serve with a graciousness and warmth that reflect the great pride they take in their participation. The decor of this peach-washed building can only be described in superlatives as elegant, rich, beautiful, and yet surprisingly comfortable and welcoming. Sitting areas both inside or outside on a garden terrace under the shade of trees or by the pool are inviting and intimate. Guestrooms, all with private bathrooms, are found either in the original building, in newly constructed wings off the reception, or in little villas. Luxurious in size and appointments, no two rooms are decorated alike—wallpapers and fabrics range from a wonderful blend of cream and reds in an array of plaids, checks, and patterns to a more dramatic finish in splashes of golds and browns. Most rooms have either a shade-covered terrace or expanse of balcony and all enjoy the quiet of the setting. Breakfast is a grand affair under the personal supervision and flourish of Michel, who creates a mood of great fun. A motto popular with the staff boasts there are "never problems, only solutions." *Directions:* Follow signs to city center and then to the Villa Gallici, traveling the road that circles the heart of Aix. At the Place Bellegarde, turn north on the Avenue Jules Isaac then left on Avenue de la Violette.

VILLA GALLICI
Hôteliers: Daniel Jouve, Gil Dez, Charles Montemarco
Avenue de la Violette
13100 Aix en Provence, France
Tel: 04.42.23.29.23, Fax: 04.42.96.30.45
E-mail: villagallici@wanadoo.fr
22 rooms, Double: 1350F–3050F
Breakfast: 130F per person
Open all year, Credit cards: all major
Restaurant for resident guests only, pool, handicap rooms
Region: Provence, Michelin Maps 245, 246
www.karenbrown.com/franceinns/villagallici.html

Le Manoir les Minimes is a lovely 18th-century manor built on the site of a 13th-century convent, convenient to the wonderful town of Amboise with its intriguing streets and shops. This newly opened hotel has a spectacular location in the shadow of the château right on the river's edge, surrounded by acres of gardens and embraced by an old stone wall. Furnishings are elegant, with antiques and attractive color schemes. The salon is spacious and formal in a wash of warm yellow, while the dining room is light and pretty (you can opt to eat in the garden when weather permits). The hotel offers eleven guestrooms in the main building and three in the facing annex. All the rooms have large beds that can convert to twins. A first-floor room is easily accessed by those who have difficulty with stairs and is also the one truly handicapped-fitted room. At the top of the first stairway is the most spectacular room (10), a corner suite decorated in beiges and creams with magnificent views both of the flowing river and up to the crowning château. There is a number of superior rooms on the second floor, which have glimpses of the Loire and are equipped with every modern convenience, while on the third floor are some great-value rooms. The three rooms in the annex are spacious but tend to be decorated in brighter colors, which contrast vividly with the stark white walls. *Directions:* Located on the riverbank on the south side of the bridge in the shadow of the castle.

LE MANOIR LES MINIMES   **New**
Directeurs: Patrice Longet & Eric Deforges
34, Quai Charles Guinot
37400 Amboise, France
Tel: 02.47.30.40.40, Fax: 02.47.30.40.77
14 rooms, Double: 590F–1,400F
Breakfast: 58F per person
Open all year, Credit cards: all major
No restaurant, enclosed parking
Region: Loire, Michelin Map 232

Located on the outskirts of Les Andelys, the Hôtel de la Chaîne d'Or looks up to the castle ruins and backs onto the Seine. Just an hour or so to the north of Paris, Les Andelys is convenient to Charles de Gaulle airport and Roissy and just a few kilometers from Giverny, Monet's home: a visit to Monet's home and the gardens that inspired his genius will prove a highlight of your trip. This hotel is managed by mother-and-daughter team Monique and Carole Foucault, who strive to excel in service and attention to detail. They take great pride in welcoming guests and overseeing the restaurant. Each year Monique redecorates a few bedrooms—soon all the accommodation will achieve her desired standard and atmosphere. The bedrooms, six with private bath, all enjoy views of the Seine and the constant, entertaining parade of barges. Carole follows in her late father's footsteps as the restaurant's baker and reason alone to overnight here would be to sample her breakfast croissants. The restaurant windows look over the Seine and across to a small island with an abandoned manor. It is an intimate and delightful place for lunch or dinner: the service is relaxed and comfortable and the menu offers an appealing selection of items. The Foucaults ask that overnight guests dine at the hotel. *Directions:* Take the D313 out of Vernon, a very scenic route, 26 km northwest to Les Andelys. La Chaîne d'Or is located in the old town, along the river's edge.

HÔTEL DE LA CHAÎNE D'OR
Hôteliers: Monique & Carole Foucault
27, Rue Grande
27700 Les Andelys, France
Tel: 02.32.54.00.31, Fax: 02.32.54.05.68
10 rooms, Double: 420F–760F
Breakfast: 75F per person
Closed January, Sunday nights & Monday
Credit cards: all major
Restaurant, riverside setting
Region: Normandy, Michelin Map 237

With the River Rhône running through it, Arles is a beautiful city, rich with Roman and medieval monuments. Just 50 kilometers from the sea, Arles has long guarded a strategic location. It is also convenient to all of Provence and an ideal base for exploring the region. The Hôtel d'Arlatan is tucked away on a small street in the center of town near the Place du Forum, within easy walking distance of all the city's major sights. In the 12th, 15th, and 17th centuries the Hôtel d'Arlatan belonged to the Counts of Arlatan de Beaumont and served as their private home. It is now the pride of Monsieur and Madame Yves Desjardin who offer an ideal retreat with charming accommodation and service. This is a quaint hotel, ornamented with antiques and pretty fabrics. Many of the bedrooms look onto a quiet inner courtyard or garden or across the tiled rooftops of Arles. No two guestrooms are alike, each with its own special charm, perhaps a sheltered patio, a lovely old fireplace, a private deck, each unique trait making a selection all the more difficult. Although there is no restaurant, a delightful breakfast can be enjoyed on the patio or in the inviting salon with a portion of its floor covered by glass to expose the excavated aqueduct. *Directions:* Arles is 36 km south of Avignon off the N570. At Place Lamartin enter the ramparts on Rue Septembre which becomes Rue du Sauvage.

HÔTEL D'ARLATAN
Hôteliers: Mme & M Yves Desjardin
26, Rue du Sauvage
13631 Arles, France
Tel: 04.90.93.56.66, Fax: 04.90.49.68.45,
E-mail: hotel-arlatan@provnet.fr
48 rooms, Double: 598F–1450F
Breakfast: 62F per person
Open all year, Credit cards: all major
No restaurant, garage: 70F, Handicap rooms
Region: Provence, Michelin Map 245
www.karenbrown.com/franceinns/hoteldarlatan.html

In the middle of the 17th century a Carmelite convent was erected in Arles by Mother Madeleine Saint Joseph. It was a residence for nuns until 1770 when the order was expelled in the midst of the French Revolution. The convent then became state property until it was purchased and transformed into a hotel in 1929. In this beautiful old convent, the Hôtel Jules César has earned a rating of four stars under the directorship of Monsieur Michel Albagnac. The hotel is situated next to and shares a courtyard with the Chapelle de la Charité, which belongs to the hotel and also dates from the 17th century. The restaurant, Lou Marquès, is air-conditioned and lovely, known for its classic and Provençal cooking. Little tables and chairs are set in the cloister, and here breakfast and light, quick lunches are served. All bedrooms are air-conditioned and spacious: room 72, with windows opening onto the garden, is an elegant, large room with two double beds. The pool is a welcome addition for those hot summer days in this region and now neighbors a beautiful Provençal garden. *Directions:* Arles is located 36 km south of Avignon traveling on the N570. The Jules César is on Boulevard des Lices, a main artery that borders the ramparts on the south.

HÔTEL JULES CÉSAR
Hôtelier: Michel Albagnac
Boulevard des Lices
BP 116, 13631 Arles, France
Tel: 04.90.93.43.20, Fax: 04.90.93.33.47
E-mail: julescesar@calva.net
58 rooms, Double: 1000F–2250F
Breakfast: 85F per person
Open December 23 to November 12
Credit cards: all major
Restaurant, garage, pool
Region: Provence, Michelin Map 245
www.karenbrown.com/franceinns/hoteljulescesar.html

The Grand Hôtel Nord-Pinus has held court on the Place du Forum for generations. It is located at the heart of Arles and has been the chosen destination of many, most colorfully the grand matadors, bullfighters en route from Paris or Spain. With a decor of terra-cotta tiles, wrought iron, and splashes of color in bountiful flower arrangements, the Nord-Pinus has served as home to many artists and writers as well. The inviting and attractive restaurant with country-motif table dressings, just off the entry, is under the supervision of the family that runs the famous L'Oustau Baumanière in nearby Les Baux. Guestrooms all have private bathrooms and vary from quite spacious to comfortable, with a decor of art deco to more traditional. Furnishings seem a bit worn, but somehow the worn look lends to the feeling of nostalgia and times past and is therefore forgiven. Choice rooms are number 4, a wonderful corner room that overlooks the plaza, and number 32, a suite, which is more modern in decor and a proven favorite of artists and photographers as it enjoys an expanse of window giving lots of light and views over the tiled rooftops of Arles. Smaller rooms such as number 7 are more reasonably priced, also nice in size, and almost always matched with a large bathroom. Breakfast is served behind arched columns on the first-floor landing or in the guestrooms. *Directions:* Travel the road that circles the heart of Arles and then follow signs to the hotel.

GRAND HÔTEL NORD-PINUS
Hôtelier: Anne Igou
Place du Forum
13200 Arles, France
Tel: 04.90.93.44.44, Fax: 04.90.93.34.00
E-mail: info@nord-pinus.com
25 rooms, Double: 840F–1700F
Breakfast: 75F or 95F per person
Open all year, Credit cards: all major
Restaurant, garage: 50F
Region: Provence, Michelin Map 245
www.karenbrown.com/franceinns/grandhotel.html

I wanted to abort my travels, unpack bags, and settle in at the beautiful Château de Vault de Lugny. I arrived on a warm spring afternoon and the obvious contentment of guests who were relaxing at tables on the front lawn was enviable. Voices were subdued and did not break the lovely quiet of the setting—perhaps because the individual desires of each guest were well tended to. It was early afternoon, yet I noticed one guest lounging over a late breakfast, a few guests sleeping with books neglected on their laps, and a foursome playing a game of cards under the shade of a large central tree. The Château de Vault de Lugny is a handsome cream-stone building with white shuttered windows and weathered-tile roof secluded by a high wall, moat, and tall gates. There are 12 bedrooms in the château, all with lovely modern bathrooms. Lavish and regal in their decor, the larger rooms are very popular. The smaller standard rooms are also charming and a better value. Meals are available at any hour, although *table d'hôte* dinners are served at a handsome trestle table set before a massive open fireplace. An added bonus for guests is the chance to ride in a hot-air balloon. *Directions:* Traveling the A6 between Paris and Beaune, take the Avallon exit and follow the direction of Vézelay west to Pontaubert, then turn right after the church. The château is on the right, 550 meters from the village.

CHÂTEAU DE VAULT DE LUGNY
Hôtelier: Elisabeth Matherat-Audan
11, Rue du Château
Pontaubert, 89200 Avallon, France
Tel: 03.86.34.07.86, Fax: 03.86.34.16.36
E-mail: hotel@lugny.com
12 rooms, Double: 950F–2500F, Breakfast: included
Open mid-March to mid-November
Credit cards: all major
Restaurant, garage: free, tennis, handicap rooms
Region: Burgundy, Michelin Map 238
www.karenbrown.com/franceinns/chateaudevaultdelugny.html

Hôtel d'Europe is a classically beautiful 16th-century mansion, formerly the home of the Marquis of Gravezon. The mansion was converted into a hotel in 1799 as it is within walking distance of the River Rhône, a prime location to attract travelers who in that period voyaged predominantly by boat. The present owner, René Daire, has completely modernized the hotel using handsome furnishings that suit the mood and complement this grand home. The walls of the marble entry hall, once an open courtyard, and the walls of the upper levels are now hung with magnificent tapestries. The bedrooms, all different in character and size, are furnished in traditional pieces and antiques. Many of the rooms are quite spacious and comfortable for extended stays. Although within the city walls of Avignon, many of the rooms overlook the hotel's courtyard and afford a quiet night's rest. You can dine in elegant formality in the hotel's fine restaurant, La Vieille Fontaine, or under the trees in the courtyard on balmy Provençal nights. *Directions:* From the A7 take the Avignon *Nord* exit towards Avignon *Centre Ville*. Follow the Rhone to the ramparts. On the right, under the bridge of Avignon follow signs to Hotel d'Europe and the entrance of Porte de l'Oulle. Just inside the ramparts, the Place Crillon is on the left.

HÔTEL D'EUROPE
Hôtelier: René Daire
Directeur: Hendrick Dandeij
12, Place Crillon, 84000 Avignon, France
Tel: 04.90.14.76.76, Fax: 04.90.14.76.71
E-mail: reservations@hotel-d-europe.fr
47 rooms, Double: 690F–3300F
Breakfast: 98F per person
Open all year
Credit cards: all major
Restaurant, garage: 55F
Region: Provence, Michelin Maps 245, 246
www.karenbrown.com/franceinns/hoteldeurope.html

La Mirande dates from the 14th century with various additions made to it in the 15th, 17th and 18th centuries. It was the residence of Cardinal Armand de Pellegrue, nephew of Pope Clement V, and later a private residence for the mayor of Avignon. The Stein family came from Germany, fell in love with the property, and converted it to a luxury hotel with a desire to improve upon the four-star hotels they had experienced in their travels. They have exceeded their goals and created a superlative property. Every luxurious detail has been well thought out and implemented, seemingly without consideration of cost—only consideration of the guests and their comfort. A multitude of public rooms and the 20 guestrooms are beautifully appointed with rich fabrics and gorgeous antiques. The dining room has an absolutely stunning 15th-century French ceiling and needlepoint carpet, an Aubusson tapestry draping an entire wall, and is warmed by a large open fireplace in winter months. Dinner is served on the terrace patio on balmy summer nights. Overlooking the palace walls, La Mirande is spacious and luxurious, an oasis for its guests. It has even been said that, "Had the Pope ended up at La Mirande instead of across the street, he might never have returned to Rome." *Directions:* Exit off A7 at Avignon *Nord*, take the gate *Porte de la Ligne* into the walled city, and follow signs to La Mirande.

LA MIRANDE
Hôteliers: Achim Stein
4, Place de la Mirande
84000 Avignon, France
Tel: 04.90.85.93.93, Fax: 04.90.86.26.85
E-mail: mirande@la-mirande.fr
20 rooms, Double: 1850F–3700F
Breakfast: 115F per person, Open all year
Credit cards: all major
Restaurant, garage: 80F, Handicap room
Region: Provence, Michelin Maps 245, 246
www.karenbrown.com/franceinns/lamirande.html

The cobblestoned town of Barbizon has attracted artists for many years, and the 19th-century timbered Hôtellerie du Bas-Bréau has had its share of famous guests. Robert Louis Stevenson wrote in *Forest Notes* about this hotel and it is often called "Stevenson's House." Famous painters who treasured this corner of the Forest of Fontainebleau include Millet, Corot, Sisley, and Monet. Some accommodations are in the main timbered house, but most are in a two-story building in the back garden. Each room is different in decor and has a bath. The restaurant is superb, drawing dinner guests from as far away as Paris. With unusually attractive flower arrangements on each table, the atmosphere of the dining room is elegant and romantic. Political leaders from Italy, Germany, Great Britain, Ireland, Greece, Luxembourg, Denmark, and the Netherlands selected the hotel as a conference location—you will understand their choice when you dine at Hôtellerie du Bas-Bréau where the menu features homegrown vegetables and herbs and specialties such as wild boar. The house wine list is incredible. *Directions:* From Paris take A6 south in the direction of Fontainebleau and exit at Barbizon. From the south on A6, exit at Fontainebleau. At the obelisk in Fontainebleau take the N7 in the direction of Paris and travel 8 km to Barbizon.

HÔTELLERIE DU BAS-BRÉAU
Hôteliers: Mme & M Jean Pierre Fava
Directeur: Tino Malchiodi
22, Rue Grande, 77630 Barbizon, France
Tel: 01.60.66.40.05, Fax: 01.60.69.22.89
E-mail: basbreau@wanadoo.fr
12 rooms, Double: 1000F–2800F
Breakfast: 100F per person
Open all year, Credit cards: AX, VS
Restaurant, garage: 70F, pool, tennis
Non-smoking and handicap rooms
Region: Île de France, Michelin Map 237
www.karenbrown.com/franceinns/hotelleriedubasbreau.html

We arrived on the doorstep of the Auberge de la Source at the most inconvenient hour, in the middle of dinner, and unintentionally put management though the most grueling "graciousness test"—they passed with flying colors. Madame Legeay, a delightful and charming hostess, met us with a smile, juggled dinner guests, directed staff, and still was able to proudly show us her home and hotel. Behind the scenes, Monsieur Legeay was in charge of the kitchen and preparation of the evening meal (a set three-course menu that changes daily), which featured his fisherman son's catch of the day. The Auberge de la Source is an enchanting inn sitting at the edge of a quiet, unspoilt Norman village. It is a complex of charming timbered buildings, the main one housing the first-floor restaurant and simple basic hotel rooms above and a second building running the length of the garden, which houses the more expensive, more commodious, more modern rooms. The gardens are peaceful, soothed by the sound of the gurgling creek and a man-made waterfall. Guestrooms are simple, attractive, comfortable, and well priced at this delightful, yet unpretentious country *auberge*. The Legeays ask that guests stay on a *demi-pension* basis, i.e., including breakfast and dinner, however long their stay. *Directions:* From Honfleur travel the D513 west along the coast in the direction of Deauville. Five km after leaving Honfleur, watch for the small road signed D62 and turn off to Barneville.

AUBERGE DE LA SOURCE   **New**
Hôteliers: Mme & M Legeay
Barneville la Bertran
14600 Honfleur, France
Tel: 02.31.89.25.02, Fax: 02.31.89.44.40
16 rooms, Double: 320F–450F*
  *price per person includes breakfast and dinner
Demi-pension required
Open February 14 to November 4, Credit cards: none
Restaurant open for dinner for residents only, parking
Region: Normandy, Michelin Map 231

L'Auberge de la Benvengudo is tucked away along the road as it winds through the valley traveling from the hillside town of Les Baux de Provence. The inn began as a family home offering rooms to friends and overnight guests. In response to the number of returning guests, as well as those who were guided here by their praise, L'Auberge de la Benvengudo has expanded from a private home into a proper hotel. Sheltered behind a vast garden, the hotel extends out from, and beautifully copies the design of the original home. Ivy has now covered the newer stucco walls as it does on the main home, and the Provençal sun has already warmed and mellowed the red-tile roofs. Green-shuttered windows open onto the surrounding rocky hillsides, low green shrubbery, the large swimming pool, tennis court, and gardens. Heavy, dark colors (very Mediterranean in flavor) are used to decorate the bedrooms. Accommodations are comfortable, basic, some quite spacious, all with modern bathrooms. Those on a longer stay might want to reserve a room equipped with a kitchenette. The restaurant is lovely and the menu is tempting in its selection. *Directions:* From Saint Rémy de Provence, travel south on the D5 to Les Baux de Provence. Turn off the D5 onto the D27. L'Auberge is located off the D27 below the village.

L'AUBERGE DE LA BENVENGUDO
Hôteliers: Beaupied Family
Vallon de l'Accoule
13520 Les Baux de Provence, France
Tel: 04.90.54.32.54, Fax: 04.90.54.42.58
23 rooms, Double: 650F–985F
Breakfast: 70F per person
Open March 15 to November 1
Credit cards: AX, VS
Restaurant closed Sunday, pool, tennis, non-smoking room
Region: Provence, Michelin Maps 245, 246

This inn nestled at the base of the village of Les Baux de Provence occupies a quiet location among olive trees surrounded by the chalky, white-rock hillsides dotted with the green shrubbery of Provence. The soft sandstone color of its exterior, dressed with soft green shutters, white trim, and a rust tile roof, was beautifully selected to blend, rather than contrast, with the warmth of its setting. The entry of the hotel is light and spacious, decorated with a mix of modern pieces and contemporary fabrics. Beams contrast with whitewashed walls and the floor is of terra-cotta tile. The lovely bedrooms are all similar in their decor with rustic oak furniture and dressed with Provençal prints and light colors. Bathrooms are spotless and modern and each room is equipped with color satellite TV, safe, mini bar, and air conditioning. A few guestrooms open onto garden terraces with their own garden entry and a lovely suite enjoys its own private garden, terrace and looks out to the olive trees. The pool with Jacuzzi offers a peaceful oasis, surrounded by a lush green lawn, and it is here that grilled meats and provençal salads are served at lunchtime. After a day of sightseeing, you can relax on a comfortable lounge, looking out to the hills of Provence. *Directions:* The entrance to Mas de l'Oulivie is located just off the D27.

MAS DE L'OULIVIE
Hôteliers: Mme & M Emmanuel Achard
13520 Les Baux de Provence, France
Tel: 04.90.54.35.78, Fax: 04.90.54.44.31
E-mail: masdeloulivie@gulliver.fr
23 rooms, Double: 620F–1400F
Breakfast: 60F or 80F per person,
Open mid-March to mid-November
Credit cards: all major, No restaurant
Garage: no charge, pool, tennis, handicap rooms
Region: Provence, Michelin Maps 240, 245
www.karenbrown.com/franceinns/masdeloulivie.html

Bayeux is renowned for being the home of the Bayeux tapestry and it is also one of France's most picturesque towns. I include the Hôtel d'Argouges as Bayeux is a wonderful town to overnight and the d'Argouges is conveniently located on one of its main squares, sheltered behind tall gates. A large courtyard and stone, semi-circular staircase lead to the front entry of the hotel. French doors in the gracious salon-library open onto the quiet back garden and terrace. Looking out over the garden or front courtyard, many of the bedrooms have exposed beams, fabric-covered walls, and comfortable furniture as well as private shower or bath and phones. There are also two suites with a small extra room for children. Additional bedrooms arc found in an adjacent home. Breakfast can be enjoyed in the privacy of your room, in the intimate breakfast salon, or on the back garden terrace overlooking Madame Auregan's brightly colored flowers. A convenient haven for travelers visiting Bayeux, the Hôtel d'Argouges offers good value in lovely surroundings plus a gracious hostess, Marie-Claire Auregan, who takes great pride in her *métier*. On a recent visit she was very proud to show me the extensive redecoration throughout so that the hotel would look fresh and pretty for the coming season. *Directions:* From Paris follow directions to *Centre Ville* and you will find yourself on Rue Saint Patrice.

HÔTEL D'ARGOUGES
Hôtelier: Marie-Claire Auregan
21, Rue Saint Patrice, 14400 Bayeux, France
E-mail: dargouges@aol.com
Tel: 02.31.92.88.86, Fax: 02.31.92.69.16
26 rooms, Double: 460F–550F
Breakfast: 45F per person
Open all year
Credit cards: all major
No restaurant, garage
Region: Normandy, Michelin Map 231
www.karenbrown.com/franceinns/hoteldargouges.html

The Château de Sully affords the traveler a luxurious base from which to explore Normandy. Just to the north of Bayeux at the end of a tree-lined drive, this beautiful 18th-century château is set on an expanse of green lawn with gorgeous gardens at the back—an elegant hotel, yet offering a genuinely warm welcome to its guests. The dining room is gorgeous, with a color scheme of blues and beiges from table linens to drapes to china, and has an enclosed outdoor terrace overlooking the garden. Public rooms run the length of the château at the back and also enjoy beautiful garden views. The games room with its billiard table is a social place to settle, the bar with its intimate clustering of tables is most attractive, and the grand sitting room is very pretty. Of the 22 guestrooms 13 are found in the main château and the additional 9 in the neighboring *Petite Manoir*. Although classification of rooms varies from standard to suite, the difference is not in the elegance, the comfort, or style of furnishings but rather in the size of room and location. There is only one suite, number 17, a romantic room with a four-poster bed draped in a handsome fabric of reds and greens. The annex rooms, which share the building with the fitness room and indoor pool, are more modern and a bit larger and two on the garden level enjoy their own terrace. *Directions*: Leave Bayeux on the D6 in the direction of Port en Bessin. The Château de Sully is located just a few kilometers north of the city limits on the east side.

CHÂTEAU DE SULLY **New**
Hôteliers: Inka & Antoine Brault
Route de Port en Bessin, 14400 Bayeux, France
Tel: 02.31.22.29.48, Fax: 02.31.22.64.77
22 rooms, Double: 520F–690F
Breakfast: 65F per person
Open March to November, Credit cards: all major
Restaurant closed for lunch on Mon & Sat
Enclosed parking, pool
Region: Normandy, Michelin Map 231

La Tonnellerie, renovated from a wine-merchant's house, is located on a quiet street near the church in the country village of Tavers. Just 3 kilometers from the medieval city of Beaugency and only an hour-and-a-half's drive from Paris by the autoroute, the Hostellerie de la Tonnellerie is an ideal starting point for visiting the châteaux of the Loire Valley. The bedrooms and suites are invitingly decorated and each has its own immaculate bathroom. Two wings of the building border a central courtyard ablaze with flowers, next to the swimming pool. On the first floor of one wing La Tonnellerie's restaurant features regional specialties as well as *nouvelle cuisine.* The atmosphere of this lovely restored home, which a century ago housed coopers making barrels for wine merchants, is enhanced by antiques, floral arrangements, lovely watercolors, and decorative wallpapers. The decor is warm and inviting and the Pouey family's welcome very gracious. *Directions:* Exit from the A10 at Meung/Beaugency, 28 km southwest of Orléans. The hotel is 3 km southwest of Beaugency on the RN152 going towards Blois.

HOSTELLERIE DE LA TONNELLERIE
Hôteliers: Marie-Christine & Alain Pouey
12, Rue des Eaux-Bleues
45190 Tavers, Beaugency, France
Tel: 02.38.44.68.15, Fax: 02.38.44.10.01
E-mail: tonelri@club-internet.fr
20 rooms, Double: 590F–1290F
Breakfast: 75F per person
Open March 1 to November 30
Credit cards: all major
Restaurant, pool
Region: Loire Valley, Michelin Map 238
www.karenbrown.com/franceinns/latonnellerie.html

In the heart of the lovely medieval town of Beaune, Le Cep offers charming and comfortable air-conditioned bedrooms decorated with elegance and taste. The Bernards' son has just returned to Beaune and settled in with his own family to take over management of Le Cep. He is charming and continues the high standard of tradition of welcome and service. The bedrooms vary in size and decor but are all handsome—highly polished wooden antique furnishings are accented by the beautiful, softly colored fabrics used for the curtains, bedspreads, and upholstery. In the bar and public areas, heavy-beamed ceilings, old gilt-framed portraits, and fresh-flower arrangements add character and elegance. The former wine cellar, a cozy room with a low, arched stone ceiling, is used as a breakfast room when the weather does not permit service outdoors in the pretty courtyard. While Beaune is a destination in itself, it is also a delightful base for touring the Burgundy wine region. Le Cep combines elegance and warmth in perfect proportions. *Directions:* Beaune is located at the heart of Burgundy, 45 km south of Dijon. Circle the town on the road that follows the ramparts. Turn left into the center of town on Rue Maufoux. Le Cep is on the right side of the road.

HÔTEL LE CEP
Hôteliers: Nerino Bernard Family
27, Rue Maufoux
21200 Beaune, France
Tel: 03.80.22.35.48, Fax: 03.80.22.76.80
E-mail: hotel-le-cep.resa@wanadoo.fr
56 rooms, Double: 800F–1800F
Breakfast: 80F per person
Open all year
Credit cards: all major
Restaurant, garage: 50F, handicap rooms
Region: Burgundy, Michelin Map 243
www.karenbrown.com/franceinns/hotellecep.html

Hôtel de la Poste is located on the old ring-road that follows the ancient city walls of Beaune. With parts of it dating back to 1660, the hotel has in recent years undergone a complete renovation including the addition of double-paned windows to eliminate all traffic noise from rooms facing the boulevard. The lobby and bar have retained their old-world ambiance, but the bedrooms are a mix of traditional as well as contemporary in their decor. This is a lovely city hotel and I am pleased each year to see that the owners have made a commitment to refurbish a few guestrooms on an ongoing basis. Although not necessarily behind the desk, the owners are ever-present and care about the welcome and level of service extended to their guests. The restaurant has maintained its standard of excellence and some of France's finest Burgundies are a perfect accompaniment to the hotel's outstanding menu selections. With Beaune as a base, you can easily venture out to explore and sample some of Burgundy's finest wines. A few minutes' walk brings you to the heart of this charming old walled town with its delightful pedestrian streets. *Directions:* Beaune is located at the heart of Burgundy, 45 km south of Dijon. Circle the town on the ring-road to Boulevard Clemenceau: the hotel is on the right-hand side of the road.

HÔTEL DE LA POSTE
Hôteliers: Mme & M Stratigos-Baboz
5, Boulevard Clemenceau
21200 Beaune, France
Tel: 03.80.22.08.11, Fax: 03.80.24.19.71
E-mail: Francoise.Stratigos@wanadoo.fr
30 rooms, Double: 680F–1500F
Breakfast: 80F per person
Open all year
Credit cards: all major
Restaurant, garage: 50F
Region: Burgundy, Michelin Map 243
www.karenbrown.com/franceinns/hoteldelaposte.html

L'Auberge de l'Abbaye is a very pretty, half-timbered inn in the picturesque village of Le Bec Hellouin. The lovely old abbey, built along a stream and surrounded by half-timbered and thatched buildings, enjoys a peaceful pastoral setting far removed from any hustle and bustle. When we entered the cozy, low-ceilinged restaurant of the 18th-century L'Auberge de l'Abbaye, we were greeted by the sight and aroma of a large, freshly baked apple tart. We were told by the welcoming owner, Madame Sergent, that her restaurant is renowned all over the world for apple tarts. Grand Marnier, a specialty of the region, is also featured here, with large bottles present on each table. The restaurant is full of old-world, country-French charm: lace curtains grace the windows, polished copper and faience ornament the walls, country-style tables are set with care, and the low-beamed ceiling adds character. A narrow little staircase leads to the bedrooms, which are small, but I was pleased to see on a recent visit that they have been redecorated with light, pretty colors and that fresh new carpets dress the hallways. Each guestroom is accompanied by a basic but spotlessly clean bathroom. Inside and out, L'Auberge de l'Abbaye is the epitome of a simple, country-French restaurant with rooms. *Directions:* Located 42 km southwest of Rouen. Take the N138 from Rouen in the direction of Alençon to Maison Brulée. Just before Brionne turn right to Le Bec Hellouin.

L'AUBERGE DE L'ABBAYE
Hôteliers: M. Sergent Family
27800 Le Bec Hellouin, France
Tel: 02.32.44.86.02, Fax: 02.32.46.32.23
10 rooms, Double: 450F–600F
Breakfast: 45F per person
Closed two weeks in January
Credit cards: all major
Restaurant, garage: no charge
Region: Normandy, Michelin Map 231
www.karenbrown.com/franceinns/aubergedelabbaye.html

The views from Domaine de Rochevilaine, perched at the end of a rocky promontory in Brittany, are stupendous, especially when the sun shines on the glistening sea or when the wind howls as the waves crash against the rocks below. The vast windows of the sitting room and the restaurant overlook a sky-wide expanse of open sea, giving the distinct sensation of being shipboard. Oriental carpets grace old polished hardwood floors and a roaring fire burns in the grate on cool days. The menu is superb, and the service is both attentive and gracious. Bedrooms are found either in the little, old stone cottages or in a new (though traditionally styled) wing of rooms near the luxurious indoor swimming pool (there's also a salt-water pool set into the rocks on the ocean's edge). All of the bedrooms enjoy dramatic sea views, several have private terraces, handsome wood floors, and mellow paneling. The most dramatic room is La Vigie (the lookout), room 11, named for its 180-degree views. Our room with its expanse of view out to the sea was a wonderful place to linger and inspired me to write. The health center offers a gymnasium, massages, and saunas. *Directions:* The Domaine de Rochevilaine is at Pointe de Pen Lan, 5 km from Muzillac on the D5. Muzillac is located 25 km southeast of Vannes on the road that travels between Vannes and Nantes.

DOMAINE DE ROCHEVILAINE
Hôtelier: Bertrand Jaquet
Pointe de Pen Lan, Billiers
56190 Muzillac, France
Tel: 02.97.41.61.61, Fax: 02.97.41.44.85
E-mail: domaine@domainerochevilaine.com
38 rooms, Double: 863F–2450F
Breakfast: 85F per person
Open all year
Credit cards: all major
Restaurant, 2 pools, health spa, handicap rooms
Region: Brittany, Michelin Map 230
www.karenbrown.com/franceinns/rochevilaine.html

Bléré is a delightful little town that is perfectly located for exploring the châteaux of the Loire Valley and quiet enough that it is not mobbed by tourists. Facing the town's pedestrian center, Le Cheval Blanc has a contemporary façade that disguises the fact that this is a very old building, once being an annex for the neighboring church. After the Revolution, the building was converted to a café-bar and remained so for almost two centuries. It was purchased by Micheline and Michel Blériot several years ago and they have converted the café into a most attractive restaurant with pretty wallpaper, wooden chairs, and tables dressed with crisp linens. For this simple country hotel, the restaurant is surprisingly elegant and the gourmet offering of the menu outstanding. An inner courtyard latticed with vines and set with white outdoor tables is a delightful spot for breakfast. Michel is the chef while Micheline looks after the front of the house. Upstairs, the bedrooms are very simply decorated, and all but one are small with either a tiny shower or bathroom. They are all spotlessly clean and provide very good value for money. *Directions:* Bléré is on the N76, 27 km east of Tours and 8 km west of Chenonceaux. The rear of the hotel faces Place Charles Bidault and the hotel's car park.

LE CHEVAL BLANC
Hôteliers: Micheline & Michel Blériot
5, Place Charles Bidault
Place de l'Église
37150 Bléré, France
Tel: 02.47.30.30.14, Fax: 02.47.23.52.80
12 rooms, Double: 350F–420F
Breakfast: 42F per person
Closed January, Credit cards: all major
Restaurant, closed Sunday night & Monday
Garage: no charge, pool, non-smoking rooms
Region: Loire Valley, Michelin Map 238
www.karenbrown.com/franceinns/chevalblanc.html

If are looking for lovely accommodations along with gourmet dining, La Bastide de Capelongue will win your heart. Nestled in the wooded hills in one of the most beautiful parts of Provence, the hotel captures the magic of this exquisitely beautiful region. This is a typical Provençal house, built of creamy white stone, accented by a rustic tiled roof, and enhanced by light-blue shutters. The dining room is especially attractive, embraced on two sides by huge arched windows capturing the special glow of the Provençal sun. The dining room opens onto a terrace and beyond, a path meanders down through fragrant beds of lavender and roses to a superb swimming pool. Just on the opposite hill, the quaint, very old village of Bonnieux clings to the hillside, almost too picture-perfect to be real. Each of the appealing guestrooms has been lovingly decorated by Madame Loubet (with the help of her daughter who painted some of the wall decorations). Luxurious fabrics, the finest linens, and highest quality amenities are found throughout. Dinner or lunch is included in the room rate, but as you savor the five-course gourmet meal while the breezes brush the pine trees on the terrace and the sun fades over the distant hills, you will never want to eat elsewhere. *Directions*: Located about 45 km northwest of Aix-en-Provence. From Cadenet, take D943 north through Loumarin. Before you come to Bonnieux there is a sign on the right that directs you to the hotel.

LA BASTIDE DE CAPELONGUE   ***New***
Hôtelier: Claude Loubet
Directrice: Marie-Pierre Le Bris
84480 Bonnieux, France
Tel: 04.90.75.89.78, Fax: 04.90.75.93.03
E-mail: bastide@francemarket.com
17 rooms, Double: 1,000F–1,200F*
*Rate per person, includes breakfast & lunch or dinner
Open mid-March to mid-November
Credit cards: all major
Restaurant, pool
Region: Provence, Michelin Map 245

Tucked 10 kilometers farther up a quiet valley from the larger town of Brantôme, Bourdeilles has an idyllic setting. I have returned numerous times over the past 23 years to the village of Bourdeilles, and the village remains as enchanting as when I first discovered it. In this old village crowned by a castle, the Hostellerie des Griffons sits next to a narrow bridge and offers accommodation in a tranquil, picture-book setting. Under new ownership, the Griffons has benefited greatly from fresh decor and refurbishments. The outside shutters are now a pretty blue and the new courtyard and rear entrance are quite attractive. This is a charming inn in an idyllic setting and it is so nice to be able to recommend it unconditionally. Guaranteeing a peaceful night's sleep, many of the bedrooms nestle under old beams and overlook the quietly flowing river—a personal favorite, number nine, is a charming corner room set under romantic beams and eaves. The restaurant is intimate and inviting, with windows opening up to the soothing sound of cascading water. Tables are set on the terrace on warm summer nights—the outdoor setting is romantic and perfect for enjoying wonderful Périgord specialties. The Hostellerie des Griffons is a delightful inn and a good value on the northern boundaries of the Dordogne. *Directions:* Bourdeilles is located 24 km northwest of Périgueux. From Périgueux take the N939 north to Brantôme and then travel 10 km west on the D78.

HOSTELLERIE DES GRIFFONS
Hôteliers: M & Mme Bernard Lebrun-Goldschmidt
Le Bourg, Bourdeilles
24310 Brantôme, France
Tel: 05.53.45.45.35, Fax: 05.53.45.45.20
10 rooms, Double: 420F–520F
Breakfast: 45F per person
Open Mar 20 to Oct 8, Credit cards: all major
Restaurant, riverside setting, non-smoking rooms
Region: Dordogne, Michelin Map 233
www.karenbrown.com/franceinns/griffons.html

Brantôme, with its Benedictine abbey tucked into the cliffs, narrow streets lined with gray-stone houses, and ancient footbridge spanning the River Dronne beside Le Moulin de l'Abbaye, offers an enchanting setting. The hotel looks across the river to the town from its picturesque riverside location. Owner Régis Bulot is president of Relais & Châteaux hotels and you can be certain that he ensures that his hotel is a flagship for this prestigious organization. Dinner is a real treat—we found it no more expensive than at far inferior places and its wine list had many well-priced wines. Dinner, whether served outdoors on the terrace or in the elegant dining room, profits from the idyllic riverside setting. The lovely bedrooms are found in three buildings: the mill, an adjacent home, and a delightful riverside house just two minutes' walk across the bridge and through the park. We particularly enjoyed our village bedroom atop a broad flight of spiral stairs. It enjoys delightful decor, views across the rooftops through tiny windows, and a luxurious bathroom with an enormous circular tub. *Directions:* Brantôme is located 27 km northwest of Périgueux on the N939. The mill is at the edge of the village on the road to Bourdeilles.

LE MOULIN DE L'ABBAYE
Hôtelier: Régis Bulot
Directeurs: Mme & M Bernard Dessum
1, Route de Bourdeilles
24310 Brantôme, France
Tel: 05.53.05.80.22, Fax: 05.53.05.75.27
E-mail: moulin@relaischateaux.fr
19 rooms, Double: 900F–1500F
Breakfast: 90F per person
Open May 2 to November 2
Credit cards: all major, handicap room
Restaurant closed Monday lunch, garage: no charge
Region: Dordogne, Michelin Map 233
www.karenbrown.com/franceinns/moulindelabbaye.html

The Château de Brélidy is located in Brittany, in an area surrounded by quiet woods and fishing streams, yet just 20 kilometers from the northern coastline. Elaine and Pierre Yoncourt are the gracious, English-speaking hosts who solicitously attend to their guests' every need. They run a professional château-hotel offering a full range of accommodation, from basic to luxurious, and a warm welcome to tourists and business travelers alike. Ten bedrooms are located in a beautifully reconstructed 16th-century wing of the castle, and although decorated with period-style furniture and tapestry-style fabrics, are modern and spotless. They all have private baths, TVs, and direct-dial phones. Guests are invited to relax in the castle's salon where tapestry chairs, a huge open fireplace, vases of fresh flowers, and *objets d'art* create a refined setting. A stay here is as comfortable as it is full of atmosphere, for although the castle dates from the 16th century, the Yoncourt-Pemezec family has worked hard to restore it to its current polished state of perfection. For travelers with smaller pocketbooks, modest bed-and-breakfast accommodation in four intimate attic rooms is available. These rooms each have private bath and toilet, are homey, comfortable, and spotlessly clean. *Directions:* From Saint Brieuc take the N12 in the direction of Brest to the D767 and exit for Lannion-Bégard, Treguier. Take the D17 to Treguier for 11 km to Brélidy.

CHÂTEAU DE BRÉLIDY
Hôteliers: Pierre & Elaine Yoncourt
22140 Brélidy, France
Tel: 02.96.95.69.38, Fax: 02.96.95.18.03
14 rooms, Double: 380F–1145F
Breakfast: 55F per person
Open April 23 to November 2
Credit cards: all major
Restaurant
Non-smoking & handicap rooms
Region: Brittany, Michelin Map 230
www.karenbrown.com/franceinns/chateaudebrelidy.html

The Château de Noirieux is exceptional. A beautiful wooded property set in the hills above Angers in the Loire Valley, it has gardens abounding with flowers, a lovely pool, tennis courts, and gorgeous river views. A charming couple, the Cômes, oversees the welcome and the exceptional kitchen. Upstairs in the château are the largest and most expensive rooms with elegant decor and views of the river. Number 1 is a corner room decorated in cascades of blue-and-cream fabric; the middle room, number 2 is decorated in a fabric of ribbons and roses in soft tones of blues and pinks; and number 3 is the smallest room but with a larger bathroom. Also in the château there are six rooms overlooking the inner courtyard, which are also lovely in decor but smaller and more moderate in price. Another ten rooms are located in the neighboring manor, all attractive and spacious. A bowl of nuts (noirieux), a basket of fruit, fresh flowers, and personalized toiletries welcome guests in each room. The ambiance in the restaurant, with its linens and drapes in soft hues of yellow, is very romantic. A pretty breakfast room, enclosed with full glass windows, is set just off the terrace. *Directions:* From the A11 from Paris exit at 14, from Angers exit at 14B, following directions to Briollay and Soucelles, on the D109.

CHÂTEAU DE NOIRIEUX
Owner: M. Shen
Hôteliers: Anja & Gerard Côme
26 Route du Moulin, 49125 Briollay, France
Tel: 02.41.42.50.05, Fax: 02.41.37.91.00
E-mail: noirieux@relaischateaux.fr
19 rooms, Double: 880F–1750F
Breakfast: 100F per person
Closed Feb 15 to Mar 15 & Nov
Credit cards: all major
Restaurant closed mid-Oct to mid-Apr, Sun & Mon nights
Tennis, pool, fishing, 20-acre park, handicap rooms
Region: Loire Valley, Michelin Map 232
www.karenbrown.com/franceinns/chateaudenoirieux.html

The atmosphere of the Middle Ages prevails in the narrow, winding, cobblestoned streets leading to the Château Grimaldi, built in 1309 by Raynier Grimaldi, the ruler of Monaco. As the streets become narrower, passing under buildings that form an archway, you arrive at Le Cagnard, a hotel that has been in operation for over 40 years. Continuing the tradition of welcome perfected by the Barel Family, their daughter and her husband, Madame and Monsieur Barel Laroche are now the resident innkeepers. Dinner on the terrace, set under a full moon, or indoors, with the atmosphere of a medieval castle with candlelight flickering against age-old walls, is a romantic experience and the presentation of the food is exceptional. The elevator is charming, presenting biblical paintings changing with each floor. Guestrooms are located either in the main building with the restaurant or tucked off cobbled streets in neighboring buildings. Rooms have a medieval flavor to their decor and are comfortable, but not overly luxurious. A few prize rooms enjoy patios with wonderful views over the tiled rooftops out to the countryside. *Directions:* If you arrive by the A8 or N7 or by N98, follow the sign *Centre Ville* along J.F. Kennedy and Marchel Juin, then *Haut de Cagnes-Château-Musée*. At the entrance to the old city you'll pass an automatic car park called *Le Planastel*, turn right; the hotel is 200 meters farther along this narrow road.

LE CAGNARD
Hôteliers: Mme & M Barel Laroche
Rue sous Barri, Haut de Cagnes
06800 Cagnes sur Mer, France
Tel: 04.93.20.73.21 & 22, Fax: 04.93.22.06.39
E-mail: cagnard@relaischateaux.fr
25 rooms, Double: 860F–1700F
Breakfast: 100F per person
Open all year, Credit cards: all major
Restaurant closed Nov 1 to Dec 20, garage
Region: Riviera, Michelin Map 245
www.karenbrown.com/franceinns/lecagnard.html

The Richeux Hôtel is situated on an old travelers' road that ran between Mont Saint Michel and Saint Malo, near the little hamlet of Saint Méloir des Ondes, just south of Cancale. Sitting high on a clifftop and surrounded by gardens, the hotel overlooks the Bay of Mont Saint Michel with the outline of its famous island in the distance. Jane and Olivier Roellinger, who have an award-winning restaurant, Maison de Bricourt, in Cancale, purchased this splendid turreted Victorian in 1992, and after a complete renovation opened it as a luxurious hotel. The comfortable sitting room and small dining rooms offer stunning sea views. We were able to see only some of the hotel's most luxurious bedrooms and found them to be absolutely divine. Galanga has a massive curved window framing Mont Saint Michel one way and Cancale the other; Anis Etoile, once an enormous bathroom, has an art-deco mosaic extending halfway up its walls; and Benso is a particularly attractive room with tall French windows and a balcony. Guests are welcomed with a personal note, fruit, an aperitif, and a serving of tea and cakes. The hotel has a small seafood restaurant or, alternatively, guests can be driven to Maison de Bricourt for dinner. *Directions:* From Cancale take the D76 towards Dol, then the first left signpost to Mont Saint Michel. The hotel is on the left upon reaching the sea.

RICHEUX HÔTEL
Hôteliers: Jane & Olivier Roellinger
1, Rue Duguesclin
Saint Méloir des Ondes
35260 Cancale, France
Tel: 02.99.89.64.76, Fax: 02.99.89.88.47
E-mail: de.Bricourt@relaischateaux.fr
19 rooms, Double: 650F–1650F
Breakfast: 90F per person
Open all year, Credit cards: all major
Restaurant
Region: Brittany, Michelin Map 230

Set in the quiet of the French countryside, Le Fleuray is a lovely soft-peach manor whose windowboxes hang heavy with geraniums. Its English owners, Hazel and Peter Newington, who settled here with their children, have decorated it with a theme of butterflies and flowers in soft muted colors of beiges and soft peach with floral and stripes both in the fabrics and wallpapers. White wicker furnishings and soft-pink carpets complement the exterior color of the building. The 11 attractive bedrooms are named after local flowers and are individualized by their beautiful hand painted name plaques. Two spacious guestrooms are located in the old barn and the Newingtons have plans once again for 2000 to add a few more rooms. The barn with its expanse of lawn and extra-large accommodation is a wonderful option for families. For meals, the Newingtons offer a lovely breakfast and dinner. Tables are set with peach-color linens in front of a gorgeous stone fireplace or under the shade of trees in the garden. The menu originated with personal favorites and has won local praise and, most importantly, patronage. In the summers they are assisted by a lovely staff of charming girls, both from the region and from England. *Directions:* Take exit 18, Amboise/Château-Renault, off the A10, and then travel south on the D31 to Autrèche, east on the D55 to Dame Marie les Bois, and south on the D74 to Fleuray. Signs direct you the entire way.

LE FLEURAY
Hôteliers: Hazel & Peter Newington
37530 Cangey, Amboise, France
Tel: 02.47.56.09.25, Fax: 02.47.56.93.97
E-mail: lefleurayhotel@wanadoo.fr
11 rooms, Double: 450F–550F
Breakfast: 68F per person
Closed Oct 25 to Nov 6, Dec 19 to Jan 4
 & Feb 12 to 28 (winter school vacations)
Credit cards: MC, VS, Restaurant, garage: no charge
Region: Loire Valley, Michelin Map 232
www.karenbrown.com/franceinns/lefleuray.html

A few years ago, the two hotels we recommended in the medieval fortress of Carcassonne, the Hôtel de la Cité and the Dame Carcas, came under new ownership, were completely renovated, and became one under the name of the Hôtel de la Cité. Predicted luxury is unfortunately at a higher price tag, but it is still memorable to settle for an evening behind the massive walls of the fortress in this lovely hotel. Recessed into the walls near the Basilica Saint Nazaire, the hotel occupies the site of the ancient Episcopal palace and offers you the refined comfort of its rooms in a medieval atmosphere. The bar is a welcome spot to settle in for a drink. Dining is an elegant and memorable experience in the hotel's restaurant, La Barbacane, or the less formal brasserie, Chez Saskie. The hotel's bedrooms, many of which open up onto the ramparts and a large enclosed garden, vary in price according to size, decor, and view. Carcassonne is a magnificent fortress, completely restored to look as it did when first constructed centuries ago. It is impressive when viewed at a distance, rising above the vineyards at the foot of the Cevennes and Pyrenees, but even more spectacular when explored on foot. *Directions:* Carcassonne is located 92 km southeast of Toulouse. Although the city is closed to all but pedestrian traffic, you can enter it by car (via Porte Narbonnaise), travel Rue Mayrevieille, Rue Porte d'Aude, and Rue Saint Louis and park at the hotel.

HÔTEL DE LA CITÉ
Hôtelier: M. Jacques Hamburger
Place de l'Église, 11000 Carcassonne, France
Tel: 04.68.71.98.71, Fax: 04.68.71.50.15
61 rooms, Double: 950F–3200F
Breakfast: 130F per person
Open January 5 to November 31
Credit cards: all major
Restaurant, garage: 90F, pool
Non-smoking & handicap rooms
Region: Languedoc, Michelin Map 235

When you visit Carcassonne, head straight for the Cité Médiévale, an 11th-century fortified town built upon a low hill overlooking the "new" town. This is an absolutely perfectly preserved walled town with a jumble of whimsical towers with peaked slate roofs, moats, drawbridges, narrow cobbled streets, and, of course, a wonderful castle. We feature in our guide the splendid, ultra-deluxe Hôtel de la Cité, but for those on a more limited budget, the Hôtel Donjon makes an excellent choice. Within this medieval building you will find the past remembered in thick walls, exposed stone, arched windows, and beamed ceilings (and even a coat of armor in the reception hall). However, nothing is dark or foreboding because skylights bring in the sunshine and the guestrooms offer all the most modern amenities such as air conditioning, cable television, and mini bar. All of the rooms are individually decorated with period furniture, some offering a traditional ambiance while others have a more contemporary feel. Some rooms have a view of the rooftops and towers, while others look down into the garden. The hotel is associated with the adjacent Brasserie Le Donjon, but for breakfast there is an intimate dining room just for guests. *Directions*: In high season you cannot bring your car into Carcassonne, so park in the lot below the ramparts and the hotel will send a mini van to pick you up. "After hours" the car can be brought to the hotel parking lot. Ask for details when making reservations.

HÔTEL DONJON   ***New***
Directrice: Anne Monnier
2, Rue Comte Roger
11000 Carcassonne, France
Tel: 04.68.71.08.80, Fax: 04.68.25.06.60
E-mail: hotel.donjon.best.western@wanadoo.fr
37 rooms, Double: 400F–765F
Breakfast: 58F per person
Open all year, Credit cards: all major
Restaurant, Brasserie Le Donjon
Region: Languedoc, Michelin Map 235

On the western outskirts of Paris, the Abbaye des Vaux de Cernay offers elegant accommodation and dining within the walls and ruins of a dramatic 12th-century abbey. Sequestered at the end of a lovely forested drive that winds through the Park Regionale de la Haute Vallée, surrounded by expanses of lawn, and fronted by a serene lake, the setting is magnificent. The Abbaye des Vaux de Cernay played an important role in French history and was restored as a family residence by the Rothschilds in the 19th century. Vaulted ceilings, arched entries, massive wood doors, lovely antiques, grand wide hallways, a handsome mix of stone, tile, and parquet floors, and old stone walls give this imposing hotel an elegant quality. The main dining room is very formal and exquisite with its intricately arched ceiling. Warmed by a large fireplace, the restaurant walls are hung with beautiful paintings and the tables are set with only the finest of linens, crystal, and silver. Sixty bedrooms are found in the main building, with the remaining rooms in the converted stables by the entrance gate. Within the grounds are tennis courts, a fishing lake, a swimming pool, and a private park. *Directions:* From Paris take the A6 then the A10 for approximately 14 km in the direction of Chartres. Take the Les Ulis exit towards Gometz along the D35 and then the D40 through Les Molières and on to Cernay la Ville. The Abbaye is west of town.

ABBAYE DES VAUX DE CERNAY
Hôtelier: André Charpentier
Cernay la Ville
78720 Dampierre-en-Yvelines, France
Tel: 01.34.85.23.00, Fax: 01.34.85.11.60
E-mail: aby-vau@club-internet.fr
120 rooms, Double: 500F–3700F
Breakfast: 80F per person
Open all year, Credit cards: all major
Restaurant, sauna, Jacuzzi, tennis, park, fishing
Non-smoking room, handicap room
Region: Île de France, Michelin Map 237
www.karenbrown.com/franceinns/abbayedesvaux.html

Chambolle-Musigny is a delightful village nestled amongst the vineyards in the heart of the Burgundy wine region. On one of the village's narrow streets, secluded behind a high wall, lies the Château-Hôtel André Ziltener, which opened as an elegant hotel in 1993. Guests can relax in the grand drawing room where tall French windows look out to the garden. Breakfast is eaten together around the large oval table in the dining room. For evening meals guests enjoy the atmosphere of the lovely wine bar where they can sample specialties and wines of the region. The bedrooms are decorated in an open and spacious manner, all with soft-beige carpets, and splendid marble bathrooms are provided with every luxurious amenity. Many of those on the top floor have high, beamed ceilings. I was impressed by the subtle elegance of this lovely château and its gorgeous surrounding gardens. Included in your hotel tariff is an informative guided tour (reserve a time for a tour in English) of the wine museum in the château's cellars and a sampling of the four grades of red wine produced in the area. *Directions:* Chambolle-Musigny is between Gevrey Chambertin and Nuits Saint Georges on the D122, a country road that parallels the N74 which runs between Dijon and Beaune.

CHÂTEAU-HÔTEL ANDRÉ ZILTENER
Hôtelier: Madame Dagmar Ziltener
Directrice: Madame Christa Cros
Rue de la Fontaine
21220 Chambolle-Musigny, France
Tel: 03.80.62.41.62, Fax: 03.80.62.83.75
E-mail: chateau.ziltener@wanadoo.fr
10 rooms, Double: 990F–1980F
Breakfast: 80F per person
Open Mar 15 to Dec 1, Credit cards: all major
Wine bar, garage: no charge
Non-smoking room, handicap room
Region: Burgundy, Michelin Map 243
www.karenbrown.com/franceinns/andreziltener.html

The Auberge du Bois Prin, nestled above world-famous Chamonix, has a breathtaking setting—looking across the valley, face-to-face with Mont Blanc. A flower-banked lane leads up to the hotel, which looks like a private home—which actually it almost was. The owner's father was planning to live here, but friends told him the view was too precious not to share, so, instead, he opened a small hotel. Built of dark wood in the local chalet style, it is picture perfect, with beautifully tended beds of colorful flowers and geraniums cascading from windowboxes and adorning all the decks. There is a most intimate charm throughout the hotel and it is truly like being a guest in a private home. In the reception area there is no formal counter, just a discreet antique desk that is used for check-in, and in one corner a cozy nook with a fireplace and a few comfortable chairs. A large deck stretches in front of the hotel where guests dine in the sunshine with the majesty of the mountains seemingly at their fingertips. All the individually decorated bedrooms capture the view of Mont Blanc. Most have either a private terrace enclosed by shrubbery or balcony. Auberge du Bois Prin is proud of their new sauna and spa as well as their reputation for quality service. *Directions:* On hillside above Chamonix. Follow signs from town center to Télécabine du Brévent and Les Moussoux.

AUBERGE DU BOIS PRIN
Hôteliers: Monique & Denis Carrier
69 Chemin de l'Hermine, Les Moussoux
74400 Chamonix, France
Tel: 04.50.53.33.51, Fax: 04.50.53.48.75
E-mail: boisprin@relaischateaux.fr
11 rooms, Double: 920F–1380F
Breakfast: 80F per person
Closed two weeks April & November
Credit cards: all major
Restaurant closed Wednesday lunch, garage: 60F
Handicap room
Region: Haute-Savoie, Michelin Map 244

Le Moulin du Roc is a small, picture-perfect 17th- and 18th-century stone mill hugging the bank of the River Dronne on the edge of the village of Champagnac de Bélair. Flower-filled gardens surround the mill and a little wooden bridge arches across the river to the swimming pool set amidst gardens on the opposite bank. The intimate dining room utilizes the weathered old beams and wooden parts and mechanisms of the original mill in its cozy decor. The atmosphere is intimate and the service is attentive. Preserving the traditions of fine gastronomy and employing established Périgord recipes and specialties, the restaurant has received accolades for its menu. The bedrooms are intimate and exquisite. One particularly enchanting suite, the Avoine, bridges the river and offers a bedroom with a marvelous canopy double bed, and an adjoining small bedroom with a single bed. The suite windows overlook the lazy River Dronne, the gardens, and the birch-lined pastures. If you want to economize, choose Blé, the least expensive guestroom. This is a small but romantic corner room overlooking the river, with a four poster bed. Maryse and Alain Gardillou succeeded their parents, Lucien and Solange, in their role as hôteliers and they promise to continue with the excellence extended to guests in this "little place of paradise." *Directions:* From Périgueux travel north on the D939 to Brantôme and on towards Angoulème. Just before you enter the village (after the cemetery) turn left and the hotel is on your right at the river.

LE MOULIN DU ROC
Hôteliers: Maryse & Alain Gardillou
24530 Champagnac de Bélair, France
Tel: 05.53.02.86.00, Fax: 05.53.54.21.31
13 rooms, Double 410F–980F
Breakfast: 75F per person
Closed January 1 to March 5
Credit cards: all major
Restaurant, pool, tennis
Region: Dordogne: Michelin Map 233
www.karenbrown.com/franceinns/moulinduroc.html

The de Valbrays are a charming, friendly, enthusiastic, and artistic young couple who truly make their visitors feel like invited guests. Their grand home dates from 1773 and has been in François's family since 1820 when his great-great-great-grandfather, the Comte de Valbray, resided here. Old family photos and portraits abound in the gracious salons. It is hard to pick a favorite bedroom, as all are furnished in keeping with the style and mood of the château; however, a bedchamber, the Rose Room, is very special: feminine in decor, it was once inhabited by François' grandmother. Also very special in their furnishings and outlook are the Lake Room and the Charles X Room. Downstairs, the parquet floors, grand chandeliers, and marble fireplaces in the public rooms attest to a very rich and elegant heritage. The elegance of a bygone era continues as guests dine at small candlelit tables dressed with family silver and china. There are billiards in the library and a swimming pool in the park available to guests. A stay of at least two days is recommended to fully appreciate the de Valbrays' hospitality and the ambiance of this aristocratic setting. The recently renovated cottage offers quiet and privacy and is ideal for those who want to settle for a week or more. *Directions*: From Angers (25 km) take the D107 north towards Cantenay Erinard, then take D768 in the direction of Feneu to Champigné. The château is signposted from Champigné, located on the D190.

CHÂTEAU DES BRIOTTIÈRES
Hôteliers: Hedwige & François de Valbray
Les Briottières, Champigné, 49330 Champigné
Tel: 02.41.42.00.02, Fax: 02.41.42.01.55
E-mail: briottieres@wanadoo.fr
12 rooms, Double: 750F–1,800F, Breakfast: 60F per person
Open all year, Credit cards: all major
Table d'hôte: 300F per person, by reservation only at 8:30 pm
Non-smoking room
Region: Loire Valley, Michelin Map 232
www.karenbrown.com/franceinns/chateaudesbriottieres.html

Every room at Royal Champagne has a private terrace and a stunning view of vineyards cascading down to the town of Épernay in the heart of the Champagne region. The decor is just as delightful as the view and the bathrooms are modern and well equipped. If you want to splurge, request the suite with its sitting room on the upper level and spiral staircase leading down to the bedroom with its dramatic two-story windows framing the countryside view. While the bedrooms are located in rows of single-story contemporary buildings, the sitting room and restaurant are found in a more traditional-style white-stucco building full of interesting military memorabilia. The hotel was at one time an inn on the post road from Reims to Lyon and many regiments both French and foreign broke their journey here (Napoleon being the most celebrated guest). Dinner and its impeccable service are a special treat in the vaulted dining room with a mural celebrating Dom Perignon's discovery of champagne. Located close to Épernay, Royal Champagne is an excellent choice for a base from which to explore the Champagne region. *Directions:* From Reims, take the N51 towards Épernay and 6 km before Épernay turn left on the Route de Champagne, the N2051. The hotel is on your right at the first corner.

ROYAL CHAMPAGNE
Hôtelier: Alain Guichaoua
Reservations Manager: Evelyne Claulin
Champillon, 51160 Ay, France
Tel: 03.26.52.87.11, Fax: 03.26.52.89.69
E-mail: royalchampagne@wanadoo.fr
29 rooms, Double: 880F–1800F
Breakfast: 90F per person
Open all year, Credit cards: all major
Restaurant, garage: no charge, tennis, driving range
Handicap room
Region: Champagne, Michelin Map 241

Haute Provence is a region of France whose beauty is bounded by the snow-covered Alps, the fields of lavender and olive trees of Provence, and the blue waters of the Riviera. Villages of soft stone and sienna-tiled roofs cluster on hilltops and dot this picturesque landscape. Haute Provence serves as an ideal resting spot when traveling between the regions that bound it. La Bonne Étape is an old coaching inn, a gray-stone manor house with a tiled roof—blending beautifully with and suited to the landscape. From its location it enjoys panoramic views over the surrounding hills. Dating from the 18th century, the hotel has eleven bedrooms and seven apartments, all attractively decorated. The restaurant is recognized for the quality of its cuisine. Pierre Gleize and his son, Jany, employ local ingredients such as honey, lavender, herbs, lemon, pork, and rabbit to create masterpieces in the kitchen. Dine in front of a large stone fireplace and sample some of their specialties. Exceeding the praise for the cuisine are the superlatives guests use to describe the hospitality extended by your charming hosts, the Gleize family. *Directions:* Château Arnoux is situated 80 km north of Aix en Provence, halfway between Albertville and Nice on the N85.

LA BONNE ÉTAPE
Hôteliers: Jany & Pierre Gleize
Chemin du Lac
04160 Château Arnoux, France
Tel: 04.92.64.00.09, Fax: 04.92.64.37.36
E-mail: info@bonneetape.com
18 rooms, Double: 850F–1800F
Breakfast: 95F per person
Open Feb 13 to Nov 28 & Dec 11 to Jan 3
Credit cards: all major
Restaurant, garage: no charge, pool
Region: Haute Provence, Michelin Map 245

We simply could not resist stopping at Les Chalets de la Serraz, drawn by the hotel's stunning setting and its incredible display of flowers. A path, bordered on both sides by an amazing riot of colorful flowers, leads down a gentle slope to the hotel which is built like a large chalet with the ubiquitous pots of geraniums draping every window and balcony. From the hotel, the slope continues downward to a lovely glacier stream that runs through the valley. Although fully reconstructed, the building dates back to 1830, when it was an old farm. Today the heritage of the hotel is carefully maintained with a sophisticated, yet rustic, elegance within. Everything is fresh and pretty, and totally pleasing in every detail. The decor is most attractive, with lots of wood used throughout, beamed ceilings, polished floors, country-style antiques, pretty fabrics, and many accents such as cow bells and bouquets of fresh flowers. The dining room is especially attractive, with windows opening to the lovely valley and mountain view. When the weather is nice, you can enjoy the same view from a large terrace. On a terrace below the hotel, there is a large swimming pool. For families or friends traveling together, there are individual wooden chalets tucked in the garden which are just as cute as can be. *Directions:* From Annecy, take D909 east for 32 km. The hotel is on D909, 4 km east of La Clusaz.

LES CHALETS DE LA SERRAZ
Hôteliers: M. et Mme. Gallay
Route du Col des Aravis
74220 La Clusaz, France
Tel: 04.50.02.48.29, Fax: 04.50.02.64.12
E-mail: serraz@hot.net
10 rooms, 3 cottages, Double: 395F–650*
*Rates per person, includes breakfast & dinner
Open November to May, June. to October
Credit cards: all major
Restaurant, garage: 65F, pool
Region: Haute-Savoie, Michelin Map 244
www.karenbrown.com/franceinns/laserraz.html

I was enchanted by the Hostellerie le Maréchal and its lovely and gracious proprietor, Madame Bomo, who extends a warm and sincere welcome while exuding a fierce pride in her home, her "dream." The hotel itself is a clustering of four charming 15th-century buildings whose common walls have been opened up to accommodate an interconnecting passageway that jogs and weaves at a slant along the various levels. Hung heavy with geraniums, the front of the inn is set back off the road behind its own gates, and the half-timbered back of the inn sits on the edge of the meandering path of the River Lauch. The hotel enjoys a lovely, picturesque setting in a quarter referred to as Colmar's "Little Venice" and is within walking distance from the heart of town. Le Maréchal's 30 guestrooms are individual in their ornate and flowery decor, and priced according to size and whether they overlook the front courtyard or the river. Set under the old beams, staggered on different levels, there are numerous niches, alcoves, and loft areas that comprise the hotel's wonderful restaurant, À l'Echevin, and deciding at which romantic spot to dine might pose a greater problem than selecting from the incredible offering of its menu! *Directions:* Easy to find following the city's signs for the hotel, the hotel is also conveniently located 1 km from the train station.

HOSTELLERIE LE MARÉCHAL
Hôteliers: M & Mme Gilbert Bomo
4–6, Place des Six-Montagnes-Noires
"Petite Venice"
68000 Colmar, France
Tel: 03.89.41.60.32, Fax: 03.89.24.59.40
E-mail: marechal@rmcnet.fr
30 rooms, Double: 600F–1600F
Breakfast: 85F per person
Open all year, Credit cards: all major
Restaurant, Non-smoking rooms
Region: Alsace, Michelin Map 242

Set on the hillside on the edge of the quiet little village of Colroy la Roche is Hostellerie la Cheneaudière, a luxurious Relais & Châteaux hotel built in recent years to resemble the surrounding Alsatian houses—the hotel blends in beautifully with the adjacent village. The hotel is a world of formal, refined elegance where either Madame and Monsieur Marcel François or Madame François-Bossée are on hand to make certain that everything is of the highest standard. Each luxurious bedroom is beautifully appointed and accompanied by a spacious bathroom—several enjoy a private patio. The largest suite is particularly impressive, with large, elegantly furnished rooms and a bathroom sporting a glinting golden-colored tub and "his and hers" sinks. The hotel has two dining rooms whose formal atmospheres are warmed by large fires. The cuisine is prepared under the supervision of Chef Jean-Paul Bossée and includes specialties such as *millefeuille de foie gras et truffes* and *tartare de saumon sauvage*. The hotel has a spacious lounge and a few elegant boutiques. Guests enjoy the large, heated indoor pool and the adjacent tennis courts. *Directions:* Colroy la Roche is located 62 km southwest of Strasbourg. Travel the D392 first in the direction of Molsheim, then Schirmeck. Beyond Schirmeck at Saint Blaise la Roche take the D424 just a few kilometers to Colroy la Roche.

HOSTELLERIE LA CHENEAUDIÈRE
Hôteliers: Mme & M Marcel François
Directrice: Mme Fabienne François-Bossée
Colroy la Roche
67420 Saales, France
Tel: 03.88.97.61.64, Fax: 03.88.47.21.73
29 rooms, Double: 630F–2700
Breakfast: 120F per person
Open all year, Credit cards: all major
Restaurant, pool, tennis, sauna, solarium, whirlpool
Region: Alsace, Michelin Map 242

Down a private drive enclosed by cornfields, Manoir d'Hautegente sits beneath shady trees in a garden bounded by stone walls, colorful flowers, and a rushing stream. The original core of this ivy-covered manor house was a forge for the local abbey and dates from the 13th century. The forge later became a mill and other sections were added with the distinctive arched windows and doors. The Hamelin family has lived here for over 300 years and the next generation is in place, as Patrick has joined his mother in the hotel and equally successful business, "Conserves Artisanales," the production and sales for many regional gourmet offerings. In the evenings Madame Hamelin is in the dining room to discuss the different menu choices prepared by Chef Dominique. Family antiques decorate the salons, halls, and bedrooms, including the tallest of grandfather clocks on the landing. With their high ceilings, fabric-covered walls, and coordinating drapes and bedspreads, the bedrooms vary greatly in size, but all enjoy river views. Bounded by a cornfield, the heated swimming pool is a perfect retreat on warm summer days. The Manoir d'Hautegente is located in quiet countryside within easy driving distance of tourist spots and is a tranquil base from which to explore the Dordogne. *Directions:* From Brive go towards Périgueux on the N89 and turn at Le Lardin in the direction of Montignac for 6 km to Condat where you turn east towards Coly on the D62. A sign before Coly directs you down a drive to the mill.

MANOIR D'HAUTEGENTE
Hôteliers: Edith & Patrick Hamelin
Coly, 24120 Terrasson, France
Tel: 05.53.51.68.03, Fax: 05.53.50.38.52
E-mail: manoir.d.hautegente.@wanadoo.fr
15 rooms, Double: 520F–1100F
Breakfast: 70F per person
Open April to November
Credit cards: all major
Restaurant, garage: no charge, pool
Region: Dordogne, Michelin Maps 233, 235

The Hostellerie de l'Abbaye, a small country hotel whose chef is also the owner, sits on a cobblestoned street just a block from the entrance of Conques. While we know they have welcomed numerous Karen Brown travelers, a photo of their most famous guest, Prince Charles, is proudly displayed at the front desk. On a recent visit the young owner, Monsieur Etourneaud, personally showed us around with much enthusiasm. Conques was one of the main stopping places on the old pilgrimage route to Santiago de Compostela in Spain (known as the Way of Saint James), and, as such, has been host to travelers for many years. While you are in Conques, if you are on a budget, the Hostellerie de l'Abbaye makes a good choice for a hotel. New modern chairs and fabrics contrast with the ancient beams and the antiques that have long graced the public rooms. Guestrooms are clean and neat, and the bathrooms are modern. All rooms are spick-and-span and carry rates appropriate for a moderately priced hotel. The restaurant is charming and the menu reflects the talents of the personable chef. *Directions:* Conques is a small village located 38 km northwest of Rodez, 57 km southwest of Aurillac. The Hostellerie de l'Abbaye is just off the main cobbled square.

HOSTELLERIE DE L'ABBAYE
Hôtelier: M Etourneaud
Rue Charlemagne
12320 Conques, France
Tel: 05.65.72.80.30, Fax: 05.65.72.82.84
8 rooms, Double: 410F–560F
Breakfast: 48F–58F per person
Open all year
Credit cards: all major
Restaurant
Region: Lot & Aveyron, Michelin Map 235
www.karenbrown.com/franceinns/delabbaye.html

The medieval village of Conques overlooks the Dourdou Gorge. Off the beaten track, the village is glorious in the gentle light of evening or in the mist of early morning. Conques' pride is an 11th-century abbey, directly across from a lovely hotel, the Sainte Foy. The shuttered windows of our room opened to church steeples and we woke to the melodious sound of bells. The decor of the bedrooms is neat and attractive and the rooms have been recently refurbished and air-conditioned. The dining rooms are a delight— tables topped with crisp linen, country-French furniture, flagstone floors, ancient stone walls, and low-beamed ceilings. In summer you can dine in the sheltered courtyard or on the rooftop terrace which overlooks the abbey. You can order *à la carte* or select from a well chosen and well priced three- or four-course fixed menu. The restaurant offers a number of regional dishes. The Roquefort cheese produced in the area is exceptional and the house *salade verte aux noix et roquefort et huile de noix* is a perfect first course to any meal. The wine list contains a wide selection of fine French wines. For recreation, you will find tennis courts and a swimming pool close by and golf just 35 kilometers away. *Directions:* From Rodez take the D901 northwest for 37 km in the direction of Decazeville and Figeac to Conques.

GRAND HÔTEL SAINTE FOY
Hôtelier: Marie France Garcenot
12320 Conques, France
Tel: 05.65.69.84.03, Fax: 05.65.72.81.04
E-mail: hotel-sainte-foy@hotelsaintefoy.fr
17 rooms, Double: 450F–1250F
Breakfast: 65F per person
Open Easter to mid-October, Credit cards: all major
Restaurant, garage: 75F, terraces, patio
Non-smokingrooms, handicap rooms
Region: Lot & Aveyron, Michelin Map 235
www.karenbrown.com/franceinns/grandhotelsaintefoy.html

Vieux Cordes is an enchanting, medieval hilltop village with the Hôtel du Grand Écuyer located at its center. Once the home and hunting lodge of Raymond VII, Comte de Toulouse, this grand hotel, which seems to improve with age, was completely redecorated with beautiful fabrics in 1999. Found along the upstairs hallway whose floors creak and slant, the bedrooms are very impressive in their decor. Decorated with period furnishings, a few of the rooms boast magnificent four-poster beds and some even enjoy large fireplaces. The bedroom windows, set in thick stone walls, open onto glorious vistas of the surrounding countryside. The reputation of the hotel's restaurant reflects the expertise of Monsieur Yves Thuriès, under whose direction and guidance selections from the menu are further enhanced by artful and creative presentation. His specialty is desserts and they are divine in taste as well as presentation. If you want to try your own talent in the kitchen, purchase a copy of his book, *La Nouvelle Patisserie*. Vieux Cordes is a gem—a medieval village that proves to be a highlight of many a trip and the Hôtel du Grand Écuyer is the extra lure that makes Cordes an ideal stopover for any itinerary. The Thuriès family has renovated the Hostellerie du Vieux Cordes, a simpler hotel at the top of this charming village. *Directions:* Cordes is 25 km northwest of Albi on the D600.

HÔTEL DU GRAND ÉCUYER
Hôtelier: Yves Thuriès
Directrice: Mme Colette Tersinier
79 Grand Rue Raimond VII
81170 Cordes-sur-Ciel, France
Tel: 05.63.53.79.50, Fax: 05.63.53.79.51
E-mail: grand.ecuyer@thuries.fr
13 rooms, Double: 500F–1300F, Breakfast: 70F p.p.
Open Apr 1 to Oct 15, Credit cards: all major
Restaurant closed Monday & Tuesday lunch
Region: Tarn, Michelin Map 235
www.karenbrown.com/franceinns/grandecuyer.html

Les Roches Fleuries is nestled in a green meadow high on a mountainside with a breathtaking view across the valley to the dramatic peaks of Mont Blanc. Like most of the buildings that dot the countryside, the hotel is like a large chalet, wrapped around with decks and balconies which in summer are one solid mass of brilliant red geraniums. The country theme continues inside, with walls paneled in light pine, rustic-style furnishings, and Provençal-print fabrics used throughout. There is a fresh, uncluttered, sunny ambiance, with light streaming in through large windows. The dining room is especially gorgeous: it has a wall of windows (draped in a beautiful blue Provençal-print fabric) capturing a stunning panorama of the mountains. There is a second, less formal dining room, La Boite aux Fromages, in an adorable rustic chalet next to the main part of the hotel. The hills beckon and walking seems to be the favorite pastime, but there is also a large swimming pool in the garden behind the hotel as well as exercise equipment, Turkish baths, and Jacuzzi for the use of guests. The bedrooms (decorated in light pine accented by pretty country-print fabrics) are all similar—only the size and color scheme vary. *Directions:* From Chamonix take A40 west to Sallanches exit. Just beyond Sallanches, look for a road going up the mountain marked to Cordon.

LES ROCHES FLEURIES
Hôteliers: Jocelyne & Gerard Picot
Cordon, 74700 Sallanches, France
Tel: 04.50.58.06.71, Fax: 04.50.47.82.30
E-mail: hotel.rochesfleuries@hot.net
25 rooms, Double: 600F–1400F
Breakfast: 65F per person
Open Dec 20 to Apr 10 & May 10 to Sep 25
Credit cards: all major
Restaurant, garage: 45F, pool, fitness room
Region: Haute Savoie, Michelin Map 244
www.karenbrown.com/franceinns/lesrochesfleuries.html

Perched on a hill in the middle of a lovely valley in Provence is the charming medieval village of Crillon le Brave—truly one of France's jewels. It is comprised of only a cluster of weathered stone houses and a picturesque church. Just below the church, terraced down the hillside, is the deluxe Hostellerie de Crillon le Brave. This small hotel exudes an aura of elegance, yet there is nothing stuffy or intimidating about staying here. The well-trained staff is friendly and the ambiance delightful. Restoration has been accomplished beautifully, maintaining all the wonderful wood and stone textures which are accented delightfully by the bold colors of Provençal-print fabric. Fine country antiques are used throughout. The guestrooms, too, are decorated in the same style and most have magnificent views of the countryside. The hillside location lends itself well to romance—the dining room is located in a medieval-looking, vaulted-ceilinged room with a massive fireplace which opens onto a splendid terrace where meals are usually served. From the terrace, a path leads down to a lower garden where a swimming pool invites you to linger on comfortable lounge chairs and soak in the view. *Directions:* In Carpentras follow signs toward Mount Ventoux and Bédoin on the D974. Travel 10 km northeast and just before the village of Bédoin, take the left turn marked Crillon le Brave.

HOSTELLERIE DE CRILLON LE BRAVE
Hôteliers: Peter Chittick & Craig Miller
Place de l'Eglise
84410 Crillon le Brave, France
Tel: 04.90.65.61.61, Fax: 04.90.65.62.86
E-mail: crillonbrave@relaischateaux.fr
23 rooms, Double: 850F–2600F
Breakfast: 90F per person
Open mid-March to end of December
Credit cards: all major
Restaurant, garage: no charge, pool
Region: Provence, Michelin Maps 245, 246
www.karenbrown.com/franceinns/hostelleriedecrillonlebrave.html

I love to drive the backcountry roads that weave through the vineyards of Burgundy and cut a path through the quiet stone villages. Not paying much attention to my course, I glimpsed a sign for an unfamiliar hotel. Following the sequence of signs, I was rewarded at their end with a new discovery. Newly constructed in the architectural style of a Burgundian farm complex, the Manassès is set on the hillside and overlooks the surrounding vineyards. The reception off the entry of the main building is just an informal desk overlooking the spacious public room where tables are set for breakfast. A handsome grandfather clock and antique bureau add richness to the spartan decor. On the second floor, down hallways with beams cleverly exposed to give an old-world look, seven guestrooms are simply furnished with a bed, desk, and chair, yet are freshly modern in decor. Three of the rooms look out to the vineyards while four overlook the central car park. Five newer bedrooms are located in a neighboring building. The Chaley family are also vintners and are happy to have you sample their wines. A quiet spot to settle, the Manassès is reasonably priced and convenient for exploring the wine region. *Directions:* Located approximately halfway between Dijon and Beaune, turn east off the N74 onto D25/D35 at Nuits St. Georges. In just a few kilometers, at Villars-Fontaine follow signage to Le Manassès.

HÔTEL LE MANASSÈS
Hôteliers: Chaley Family (Yves, Françoise & Cécile)
Curtil-Vergy
21220 Gevrey-Chambertin, France
Tel: 03 80 61 43 81, Fax: 03 80 61 42 79
12 rooms, Double: 430F–700F
Breakfast: 50F per person
Open March to December
Credit cards: all major
No restaurant, courtyard parking, wine museum
Non-smoking rooms
Region: Burgundy, Michelin Map 243

Dinan is a magnificent old city of timbered houses and cobbled streets that rise from its old port to the fortification above. With its multitude of shops, galleries, art studios, restaurants, and sidewalk cafés, Dinan is fun to explore and understandably attracts many visitors. In search of a hotel that would allow more than an afternoon visit, I was thrilled to happen upon the comfortable and charming d'Avaugour. Set on the main road within steps of the heart of the cobbled old quarter, this is a small, city, three-star hotel with character. You enter off the street into an attractive lobby with a sitting area and exposed beams. A modern bar is accessed off the entry or through another entrance off the street. With lots of plans and dreams, Monsieur Caron, who has been director of some of Paris's finest hotels, is in the process of fully modernizing and revamping bathrooms and redecorating guestrooms, and everything I saw looked modern and extremely comfortable. His choice of decor is traditional though, perhaps because of the newness, not quite as charming as that of older rooms, but definitely superlative in terms of comfort. One of the hotel's greatest features is its wonderful garden, which extends out back. Here guests can enjoy breakfast on the terrace, wander the paths, and enjoy unobstructed views of Dinan's castle and a panoramic outlook over the countryside. *Directions:* On the road that circles the heart of the old town, on the south side, just up from the château.

L'HÔTEL D'AVAUGOUR   **New**
Hôtelier: Nicolas Caron
1, Place du Champ, 22100 Dinan, France
Tel: 02.31.89.25.02, Fax: 02.96.85.43.04
21 rooms, Double: 700F–800F
Breakfast: 52F per person
Closed mid-November to mid-December
Credit cards: MC, VS
No restaurant, parking, garden terrace
Region: Brittany, Michelin Map 230

This pretty château-in-miniature enjoys an idyllic setting above the River Rance and looking out to sea. Your first impression of the home is of its gorgeous gardens and profusion of flowers lining the entry drive and it is not until you are actually inside the hotel that you can quite appreciate the spectacular setting and water views. This intimate, whitewashed, two-story manor with gray-slate roof and single distinctive turret is owned and run fastidiously by Madame Jasselin. Feminine touches abound, as does her attention to detail. The entry is very inviting with its family antiques—a gorgeous Breton grandfather clock, a handsome armoire, and a dramatic, enormous copper tub filled with silk flowers. Off the entry breakfast tables set in the conservatory take full advantage of the view of sea. The salon is a comfortable place to settle, with pretty fabrics framing large picture windows and games placed on tables for anyone to enjoy. There is also a small bar area set with leather chairs. In warm weather, guests enjoy both breakfast and afternoon tea at tables on the garden terrace. Guestrooms, all but two of which enjoy a glimpse of the water, vary from simple, basic accommodation to spectacular large rooms such as 1 and 5 with banks of window and unobstructed sea views. *Directions*: From Dinard travel south on the D266 in the direction of Dinan to Pleurtuit and then find the small road that travels northeast (the D5) to La Jouvente and the hotel.

*MANOIR DE LA RANCE   **New***
Hôtelier: Mme Jasselin
La Jouvente
35730 Pleurtuit, Dinard, France
Tel: 02.99.88.53.76, Fax: 02.99.88.63.03
9 rooms, Double: 450F–800F
Breakfast: 50F per person
Open mid-March to end of December
Credit cards: MC, VS
No restaurant, parking, garden
Region: Brittany, Michelin Map 230

The River Dordogne makes a panoramic journey through a rich valley studded with castles. The ancient village of Domme has for centuries stood guard high above the river and commands a magnificent panorama. The town itself is enchanting, with ramparts dating from the 13th century and narrow streets that wind through its old quarter and past a lovely 14th-century Hôtel de Ville. Visitors come to Domme for its spectacular views of the Dordogne river valley and the best vantage point is from the shaded terrace of the Hôtel de l'Esplanade, located on the outside edge of the village. Staying at this hotel enables you to savor the village long after the tour buses have departed. The Gillards extend a warm and friendly greeting and René Gillard is both your host and chef—in either of the two dining rooms, charmingly country in their decor, he'll propose some excellent regional specialties. Bedrooms in the main building of the hotel are found down narrow, ornately decorated hallways, and a few open onto unobstructed, million-dollar views of the Dordogne. Other guestrooms of the hotel are found in annexes down cobbled streets in neighboring buildings in the village. Most annex accommodations are housed behind old stone walls and, although attractively decorated and comfortable, are not luxurious. *Directions:* Domme is located 75 km southeast of Périgueux. From Sarlat take the D45 for 12 km to Domme.

HÔTEL DE L'ESPLANADE
Hôteliers: René Gillard & Family
24250 Domme, France
Tel: 05.53.28.31.41, Fax: 05.53.28.49.92
25 rooms, Double: 350F–900F
Breakfast: 60F per person
Open February 14 to November 3
Credit cards: all major
Restaurant, closed Monday off season
Region: Dordogne, Michelin Map 235

At first glance this hotel appears as a typical French roadside restaurant with natural-wood shutters and flowerboxes overflowing with a profusion of red, pink, and white geraniums. The wonderful surprise is that behind a simple exterior lies a sophisticated hotel and gourmet restaurant run by Jean-Paul Perardel and his charming wife Denise. Bedrooms are located in quiet wings that stretch behind the hotel. The smaller, less expensive, rooms are decorated in what Denise Perardel terms a "rustic" style. Larger rooms are more county-house style in their decor. All are accompanied by an immaculate bath or shower room and are outfitted with telephone, TV, and mini bar. Sixteen plainer rooms are found in a modern house in the village. Gilles Blandin presides in the kitchen and his appealing cuisine ensures that the restaurant attracts a great many local patrons. The hotel is located in a farming region a half-hour's drive from the vineyards of Champagne. *Directions:* From Reims take the N44 south to Châlons sur Marne and then the N3 east in the direction of Metz for 8 km.

AUX ARMES DE CHAMPAGNE
Hôteliers: Denise & Jean-Paul Perardel
31, Avenue du Luxembourg
51460 L'Épine, France
Tel: 03.26.69.30.30, Fax: 03.26.69.30.26
E-mail: aux.armes.de.champagne@wanadoo.fr
37 rooms, Double: 880F–1350F
Breakfast: 70F per person
Closed January 1 to February 10
Credit cards: all major
Restaurant, tennis, mini-golf
Region: Champagne, Michelin Map 241
www.karenbrown.com/franceinns/auxarmes.html

The vine-covered Hôtel Cro-Magnon was built on the site where the skull of a prehistoric Cro-Magnon man was unearthed and, appropriately, a beautiful collection of prehistoric flints is on display in the hotel. Managed by the third generation of the Leyssales family, this is a tranquil country-style hotel with beautiful furnishings from the Périgord region. The hotel has a large swimming pool, perfect for warm summer days, and a park of 4 acres. There are 22 rooms, some of which are in the annex. Rooms are priced according to their location and size. Back bedrooms in the annex look out through shuttered windows onto the expanse of colorful garden and pool. The restaurant is truly delightful in its country-French decor and the menu features Périgordian specialties that are a prime attraction of the region. The hotel's front terrace is set under the shade of draping vines and is an ideal place to linger over lunch or enjoy an aperitif. Les Eyzies is a popular tourist destination and the town is rich in accommodation. The Cro-Magnon hotel proves to be a choice and favorite of many, which is a direct reflection on the standards of service and welcome set by the Leyssales—we continue to receive only words of praise from our readers who have experienced the family's hospitality in this lovely hotel. *Directions:* Les Eyzies is located 45 km southeast of Périgueux.

HÔTEL CRO-MAGNON
Hôteliers: Christiane & Jacques Leyssales
24620 Les Eyzies, France
Tel: 05.53.06.97.06, Fax: 05.53.06.95.45
E-mail: cromagnon@minitel.net
22 rooms, Double: 350F–850F
Breakfast: 50F per person
Open May 10 to October 8
Credit cards: all major
Restaurant, pool
Region: Dordogne, Michelin Map 233
www.karenbrown.com/franceinns/hotelcromagnon.html

For more than a thousand years this majestic château has soaked up the sun and looked across the beautiful blue water of the Mediterranean. Rising 400 meters above sea level, the medieval village of Èze looks down upon Cap Ferrat and Nice. You can happily spend an entire afternoon on the secluded hotel terrace overlooking the pool and the stunning coastline vistas and in the sparkle of evening lights, the coastal cities seem to dance along the waterfront. The hotel's bedchambers open onto views of the Riviera or surrounding hillsides. Housed within the old stone walls of this medieval village, the rooms are not especially large, but tastefully appointed, having been recently redecorated, with modern conveniences. Enjoy a drink in the bar just off the pool while studying the day's menu selections. For lunch or dinner, a meal at the Château de la Chèvre d'Or is a wonderful experience, a combination of marvelous cuisine and incredible views. The restaurant is popular with the local community and the many celebrities who have homes on the Riviera, so reservations are a must. Attentive service, superb cuisine, beautiful views, and a serene, medieval atmosphere make the Château de la Chèvre d'Or a hotel to which you will eagerly return. *Directions:* Èze Village is located on the *Moyenne Corniche*, the N7, between Nice and Monaco (13 km east of Nice). Exit the Autoroute, A8, at La Turbie.

CHÂTEAU DE LA CHÈVRE D'OR
Hôtelier: Thierry Naidu
Rue du Barri, 06360 Èze Village, France
Tel: 04.92.10.66.66, Fax: 04.93.41.06.72
E-mail: chevredor@relaischateaux.fr
31 rooms, Double: 1500F–5500F
Breakfast: 120F per person
Open March to November
Credit cards: all major
Restaurant, pool
Region: Riviera, Michelin Map 245
www.karenbrown.com/franceinns/chevredor.html

Owners Patti and Terry Giles entirely redecorated Prince William of Sweden's former château, making this magnificent residence and hotel even finer. The Château Eza is located in the medieval village of Èze, perched 400 meters above the coastline of the Riviera. The hotel's bedrooms are found in a cluster of buildings that front onto Èze's narrow, winding, cobblestoned streets. Most have a private entry and blend in beautifully as part of the village scene. Although limited in comfort and light because of the old medieval walls, accommodation is extremely luxurious with stunning decor, priceless antiques, and Oriental rugs. Each room enjoys spectacular views and wood-burning fireplaces and most have private terraces, with views extending out over the rooftops of the village. The Château Eza has a renowned restaurant with views and service to equal the excellent cuisine. A multi-level tea room with hanging garden terraces is a delightful and informal spot for afternoon tea or a light meal. The Château Eza is a wonderful final splurge before leaving France—the airport at Nice is just 15 minutes away. As Èze is closed to cars, look for the reception at the base of the village: the two donkeys, *les bagagistes*, stabled out front. *Directions:* Èze Village is on the *Moyenne Corniche*, the N7, between Nice and Monaco. Exit the Autoroute, A8, at La Turbie.

CHÂTEAU EZA
Hôteliers: Patti & Terry Giles
Directeur: Jesper Jerrik
06360 Èze Village, France
Tel: 04.93.41.12.24, Fax: 04.93.41.16.64
E-mail: chateza@webstore.fr
10 rooms, Double: 2000F–4000F
Breakfast: included
Open April to November
Credit cards: all major
Restaurant
Region: Riviera, Michelin Map 245
www.karenbrown.com/franceinns/chateaueza.html

William the Conqueror, the famous Frenchman who conquered England, was born in the town of Falaise's mighty fortress. Just a five-minute drive from the castle's ramparts you come to Château du Tertre, a stylish little 18th-century château set in parklike grounds. Vivacious Nathalie Gay manages the château. Owner Roger Vickery, a transplanted Englishman, chose to go with an uncluttered decor, mixing contemporary and traditional in a very pleasing way which gives the hotel a very sophisticated look. In the evenings, guests enjoy drinks in a clubby little parlor or the elegant grand salon before going into town for dinner. Each bedroom is named after a famous French writer who wrote about Normandy. We particularly enjoyed Madame Bovary, which can be a suite of rooms when joined with the adjacent room, Gustave Flaubert. We found Alphonse Allais to be a little too busy for our taste, but would gladly have settled into any of the other rooms. All but one of the bathrooms has a vast Victorian claw-foot tub. The staff is young and very enthusiastic. *Directions:* Leave Falaise on D5111 toward Pont d'Oully. After 1 km, at the roundabout, take D44 toward Fourneaux le Val and the château is on your right after 1 km.

CHÂTEAU DU TERTRE
Hôtelier: Roger Vickery
Directrice: Nathalie Gay
Saint Martin de Mieux,
14700 Falaise, France
Tel: 02.31.90.01.04, Fax: 02.31.90.33.16
9 rooms, Double: 590F–1400F
Breakfast: 70F per person
Closed November to end of February
Credit cards: all major
Restaurant closed Sunday evening & Monday
Garage: no charge
Region: Normandy, Michelin Map 231

The Château de Fère is a delightful château-hotel an hour's drive from Charles de Gaulle-Roissy airport. Set in parklike grounds, there are actually two castles. One built in 1206 by Robert de Dreux is now in ruins and serves as a background to the second, the 16th-century Château de Fère. The owner, Richard Bliah, is an architect, and he has remodeled and decorated his hotel in a style that he finds pleasing, with fabric-covered walls and matching draperies and bedspreads. Some of his choices are delightful pastels while others are very flowery or very dark in color. We particularly enjoyed our bedroom (25) with its heavy beams and pale-yellow walls. Other favorites include the dramatic suite (33) with its huge circular tub and two bedrooms, and rooms 15, 17, 20, 36, and 25. Most bedrooms have twin beds that can be made into one large bed. The restaurants look out to the wooded grounds through tall windows, and display elegant linens, silver, and crystal. Ask for a seat in the pine-paneled restaurant if the large folklore animal murals in the main restaurant are not to your taste. A magnificent menu and an excellent wine list are offered with the estate's champagne being a specialty. *Directions:* From Paris take A4 and exit at Château Thierry following directions to Soissons, then take D967 north to Fère en Tardenois. The Château de Fère is located 3 kilometers outside Fère en Tardenois.

CHÂTEAU DE FÈRE
Directrice: Jo-Andréa Finck
02130 Fère en Tardenois, France
Tel: 03.23.82.21.13, Fax: 03.23.82.37.81
E-mail: chateau.fere@wanadoo.fr
25 rooms, Double: 800F–1950F
Breakfast: 95F per person
Closed mid-January to mid-February
Credit cards: all major
Restaurant, pool, tennis, handicap rooms
Region: Champagne, Michelin Map 237

La Régalido, converted from an ancient oil mill, is a lovely Provençal hotel, with its cream-stone façade, sienna-tiled roof, and shuttered windows peeking out through an ivy-covered exterior. Running the length of this hotel is a beautiful garden bordered by brilliantly colored roses. In the entry, lovely paintings and copper pieces adorn the walls, and plump sofas and chairs cluster before a large open fireplace. An arched doorway frames the dining room, which opens onto a verandah and the rose garden. The restaurant, with its tapestry-covered chairs placed around elegantly set tables, is renowned for its regional cuisine and its wine cellar. Monsieur Michel spends much of his day tending to the kitchen and is often seen bustling about the hotel, dressed in his chef's attire, but is never too busy to pause for a greeting. His wife's domain is the garden—the French say that she has a "green hand" instead of just a "green thumb," and it shows. The bedrooms of La Régalido are very pretty in their decor and luxurious in size and comfort. About half of the rooms have terraces that look out over the tile rooftops of Fontvieille. *Directions:* From Avignon take N570 south in the direction of Arles. Ten km before Arles turn southeast on the D33 to Fontvieille.

LA RÉGALIDO
Hôteliers: Mme & M Jean-Pierre Michel
Rue Frédéric Mistral
13990 Fontvieille, France
Tel: 04.90.54.60.22, Fax: 04.90.54.64.29
E-mail: regalido@avignon.pacwan.net
15 rooms, Double: 750F–1680F
Breakfast: 43F, 85F, or 105F per person
Open mid-February to end-December
Credit cards: all major
Restaurant closed Monday & Tuesday lunch,
  & Monday dinner in low season
Region: Provence, Michelin Maps 245, 246
www.karenbrown.com/franceinns/laregalido.html

The 12th-century Auberge du Vieux Fox is an appealing, moderately priced hotel dominating a tiny village perched on a wooded bluff that was once a Roman encampment. In 1995 Nicole and Rudolf bought the auberge and spent several years totally renovating it to their high standard of perfection. This is not a fancy, deluxe hotel, nor is it meant to be. Instead, it exudes a rustic simplicity that is most appropriate to its rugged stone structure. The guestrooms are all different, but similar in mood, with sturdy, hand-hewn-looking wood furniture. The well-equipped bathrooms are spacious and large towels are provided. A major appeal of the hotel is its restaurant. The decor here is cozy, with a thick-beamed ceiling, cream-colored walls, red-tiled floor, a grandfather clock on one wall, and pretty blue-and-white porcelain above the mantel. When the weather is balmy, guests dine outside, either in the romantic walled garden brightly accented by geraniums, or on the lower terrace with its sweeping view of the valley and beyond to the wooded hills. Be sure to make a reservation to dine when you book your room because the food is delicious—the unpretentious menu features simple, tasty, hearty meals prepared from local produce. *Directions*: From A8, take exit 36 to Draguignan then follow signs to Flayosc. Continue on D560 past Salernes to Sillans la Cascade. Take D32 to the Fox-Amphoux turnoff.

AUBERGE DU VIEUX FOX
Hôteliers: Nicole & Rudolf Staudinger
Place de l'Eglise
83670 Fox-Amphoux, France
Tel: 04.94.80.71.69, Fax: 04.94.80.78.38
8 rooms, Double: 380F–500F
Breakfast: 40F per person
Open all year
Credit cards: all major
Restaurant
Region: Haut Provence, Michelin Map 245

Set across the street from a stretch of lawn that borders the meandering River Loire, this is an attractive city hotel known for its restaurant. We chose to overnight in Gien to be first in line to visit the Gien Faience Museum and Factory, which opens at 9 am. The hotel looked as if it might be the best in town, and although we were just looking for a comfortable overnight, we were surprised and rewarded with exceptionally courteous service and a very attractive room. All employees of the hotel seem to have taken a course in hospitality—from the girls cleaning the rooms who always wear a warm smile, to the young man who appeared from the kitchen with a cold bottle of Evian, prompted only by the fact that he had seen us discard an empty bottle. This restaurant with rooms is reasonably priced, and the deluxe apartments are spacious. Our room, which overlooked the back parking area, was quiet. The rooms at the front enjoy river views and have double-glazed windows to block out traffic noise. *Directions:* Gien is located on the Loire, 64 km southeast of Orléans. Arriving from the northwest, follow the D952 as it parallels the river through town. Just past the center of town, look for the Hôtel du Rivage on the left-hand side opposite the river.

HÔTEL DU RIVAGE
Hôteliers: Mme & M Christian Gaillard
1, Quai de Nice
45500 Gien, France
Tel: 02.38.37.79.00, Fax: 02.38.38.10.21
19 rooms, Double: 380F–690F
Breakfast: 48F per person
Open all year
Credit cards: all major
Restaurant closed mid-February to mid-March
Garage: no charge
Region: Loire Valley, Michelin Map 238

In a tranquil setting of 5 hectares of pasture, orchard, and neighboring forest, La Réserve is a beautiful amber-wash, two-story manor just a short drive from the town of Giverny, whose owners offer guests a most enthusiastic and genuine welcome. Unbelievably, the building is of new construction—with much hard work and love, Marie Lorraine and Didier built it themselves, repaired furniture, and made all the curtains. The result is a gorgeous, elegant, and wonderfully comfortable hotel with exceptional accommodation. On the ground floor you find a beautiful salon with fireplace and old pool table, a gorgeous dining room, and an adorable guestroom tucked just below the stairs looking out through large windows across to the orchards and the fields grazed by cattle. Upstairs, guestrooms under high, beamed ceilings are magnificent. Twin or queen beds are set on wooden floors that creak and are topped with attractive throw rugs, while large, shuttered windows open onto greenery and seem almost to frame a painting worthy of Monet. Just 45 minutes from CDG airport, this would be a convenient beginning or end to a trip. From here you can easily explore Normandy, take a day to experience Giverny, a day to visit the American Museum, and at least one day to laze in the countryside. *Directions*: Depending on the approach, either turn right past the American Museum or left past the church at the *charcuterie* and travel up the hill (C3) 900 meters until you see Didier's white arrows. Turn left, follow the lane and then go left again on the drive just past the orchard.

LA RÉSERVE   *New*
Hôteliers: Marie Lorraine & Didier Brune
27620 Giverny, France
Tel & fax: 02.32.21.99.09, Cellular: 06.11.25.37.44
5 rooms, Double: 450F–650F, Breakfast: included
Open April to October, in winter by reservation
Credit cards: none
No restaurant, parking, bicycles
Region: Normandy, Michelin Map 237
www.karenbrown.com/franceinns/lareserve.html

La Bastide was opened in recent years right at the heart of the medieval village of Gordes, and from the distance appears to be terraced into the hillside, with its striking pool set against the old stone walls. You enter off the street into a lovely and elegant reception. Guestrooms overlook either the valley or the village street but double-glazed windows block out any noise and in the evening there is very little traffic. Rooms overlooking the valley are priced at a premium, but some of the smaller rooms on the village side are extremely good value. All the rooms are very similar in decor with an attractive rust-and-brown fabric used throughout and some rooms are equipped with king beds (rare to find in Europe). From the entry and living room you can enjoy views from tables set narrowly on an outstretched arm of the medieval wall—an ideal spot for enjoying breakfast or an evening drink. Views look out spectacularly across the valley and down to the hotel's pool. From the terrace you can descend down a circular stone staircase to the pool and sauna and fitness room. One guestroom is located on the lower level, opening onto the lawn that stretches to the pool and enjoying lounge chairs and tables set just outside its door. Guests now enjoy a new terrace restaurant with memorable views overlooking the valley and surrounding mountains. Twelve rooms and two suites have also recently been added. *Directions:* As you enter the village, La Bastide is the first hotel on the right.

LA BASTIDE DE GORDES
Hôtelier: L. Mazet
Le Village, 84220 Gordes, France
Tel: 04.90.72.12.12, Fax: 04.90.72.05.20
E-mail: bastide-gordes@avignon.pacwan.net
45 rooms, Double: 840F–1970F
Breakfast: 105F per person
Open March 3 to November 30
Credit cards: all major, handicap rooms
Restaurant, pool, parking, local golf privileges
Region: Provence, Michelin Maps 245, 246

Hôtel les Bories has a quiet and restful setting on the outskirts of Gordes overlooking terraced gardens planted in typical Provence style with olive trees, shrubs, and lavender and out to the surrounding countryside of the Luberon. Ten new guestrooms, which have converted what was principally a "restaurant with rooms" into a small hotel, are found in a wing off the reception area. Nine are identical in size, equipped with TV, air conditioning, and mini bar—all similar in their functional but attractive decor and each with either a garden patio or upstairs balcony and lovely modern, marble bathroom. One larger room, the only suite, enjoys a bedroom, smaller adjoining bedroom, common sitting room, and an especially large terrace. In the new wing there is a lovely indoor as well as a wonderful, large outdoor pool tucked below. Three of the rooms are original to the inn and are very cozy, set under the beams in one of the original farmhouses. Five rooms are found in another separate annex with lovely tiled floors and "Juliet" balconies. The unique restaurant is a narrow room under a pitched roof, rather like a cave—intimate and cozy—but it is used only in cooler months. In warm Provençal summers, dinner is served on the garden terrace. Ambitious plans are in place to add 16 more rooms and a full-service spa in the year 2000. *Directions:* On the approach to town, follow signs to Sénanque and the hotel. Gordes is about 45 km west of Avignon, off the D2.

HÔTEL LES BORIES
Hôtelier: Mme Françoise Gallon
Route de l'Abbaye de Sénanque
84220 Gordes, France
Tel: 04.90.72.00.51, Fax: 04.90.72.01.22
E-mail: lesbories@wanadoo.fr
18 rooms, Double: 860F–2950F
Breakfast: 105F per person
Open April 1 to October 31, Credit cards: all major
Restaurant, garage: no charge, pools, tennis court
Non-smoking rooms
Region: Provence, Michelin Maps 245, 246

When the Konings family (from Holland) asked a realtor to find a place for them to retire to in Provence, they expected the search to take years. To their delight, the perfect property, a very old stone farmhouse with great potential charm, was found almost immediately. The Konings bought the farmhouse and restored it into an absolute dream. The nine guestrooms are in a cluster of weathered stone buildings forming a small courtyard. The name of each room gives a clue as to its original use, such as The Old Kitchen, The Hayloft, and The Wine Press. Arja Konings has exquisite taste and each room is decorated with country antiques and Provençal fabrics. The Konings' son, Gerald (who was born in the United States), is a talented chef. He oversees the small restaurant which is delightfully appealing, with massive beamed ceiling, tiled floor, exposed stone walls, and country-style antique furnishings. The dining room opens onto a terrace which overlooks the swimming pool. *Directions:* Gordes is located about 38 km northeast of Avignon. From Gordes go towards Apt on D2 for about 3 km. Turn right (south) on D156 and in two minutes you will see La Ferme de la Huppe on your right.

LA FERME DE LA HUPPE
Hôteliers: Konings Family
Route D156, 84220 Gordes, France
Tel: 04.90.72.12.25, Fax: 04.90.72.01.83
E-mail: Gerald.konings@wanadoo.fr
9 rooms, Double: 400F–750F
Breakfast: included
Open March 29 to December 20
Credit cards: MC, VS
Restaurant closed Thursday, non-smoking rooms
Region: Provence, Michelin Maps 245, 246
www.karenbrown.com/franceinns/lafermedelahuppe.html

The Château de Locguénolé, isolated by acres of woodland, presents an imposing picture as it sits high above the River Blavet with lawns sloping down to the water's edge. This magnificent château has been the family home of the de la Sablière family since 1600 and today Madame de la Sablière and her son Bruno run it as an elegant Relais & Châteaux hotel. Family antiques abound in the four elegant salons. Down the grand curving staircase is the restaurant where Chef Philippe Peudenier presents a wonderful menu complemented by an excellent wine list. The principal bedrooms are grand, lofty, and high-ceilinged, overlooking a panorama of lawn, forest, and river. It is hard to beat the luxury offered by room 2, a decadent suite, and rooms 4 and 1, large rooms with massive bay windows. The low-beamed-ceiling attic rooms are delightful, but Bruno assured me that Americans prefer the cozy, comfortable rooms in the adjacent manor. With its close proximity to the coast, Château de Locguénolé offers exceptional accommodation and a lovely spot for exploring Brittany's coastline as well as visiting its historic hinterland. *Directions:* Hennebont is 10 km east of Lorient on N165. On the approach to Lorient, take the Port Louis exit from D781 for 2.5 km and then travel south away from Hennebont to the château.

CHÂTEAU DE LOCGUÉNOLÉ
Hôteliers: Mme & Bruno de la Sablière
Route de Port Louis
56700 Hennebont, France
Tel: 02.97.76.76.76, Fax: 02.97.76.82.35
E-mail: locguenole@relaischateaux.fr
22 rooms, Double: 820F–2300F
Breakfast: 90F per person
Open February 11 to January 3
Credit cards: MC, VS
Restaurant, closed Monday, pool, tennis, sauna
Region: Brittany, Michelin Map 230
www.karenbrown.com/franceinns/locguenole.html

Narrow cobbled streets lined with ancient houses wind up from the picturesque sheltered harbor in Honfleur. Just a short stroll from the bustle of Saint Catherine's Square, you find yourself on the quiet cobbled street that leads to Hôtel l'Écrin. Set behind tall gates and fronted by a large courtyard, Hôtel l'Écrin was once a grand home and it retains that feel today. The decor, to say the least, is flamboyant—red velvet and gilt, lavishly applied, the fanciest French furniture, a multitude of paintings of all sizes and descriptions, and a wide assortment of decorations including stuffed birds, a larger-than-life-size painted statue of a Nubian slave, and two enormous wooden Thai elephants. The same lavish taste extends to the bedrooms in the main house where several large high-ceilinged rooms are decorated ornately. The bathrooms are modern and well equipped. On either side of the courtyard are additional, less ornate bedrooms. The staff is friendly, helpful, and always happy to recommend restaurants to fit your budget. Honfleur is truly one of France's most picturesque port towns and the Hôtel l'Écrin offers quiet, convenient, moderately priced, colorful accommodation. *Directions*: From Paris (180 km) take the Autoroute A13 in the direction of Caen via Rouen. Exit A13 at Beuzeville, travel north on D22, then west on D180 to Honfleur.

HÔTEL L'ÉCRIN
Hôtelier: Mme Lucienne Blais
19, Rue Eugéne Boudin
14600 Honfleur, France
Tel: 02.31.14.43.45, Fax: 02.31.89.24.41
26 rooms, Double: 420F–980F
Breakfast: 55F per person
Open all year
Credit cards: all major
No restaurant, private parking (closed at night)
Region: Normandy, Michelin Map 231
www.karenbrown.com/franceinns/hotellecrin.html

Set on the coastal hills just outside the picturesque port town of Honfleur, La Ferme Saint Siméon is a lovely 17th-century Normandy home with flowerboxes adorning every window. In the garden where painters such as Monet, Boudin, and Jongkind set up their easels, 17 rooms have been added. Of these new rooms, three are suites and, like the other rooms, all are individually styled and handsomely decorated with fine antiques. The intimate decor of the restaurant is beautifully accented by a beamed ceiling and colorful flower arrangements decorate each table. The chef, Denis Le Cadre, has earned recognition in some of France's most prestigious restaurants. He uses only high-quality fresh produce, for which the region is famous, to create exquisite dishes. Offered on an à-la-carte basis, the cuisine is delicious and expensive. Reservations for the hotel and the restaurant are a must and should be made well in advance. La Ferme offers a convenient and luxurious base from which to explore enchanting Honfleur. The D-Day beaches and Monet's home at Giverny are both just an hour's drive away. *Directions:* From Paris (180 km) take the Autoroute A13 in the direction of Caen via Rouen. Exit A13 at Beuzeville, travel north on D22, then west on D180 to Honfleur. La Ferme is located just beyond the town on the coastal road (D513) going towards Deauville.

LA FERME SAINT SIMÉON
Hôteliers: Boelen Family
Rue Adolphe-Marais
14600 Honfleur, France
Tel: 02.31.89.23.61, Fax: 02.31.89.48.48
34 rooms, Double: 790F–5100F
Breakfast: 95F–175F per person
Open all year
Credit cards: all major
Restaurant, pool, sauna
Region: Normandy, Michelin Map 231
www.karenbrown.com/franceinns/lafermesaint.html

Le Manoir du Butin is nestled against the forest just off the road on the left as you leave Honfleur in the direction of Deauville. It is a lovely, small, intimate home of three stories with stone detailing the exterior of the first floor and gray-blue timbers dramatically etching the top two. Views are across the lawn and west to ocean and sand unmarred by the towering chimney and factory stacks near Honfleur. Beautiful tiles warm the entry and to the right curtains open onto a gorgeous salon warmed by a large open fireplace. Tables in the dining room are dressed with soft yellows and are arranged to maximize the enjoyment of the view across the expanse of lawn to the sea. There are nine guestrooms in the house but since it was a holiday I saw just a sampling of them—two of the small suites. On the third floor at the front of the house, room 7 offers a queen bed set opposite the view and chairs placed in front of the French doors and balcony. In a decor of creams and blues, this room was very appealing and restful and the marble bathroom with tub and shower spoke of luxury. On the second floor the larger room 2, in creams and reds, enjoys the same orientation out to the sea but has no balcony. Breakfast is served either in the dining room or in the privacy of your room. *Directions:* Leave Honfleur traveling west on the D513 in the direction of Deauville. The manor is beyond La Ferme St. Simeon, on the south side of the road.

LE MANOIR DU BUTIN　　　**New**
Hôtelier: Hervé Delahaye
Phare du Butin
14600 Honfleur, France
Tel: 02.31.81.63.00, Fax: 02.31.89.59.23
9 rooms, Double: 640F–1970F
Breakfast: 65F per person
Open Jan 20 to Nov 15 & Dec 10 to Jan 3
Credit cards: all major
Restaurant closed Mon & Tues lunch
Parking, tennis
Region: Normandy, Michelin Map 231

The village of Itterswiller, nestled on the hillside amongst the vineyards, is a wonderful base from which to explore the region of Alsace and the Hôtel Arnold is a simple country hotel. The accommodation and restaurant are in three separate buildings. The color wash of the individual buildings varies from white to soft yellow to burnt red but all are handsomely timbered and windowboxes hang heavy with a profusion of red geraniums. Most bedrooms are located in the main building of the Hôtel Arnold, set just off the road on the edge of the village. All the guestrooms are basic and simple in comfort and in their decor, and those at the back overlook the vineyards. I was pleased to learn after our recent visit that the rooms in the main hotel were refurbished late Spring of last year and decorated with an Alsatian theme. When the main building is full, a few additional rooms are rented in a delightful little home, La Reserve, next to Weinstube Arnold, the hotel's restaurant. Weinstube Arnold, set under lovely old beams with pretty cloths and decorative flower arrangements adorning the tables, is an appealing place to dine on regional specialties and to sample the estate's wines. Arnold's also has a delightful gift shop. *Directions:* From the A4, Paris-Strasbourg, take the A35 to the Epfig exit, then travel the N422 to Epfig and take the first right on D335. From the N83, Mulhouse-Sélestat, exit at Obernai/Dambach, then take the N422 to Epfig and leave the village on D335.

HÔTEL ARNOLD
Hôteliers: Marlène & Gérard Arnold
98 Route du Vin
67140 Itterswiller, France
Tel: 03.88.85.50.58, Fax: 03.88.85.55.54
29 rooms, Double: 510F–980F
Breakfast: 50F per person
Open all year, Credit cards: all major
Restaurant closed Sun evenings & Mon, handicap room
Region: Alsace, Michelin Map 24
www.karenbrown.com/franceinns/hotelarnold.html

The Château du Plessis is a lovely, aristocratic country home, truly one of France's most exceptional private château-hotels, and a personal favorite. Madame Benoist's family has lived here since well before the Revolution, but the antiques throughout the home are later acquisitions of her great-great-great-grandfather. The original furnishings were burned on the front lawn by revolutionaries in 1793. Furnishings throughout the home are elegant, yet the Benoists have established an atmosphere of homey comfort. Artistic fresh-flower arrangements abound and you can see Madame's cutting garden from the French doors in the salon that open onto the lush grounds. The well-worn turret steps lead to the beautifully furnished accommodations. In the evening a large oval table in the dining room provides an opportunity to enjoy the company of other guests and the country-fresh cuisine of Madame Benoist. She prepares a four-course meal and Monsieur Benoist selects regional wines to complement each course. Advance reservations must be made. The Benoists are a handsome couple who take great pride in their home and the welcome they extend to their guests and they are pleased to announce that their daughter, Valerie, and her family will soon join them. *Directions*: Travel north of Angers on N162. At the town of Le Lion d'Angers clock the odometer 11 km farther north to an intersection, Carrefour Fleur de Lys. Turn east and travel 2½ km to La Jaille-Yvon and its southern edge.

CHÂTEAU DU PLESSIS
Hôteliers: Simone & Paul Benoist
49220 La Jaille-Yvon, France
Tel: 02.41.95.12.75, Fax: 02.41.95.14.41
E-mail: plessis.anjou@wanadoo.fr
8 rooms, Double: 650F–1200F, Breakfast: included
Open April to November, Credit cards: all major
Restaurant for guests only, closed Sunday
Region: Loire Valley, Michelin Map 232
www.karenbrown.com/franceinns/chateauduplessis.html

The exterior of the Hôtel l'Arbre Vert with its shuttered windows, fragrant wisteria, and windowboxes brimful of flowers is picture-book perfect. The interior is also attractive with a rustic breakfast room, a sophisticated restaurant, and, upstairs, basic bedrooms with sprigged wallpaper and country pine furniture. In summer, request one of the six smaller, contemporary rooms with terraces, each just large enough for a table and two chairs. The atmosphere is very friendly and the Kieny and Wittmer families extend a personal welcome. Monsieur Kieny, who supervises the kitchen, offers a number of interesting Alsatian specialties complemented by the regional wines. The hotel also has a cozy wine cellar where you can sample some famous as well as local Alsatian wines. Should the Hôtel l'Arbre Vert be full, the family uses the more modern-looking building across the street, the Hôtel la Belle Promenade (tel: 03.89.47.11.51), for overflow. Although its exterior is more nondescript than L'Arbre Vert, the guestrooms have recently been redecorated and are more appealing in their traditional Alsatian decor and touches. Kaysersberg's streets are lined with colorful old houses, many of which date back to the 16th century. *Directions:* Kaysersberg is located 11 km northwest of Colmar by traveling on N83 and N415. L'Arbre Vert is located in Haute Kaysersberg. Once in town, follow the hotel's signposts through the town's narrow streets up to Haute Kaysersberg and to the hotel.

HÔTEL L'ARBRE VERT
Hôteliers: Kieny & Wittmer Families
1, Rue Haute du Rempart
68240 Kaysersberg, France
Tel: 03.89.47.11.51
23 rooms, Double: 350F–400F
Breakfast: 43F per person
Closed: January
Credit cards: MC, VS
Restaurant closed Monday
Region: Alsace, Michelin Map 242

Just inside the walls of the charming town of Kaysersberg sits the Résidence Chambard. The inn was built in 1981 and is a definite mix of modern with old. The owners must prefer the modern, because with each visit I see another renovation whose results are modern dominating the more traditional. Guestrooms are standard hotel rooms and found down a maze of corridors and hallways. One main entrance services the hotel, restaurant, and bistro. Although, showing a bit of wear, part of the entrance hall is a large attractive lounge and at the front of the hotel is the charming bistro. The bistro is conveniently open six days a week and offers a light, enticing menu. The Restaurant Chambard, Pierre Irrmann's pride and joy, is found in what once was the basement. The decor is handsome and specialties of the house include *foie gras frais en boudin*, *pot au feu de foie d'oie*, *medaillons de chevreuil poivrade,* and *mousses chambard*. The wine list highlights some delicious Rieslings and Pinot Gris. *Directions:* Kaysersberg is located 11 km northwest of Colmar by traveling on N83 and N415. The Hôtel Résidence is on the main strect just inside the town gates.

HÔTEL RÉSIDENCE CHAMBARD
Hôtelier: Pierre Irrmann
13, Rue du Général de Gaulle
68240 Kaysersberg, France
Tel: 03.89.47.10.17, Fax: 03.89.47.35.03
20 rooms, Double: 650F–750F
Breakfast: 80F per person
Closed March 1 to 21, Credit cards: all major
Restaurant closed Monday & Tuesday midday
Bistro open Monday & Tuesday midday
Region: Alsace, Michelin Map 242
www.karenbrown.com/franceinns/chambard.html

Perched above the flowing River Dordogne and backed by formal French gardens and acres of parkland, the Château de la Treyne has been renovated and returned to its earlier state of grandeur. Michèle Gombert-Devals has opened her home as a luxury Relais & Châteaux hotel. A fairy-tale fortress, the château will enchant you with its presence, its grace, its regal accommodation, and excellent restaurant. Inside, heavy wood doors, wood paneling, and beams contrast handsomely with white stone walls and the rich, muted colors of age-worn tapestries. Public rooms are furnished dramatically with antiques and warmed by log-burning fires. The resident dog usually lounges lazily in front of one of those crackling fires, adding a touch of homeyness to this elegant ambiance. In summer, tables are set on a terrace with magnificent views that plunge down to the Dordogne. On brisk nights a fire is lit in the beautiful Louis XIII dining room, the tables are set elegantly with silver, china, and crystal, and a pianist plays the grand piano softly. Up the broad stone staircase the château's bedrooms are all luxuriously appointed and furnished. Individual in their decor, size, and location, the bedrooms have windows opening onto either dramatic river views or the lovely grounds. *Directions:* From Souillac on the N20 take D43 for 3 km west towards Lacave and Rocamadour. Cross the Dordogne river and the gates to the château are on your right.

CHÂTEAU DE LA TREYNE
Hôtelier: Mme Michèle Gombert-Devals
Directeur: Philippe Bappel
Lacave, 46200 Souillac, France
Tel: 05.65.27.60.60, Fax: 05.65.27.60.70
E-mail: treyne@relaischateaux.fr
16 rooms, Double: 950F–2650F, Breakfast: 80F p.p.
Closed mid-Nov to Easter, Credit cards: all major
Restaurant, closed Tuesday & Wednesday lunch
Pool, tennis, elevator, non-smoking rooms
Region: Dordogne, Michelin Map 239
www.karenbrown.com/franceinns/latreyne.html

evernois is a country village located just five minutes by car on D970 from Beaune. Here the ivy-clad Hôtel le Parc offers a delightful alternative to Beaune for those travelers who prefer the serenity of the countryside. Christiane Oudot owns and manages this delightful hotel which is comprised of two lovely ivy-covered homes facing each other across a courtyard. Guests congregate in the evening in the convivial little bar, just off the entry salon or at tables in the lovely, shaded courtyard garden. (Note: The owners prefer that guests purchase beverages from them rather than bring their own, if they drink in public areas.) In the summer, breakfast is also offered in the courtyard; in winter guests are served in the attractive breakfast room. Breakfast is the only meal served. Wide, prettily papered hallways lead to bedrooms in the main building. The rooms are very attractive and simply decorated; all but two have their own spotlessly clean bath or shower. Across the courtyard are the larger bedrooms (number 23 a queen and number 24 with twin beds) furnished with attractive pieces of antique furniture. Reserve early to enjoy the warm hospitality of Madame Oudot in this tranquil setting. *Directions:* Travel 3 km southeast of Beaune on Route de Verdun-sur-le-Doubs D970 and D111.

HÔTEL LE PARC
Hôtelier: Mme Christiane Oudot
Levernois
21200 Beaune, France
Tel: 03.80.24.63.00 & 03.80.22.22.51
Fax: 03.80.24.21.19
25 rooms, Double: 200F–520F
Breakfast: 37F per person
Closed December 1 to January 15
Credit cards: MC
No restaurant
Region: Burgundy, Michelin Map 243
www.karenbrown.com/franceinns/hotelleparc.html

In a Renaissance setting, encased within the walls of Old Lyon, this hotel is unique in Europe and has been described as an architectural masterpiece. Housed in four buildings that once belonged to the Lord of Burgundy, Claude de Beaumont, the decor of the Cour des Loges is a stunning contrast of modern and old. Old stone walls and massive beams stage a backdrop for bright fabrics, chrome, glass, and dried flowers. Salon Piano is the hotel's one informal restaurant and offers fine light cuisine. Double windows buffer city noises, automatic shutters block out the light, televisions offer CNN, mini bars are stocked with complimentary beverages, and bathrooms are ultra modern. Accommodations are expensive and surprisingly varied in size and appointments, from a small duplex tucked under beamed ceilings, to a junior suite overlooking gardens, or an apartment in a more classical layout. In some cases the bathrooms are located on a terraced level in the room—not for the modest. This hotel is perfect for tourists since it is in the heart of this lovely old city. *Directions:* From A6 going south exit *Vieux Lyon* (after Tunnel Fourvière). Follow the Quai Fulchiron to where it becomes the Quai Romain Rolland. At the bridge turn left on Rue Octavio-Mey, then first left on Rue de l'Angile. At the end of the street on the right is a "welcome" (*accueil*) garage where an employee will open the barrier so you can drive to the hotel.

COUR DES LOGES
Hôtelier: Jean-François Piques
2,4,6,8 Rue du Boeuf
69005 Vieux Lyon, France
Tel: 04.72.77.44.44, Fax: 04.72.40.93.61
E-mail: contact@courdesloges.com
63 rooms, Double: 1212F–3000F
Breakfast: 110F per person
Open all year, Credit cards: all major
Restaurant, garage: 120F, pool, sauna
Region: Rhône Valley, Michelin Maps 244, 246

The Basilique de Fourvière dominates the wonderful old quarter of Vieux Lyon. Set just in its shadow is the recently opened Villa Florentine, whose seemingly perched location affords it an unrivaled setting and dramatic, sweeping vistas of the city. With an exterior wash of soft yellow-cream and salmon, its feeling is reminiscent of Italy. Inside, the Florentine's decor is very traditional and grand, with a stunning contrast of modern furnishings and appointments against old beams and walls. High ceilings, chandeliers, and a marble floor grace the entry off which is a lovely pool, which seems to extend out to the vista's edge. One can enjoy breakfast or an aperitif at tables set on the sweeping expanse of patio. The hotel has a fine dining room on the landing off the reception for winter months, while in the summer guests sit at tables on the verandah and terrace, enjoying gorgeous views. Guestrooms are all very similar in their hotel-style decor—attractive, with modern furnishings and traditional fabrics—though rooms on the sixth floor have the added charm of wonderful wooden floors under lovely beams. Rooms 4, 7, and 8 have particularly breathtaking views. The hotel's multi-lingual staff is very professional, and if you are traveling by train, they will arrange to have you met at the station. *Directions:* Follow signs for *Vieux Lyon Centre Ville* and then Saint Paul to the Montée Saint Barthélémy.

LA VILLA FLORENTINE
Managers: Eric Giorgi, Mme A. Blancardi or
* Anne Christensen (English contact)*
25–27 Montée Saint Barthélémy
69005 Lyon, France
Tel: 04.72.56.56.56, Fax: 04.72.40.90.56
E-mail: florentine@relaischateaux.fr
19 rooms, Double: 1600F–2100F
Breakfast: 110F per person
Open all year, Credit cards: all major
Restaurant, pool
Region: Rhône Valley, Michelin Maps 244, 246

The Domaine du Colombier is a most appealing small hotel with an extraordinary warmth of welcome. What makes a stay at this handsome, 12th-century stone farmhouse outstanding is that it is definitely a family business and, as such, exudes a friendly, homey atmosphere. Anne Chochois, who took over the operation of the hotel from her parents, will probably be at the front desk to greet you. Her cheerful manner and contagious laughter will make you feel instantly welcome. Max, the huge, friendly Swiss mountain dog, is always around to give his special greeting to children. Anne's husband, Thierry, is a talented chef, and a great addition to this family enterprise. The reception lounge has pretty blue-and-yellow slip-covered chairs and the dining room is especially attractive, with creamy-white walls setting off pretty provincial-style blue chairs and tables set with colorful cloths. The dining room opens onto an interior courtyard where meals are served when the weather is fine. Each of the guestrooms is individually decorated as in a home and some have extra sleeping space, very convenient for families traveling with children. Spacious meadows surround the property and beside the house is a large swimming pool. *Directions:* From the A7 take the Montélimar Sud exit (exit 19), following signs to Malataverne. From Malataverne, follow signs to the Domaine du Colombier, which is located on the road to Denzere.

DOMAINE DU COLOMBIER
Hôteliers: Anne & Thierry Chochois
26780 Malataverne, France
Tel: 04.75.90.86.86, Fax: 04.75.90.79.40
25 rooms, Double: 480F–1300F
Breakfast: 70F per person
Open all year
Credit cards: all major
Restaurant, pool, non-smoking rooms
Region: Provence/Drôme, Michelin Map 245

Château de la Caze is a fairy-tale 15th-century castle, majestically situated above the Tarn. With its heavy doors, turrets, and stone façade, it is a dramatic castle, yet intimate in size. It was not built as a fortress, but rather as a honeymoon home for Soubeyrane Alamand. She chose the idyllic and romantic location and commissioned the château in 1489. Now a hotel, its grand rooms with their vaulted ceilings, rough stone walls, and tiled and wood-planked floors are warmed by tapestries, Oriental rugs, dramatic antiques, paintings, copper, soft lighting, and log-burning fires. Each bedroom in the castle is like a king's bedchamber. Room 6, the honeymoon apartment of Soubeyrane, is the most spectacular room, with a large canopied bed and an entire wall of windows overlooking the Tarn and its canyon. Another room has a painted ceiling depicting the eight very beautiful sisters who later inherited the château. Just opposite the château, La Ferme offers six additional, attractive apartments. The restaurant enjoys spectacular views of the canyon. We have received only wonderful feedback on the welcome extended by the Lecroqs. It is nice to know that one of our favorites remains as magnificent as its setting. *Directions:* La Malène is located 42 km northeast of Millau traveling on N9 and D907. From La Malène travel northeast 5½ km on D907.

CHÂTEAU DE LA CAZE
Hôteliers: Mme & M Jean Paul Lecroq
La Malène
48210 Sainte Enimie, France
Tel: 04.66.48.51.01, Fax: 04.66.48.55.75
E-mail: chateau.de.la.caze@wanadoo.fr
19 rooms, Double: 600F–1400F
Breakfast: 70F per person
Open March 15 to November 15
Credit cards: all major
Restaurant closed Wed in low season, handicap room
Region: Tarn, Michelin Map 240
www.karenbrown.com/franceinns/chateaudelacaze.html

The Château de Montlédier is a medieval 12th-century castle tucked away in a beautiful woodland setting on a cliff overlooking the Arn river valley in the quiet of the Black Mountains. The backdrop of the castle is a vista of unspoilt forest with a superlative view of the River Arn running through a deep gorge. The castle has witnessed centuries of the history of the Haut Languedoc. If you are looking to experience the glories of the past, the château invites you to share the delights of its atmosphere and setting. Once you've arrived at the Château de Montlédier and developed a taste for the splendor and elegance it offers, you will not want to leave, and when you do, you will resolve to return. With just 16 guestrooms, this hotel is intimate in size and atmosphere. The accommodations are magnificent in their furnishings, luxuriously appointed, with commodious, modern bathrooms. Raymond, with its two stunning canopied beds, is one of the loveliest bedrooms. The hotel's restaurant is in the cellar—cozy and intimate, it is a romantic setting in which to sample the excellent cuisine. The château also has a lovely swimming pool with views of the surrounding woodlands. The Château de Montlédier is a delightful hotel and has recently changed ownership. We would welcome feedback from our readers as we have yet, personally, to meet the new hôteliers. *Directions:* Mazamet is located 47 km north of Carcassonne. From Mazamet take N112 in the direction of Béziers—the Château de Montlédier is 5 km farther on.

CHÂTEAU DE MONTLÉDIER
Hôteliers: James & Mida Conway
Route d'Anglès, Mazamet
81660 Pont de Larn, France
Tel: 05.63.61.20.54, Fax: 05.63.98.22.51
E-mail: montledier@infonie.fr
16 rooms, Double: 450F–750F, Breakfast: included
Closed January, Credit cards: all major
Restaurant closed Sunday evening & Monday, pool
Region: Tarn, Michelin Map 235
www.karenbrown.com/franceinns/chateaudemontledier.html

Le Fer à Cheval is an absolute gem, abounding with romantic charm. A feeling of intimacy and genuine hospitality prevails, untainted by any hint of ostentatious grandeur. There are many cozy nooks, each decorator-perfect. Throughout, you find walls and ceilings paneled with wood gleaming with the patina of age, fine oil paintings, grandfather clocks ticking in every room, cozy fireplaces, fabulous country antiques, and gorgeous Provençal fabrics. Isabelle Sibuet, who is extraordinarily gifted, has decorated all the rooms and, what is truly astounding, has sewn the innumerable pillows, curtains, bed coverings, and tablecloths. The bedrooms exude the same quality and country charm, with antiques, pine paneling, and puffy down comforters on the beds. Nestled in the garden at the back of the hotel is a swimming pool and, next to it, a terrace, a favorite spot to dine when the weather is warm. However, you must not miss the dining room: it is a dream, with low, paneled ceiling, paneled walls, red-checked chair cushions, a large fireplace, lovely linens, soft candlelight, and Limoges china. Best of all, the food is fantastic. Le Fer à Cheval offers excellent value when considering the exceptional quality displayed in every detail of this ever-so-charming hotel. *Directions:* From Chamonix take A40 west to the Sallanches exit. From Sallanches take N212 south for 13 km to Megève.

LE FER À CHEVAL
Hôteliers: Isabelle & Marc Sibuet
36 Route du Crêt d'Arbois
74120 Megève, France
Tel: 04.50.21.30.39, Fax: 04.50.93.07.60
47 rooms, Double: 1520F–1960F*
*Rate includes breakfast & lunch or dinner
Open Dec 15 to Apr 15 & Jun 15 to Sep 15
Credit cards: all major
Restaurant, garage: no charge, pool, handicap rooms
Region: Haute-Savoie, Michelin Map 244
www.karenbrown.com/franceinns/leferacheval.html

Jocelyne and Jean-Louis Sibuet are masters in the hotel business, owning several premier hotels in the lovely mountain village of Megève—but for sheer drama, none can surpass Les Fermes Marie. This is definitely no ordinary hotel, but rather a cluster of antique chalets put together to look like a typical Haute-Savoie village. The owner, Jean-Louis Sibuet, spent five years combing the countryside for marvelous old farmhouses which he brought back and reconstructed in a two-acre park and meadow on the outskirts of Megève. While Jean-Louis was busy searching for buildings, his talented wife, Jocelyne, was scouting the region for antique artifacts and furniture. When the houses were in place, Jocelyne added her magic decorating touch. Every room is filled with antiques and many whimsical accessories such as cute paintings of geese and contented cows. The bedrooms are each individually furnished, but have the same "country-cozy" charm. There is an abundance of paneled walls, open-beamed ceilings, and pretty fabrics throughout. Although the hotel has a rustic ambiance, its top-notch amenities appeal to the most sophisticated traveler, with excellent bathrooms, a health and beauty-care center, and an indoor swimming pool. *Directions:* From Chamonix take A40 west to Sallanches exit. From Sallanches take N212 south 13 km to Megève.

LES FERMES MARIE
Hôteliers: Jocelyne & Jean-Louis Sibuet
Chemin de Riante Colline
74120 Megève, France
Tel: 04.50.93.03.10, Fax: 04.50.93.09.84
E-mail: contact@fermesdemarie.com
69 rooms, Double: 1190F–1400F*
*Rate is per person including breakfast, dinner & spa
Open mid-Jun to mid-Sep & mid-Dec to mid-Apr
Credit cards: all major
3 restaurants, garage, indoor pool, sauna, Jacuzzi
Region: Haute-Savoie, Michelin Map 244
www.karenbrown.com/franceinns/lesfermesmarie.html

Hôtel Mont-Blanc is in the heart of Megève's pedestrian zone, facing onto the square in front of the church. The exterior looks similar to many chalet-style hotels but once you are inside, enchantment begins. The decor blends the ambiance of an elegant chalet with that of a private English club. You enter into a cozy lounge with polished wood floors and ceiling and walls completely paneled in gorgeous antique pine. The focal point of the room is a large fireplace with bookshelves on either side, flanked by comfortable sofas. The color scheme is where the "clubby" look comes in: rich "racing-green" drapes are tied back with crimson sashes, the chairs are slip-covered in greens and reds, and the handsome wing-back chairs are done in green-and-red plaid. Antiques abound—a beautiful writing desk, handsome oil paintings, beautiful chests of drawers, grandfather clocks, to name only a few. In the breakfast room the mood changes from slightly formal to definitely country-cozy, with wooden carved chairs and Provençal-print fabrics. The guestrooms continue the charming rustic ambiance. Each has its own personality, but all are similar in style with an abundant use of pretty country-print fabrics and lots of mellow woods. *Directions:* From Chamonix take A40 west to the Sallanches exit. From Sallanches take N212 south for 13 km to Megève.

HÔTEL MONT-BLANC
Hôteliers: Jocelyne & Jean-Louis Sibuet
Place de l'Eglise
74120 Megève, France
Tel: 04.50.21.20.02, Fax: 04.50.21.45.28
E-mail: contact@hotelmontblanc.com
40 rooms, Double: 1060F–3320F
Breakfast: 80F per person
Closed May 1 to June 10
Credit cards: all major
No restaurant, spa, pool
Region: Haute-Savoie, Michelin Map 244

There is an enchantment about this beautiful castle high above Mercuès and the Lot Valley. Once you have seen it, you will not be able to take your eyes away or to drive through the valley without stopping—it appears to beckon you. Here you can live like royalty with all the modern conveniences. The château has been restored and decorated in keeping with formal tradition. Accommodation is dramatic and memorable: the 30 guestrooms are magnificent—the furnishings are handsome and the windows open to some splendid valley views. Unique and priced accordingly, room 19 (in a turret) has windows on all sides and a glassed-in ceiling that opens up to the beams. Enjoy a marvelous dinner in the elegantly beautiful restaurant. The Vigouroux family owns vineyards which produce sumptuous wines bottled under the *Château de Haute Serre* and *Château de Mercuès* label and they have just built some large cellars under the gardens with a connecting underground passage to the château to store their produced and acquired wines. *Directions:* Located 6 km from Cahors. Take D911 from Cahors to Mercuès and then turn right at the second light in the village of Mercuès.

CHÂTEAU DE MERCUÈS
Hôtelier: Georges Vigouroux
Directeur: Bernard Denegre
Mercuès, 46090 Cahors, France
Tel: 05.65.20.00.01, Fax: 05.65.20.05.72
E-mail: mercues@relaischateaux.fr
30 rooms, Double: 850F–2250F
Breakfast: 90F per person,
Open April 1 to October 31
Credit cards: all major
Restaurant closed for lunch Mon & Tues except
  July & August, pool, tennis, handicap room
Region: Lot, Michelin Map 235

In one of Burgundy's most elegant wine villages, Les Magnolias is a handsome 18th-century complex that served as a private residence until it was converted to a hotel in 1989. Your host Monsieur Delarue is charming, and the home reflects both his French and English origins. At the time of our spring visit, the cream stone building hung heavy with roses. Tall trees frame the entry and teal blue shutters adorn the windows. (The shutters are used during hot summer months as the hotel does not have air conditioning other than the natural thick walls.) The largest building in the complex accommodates eight charming, but simple guestrooms, sweet in the fabrics selected and comfortable with good mattresses and large square pillows. Guests enjoy an intimate sitting room just of the entry. A smaller building houses three rooms and one suite—again, rooms are simple in their appointments and decor. Breakfast is enjoyed in the privacy of one's guestroom or, when weather cooperates, at tables set in the yard behind the entry gates. Les Magnolias is not luxurious, but decorated like a stately country home and has the atmosphere of a private residence. Thoughtful touches such as fresh flowers in the bedroom and posies in the bathroom make one feel both appreciated and cared for. *Directions:* Leave the A6 at Beaune and follow signs to Chalon sur Saone or Lyon on the N74 then wind through the vineyards on the D973 to Meursault.

HÔTEL LES MAGNOLIAS
Hôtelier: Antonio Delarue
8, Rue Pierre Joigneaux
21190 Meursault, France
Tel: 03.80.21.23.23, Fax: 03.80.21.29.10
12 rooms, Double: 570F–850F
Breakfast: 48F per person
Open March 15 to December 1
Credit cards: all major
No restaurant, off-street parking
Non-smoking rooms, handicap rooms
Region: Burgundy, Michelin Map 243

The Château de Meyrargues is a stunning castle, once the stronghold of the mightiest lords in Provence, perched on a hill overlooking the village below that bears its name. This outstanding property has always been one of our favorites, so we were eager to see what transformation had taken place when it reopened after being closed for four years for renovation. What a pleasure to find that it is more outstanding than ever. The hotel wraps around a courtyard where a terrace extends to a stone balustrade from which you can admire a panoramic view of forested hills. Although this is a huge château, once you enter, a cozy warmth prevails in the intimate lounges and beautiful small dining rooms. And, although the hotel looks like it might have many bedrooms, there are remarkably only eleven, and each guest is welcomed warmly as an individual. Each of the bedrooms is beautifully decorated. No two are alike, but each one is gorgeous—all the fabrics are color-coordinated and every detail in the rooms obviously chosen with loving care. The suites are very grand, but even the less expensive rooms are perfect in every detail. The charming owner, Maurice Binet, is also the director, and is constantly about, making sure that guests are well looked-after. *Directions*: Going north from Aix-en-Provence on the A51, take exit 14 marked Meyrargues, following signs to the village center. Before reaching the village, take the road on the right marked to the hotel.

CHÂTEAU DE MEYRARGUES   **New**
Hôtelier: Maurice Binet
13650 Meyrargues, France
Tel: 04.42.63.49.90, Fax: 04.42.63.49.92
13650 Meyrargues, France
8 rooms, 3 suites, Double 700F–2000F
Breakfast: 65F–100F per person
Open all year
Credit cards: all major
Restaurant open daily in season, swimming pool
Region: Provence, Michelin Map 245

Overpowered by the walls of the towering Jonte Canyon, the picturesque houses of Meyrueis huddle along the banks of the River Jonte. From this quaint village you take a farm road to the enchanting Château d'Ayres. A long wooded road winds through the grounds and, hidden behind a high stone wall, the château has managed to preserve and protect its special beauty and peace. Built in the 12th century as a Benedictine monastery, burned and ravaged over the years, it was at one time owned by an ancestor of the Rockefellers. In the late 1970s the property was sold to an enthusiastic couple, Chantal and Jean-François de Montjou, under whose care and devotion the hotel is managed today. A dramatic wide stone stairway sweeps up to the handsome bedchambers. Rooms vary in their size and bathroom appointments, which is reflected in their price, but all enjoy the quiet of the park setting. The decor throughout the château is lavished with personal belongings and is well worn, comfortable, and homey. Instead of having one large formal room, tables are intimately set in a few small cozy niches in rooms that serve as the restaurant. Works of culinary art are created in the kitchen daily. The Château d'Ayres is a lovely and attractive hotel. *Directions:* From Millau take N9 (signposted Clermont) for 7 km to Aguessac where you turn right (signposted Gorges du Tarn).

CHÂTEAU D'AYRES
Hôteliers: Chantal & Jean-François de Montjou
48150 Meyrueis, France
Tel: 04.66.45.60.10, Fax: 04.66.45.62.26
E-mail: alliette@wanadoo.fr
27 rooms, Double: 550F–950F
Breakfast: 67F per person
Open March 27 to November 20
Credit cards: all major
Restaurant, pool, tennis
Region: Tarn, Michelin Map 240
www.karenbrown.com/franceinns/chateaudayres.html

Relais la Métairie is a charming country hotel nestled in one of the most irresistible regions of France, the Dordogne. La Métairie is an attractive soft-yellow-stone manor set on a grassy plateau. Views from its tranquil hillside location are of the surrounding farmland and down over the *Cingle de Trémolat,* a scenic loop of the River Dordogne. The nine bedrooms and one apartment are tastefully appointed and benefit from the serenity of the rural setting. Rooms open onto a private patio or balcony terrace. The bar is airy, decorated with white wicker furniture. The restaurant is intimate and very attractive with tapestry-covered chairs, and a handsome fireplace awaits you in the lounge. In summer, grills and light meals are served on the terrace by the swimming pool. Relais la Métairie is found on a country road that winds along the hillside up from and between Mauzac and Trémolat. Without a very detailed map, it is difficult to find. However, it is worth the effort, as this is a lovely country inn with an idyllic, peaceful setting. *Directions:* From Trémolat travel west on C303 and then C301 to La Métairie. Both Trémolat and Millac are approximately 50 km south of Périgueux. Follow signs for Cingle de Trémolat up from Mauzac.

RELAIS LA MÉTAIRIE
Hôtelier: Heinz Johner
Directeur: Daniel Schmid
Millac, 24150 Mauzac, France
Tel: 05.53.22.50.47, Fax: 05.53.22.52.93
E-mail: bristol@bluewin.ch
11 rooms, Double: 550F–1050F
Breakfast: 60F per person
Open March 15 to November 15
Credit cards: MC, VS
Restaurant, pool, non-smoking rooms
Region: Dordogne, Michelin Map 235
www.karenbrown.com/franceinns/lametairie.html

A glimpse of the dramatic Château de la Bretesche with its clustering turrets will draw you through the gates but it is the luxury of accommodation at the neighboring hotel that will tempt you to settle. The hotel is distanced from the château by the encircling waters of La Bière and elegantly housed in what were once the château's stables and farm buildings. Its 200-hectare grounds back onto its own golf course, which weaves through the lush and beautiful national park. Off the handsome, stone-tiled entry a very attractive bar is cleverly incorporated into the former stables, with individual groupings of tables in each stall and old wood, troughs, and implements attractively featured in the decor. Tables are set in the gourmet restaurant facing floor-to-ceiling windows, which afford views of the water. The friendly clubhouse just across the courtyard offers a more casual ambiance and lighter fare at lunchtime. The hotel has four categories of guestrooms in the principal building and less expensive rooms in the *Résidence* wing. The rooms vary in size of room, size of bed, and bathroom appointments. The hotel has a wonderful tranquil setting, is convenient to the rugged beaches of Brittany yet removed from the often harsh winds, and offers perhaps an ideal spot in which to break your more traditional sightseeing travels to play some golf or tennis or lounge by the gorgeous outdoor pool. *Directions:* Halfway between La Roche Bernard and Pontchâteau on the E60, turn north at Missillac. The Hôtel de la Bretesche is just off the autoroute on D2.

HÔTEL DE LA BRETESCHE   **New**
Directeur: Christophe Delahaye
44780 Missillac, France
Tel: 02.51.76.86.96, Fax: 02.40.66.99.47
E-mail: hotel@bretesche.com
29 rooms, Double: 450F–1500F
Breakfast: 80F per person
Open January, March 6 to December 31
Credit cards: all major
Restaurant, golf, tennis, pool
Region: Brittany, Michelin Map 230

On a recent visit I was thrilled to find Les Moulins du Duc closed for renovation as, just a few years ago, I sadly had to pull it from our guide when it no longer met our standards. I don't honestly know what made me take the time to detour back to see the mill as, at the time, I wasn't aware of the change of ownership. This charming 16th-century complex of mills and little cottages beside a peaceful lake and rushing stream is absolutely picture-perfect and I am delighted to once again be able to recommend it. The new owners are young and charming and were hard at work painting and redecorating with a scheduled opening in just a few weeks' time. The largest mill is reflected in the pond that fronts it and also sits right up against the river at its side. It houses an attractive reception area, cozy sitting rooms (one of which incorporates the grinding machinery), and a charming dining room overlooking the rushing water of the millstream. The interior is romantic and intimate under the old exposed beams of the working mill. The 27 guestrooms are dispersed amongst the various buildings and vary in price according to size and comfort of amenities. *Directions:* Moëlan sur Mer is located 7 km south of Riec sur Bélon on the D24. The mill is on the outskirts of town nestled on the tip of the inlet. On the Michelin map the location is actually noted by the symbol of a small box within a box (indicating a remote hotel) on a small unmarked road that winds north to the D783.

LES MOULINS DU DUC   ***New***
Hôteliers: Thierry Quilfen & Angel Divovic
Route des Moulins
29350 Moëlan sur Mer, France
Tel: 02.98.96.52.52, Fax: 02.98.96.52.53
27 rooms, Double: 480F–930F
Breakfast: 50F per person
Open Feb 15 to Nov 15 & Dec 15 to Jan 5
Credit cards: all major
Restaurant, indoor pool, sauna, gardens
Region: Brittany, Michelin Map 230

Haute Provence is a beautiful region of rugged terrain and villages of warm sandstone buildings and tiled roofs, nestled between the Riviera, the Alps, and Provence. The Bastide du Calalou was built in the shadow of Moissac to match the village architecturally and blend beautifully into the landscape. New owners, Monsieur and Madame Vandevyver keep the property clean, the public areas fresh, the garden immaculately groomed, and the terrace swept. The Vandevyvers extend a gracious welcome and their staff is accommodating. The bedrooms are freshly decorated, simple, and basic in their decor, and have very comfortable beds and modern bathrooms. The rooms look out over the swimming pool to spectacular valley views or open onto a private terrace. You can dine either in the glass-enclosed restaurant, a smaller, more intimate dining room, or on the garden terrace. During high season, May through mid-September, the Vandevyvers request that guests stay at Le Calalou on a *demi-pension* basis. Off season, take advantage of the hotel's proximity to the village of Tourtour, *village dans le ciel*, and discover its many charming restaurants along medieval streets. *Directions:* Moissac Bellevue is about 86 km from Aix. From Aix take the A8 to Saint Raximin and follow the D560 northeast through Barjols to Salernes where you take the D31 north to Aups and D9 to Moissac Bellevue.

BASTIDE DU CALALOU
Hôteliers: Mme & M Vandevyver
83630 Moissac Bellevue, France
Tel: 04.94.70.17.91, Fax: 04.94.70.50.11
E-mail: bastide.du.calalou@wanadoo.fr
34 rooms, Double: 550F–800F
Breakfast: 65F per person
Open February 14 to November 1
Credit cards: all major
Restaurant, garage, pool, tennis, non-smoking rooms
Region: Haute Provence, Michelin Map 245
www.karenbrown.com/franceinns/bastideducalalou.html

Monpazier is a delightful town with cobbled streets, arched gateways, and a central square with old beams supporting a roof for the local market—arched columns ring the market square. I was pleased to discover the town and just as pleased to find a hotel whose comfort and charm will tempt you to explore and linger in Monpazier. A beautiful, ornate, cream-stone château, the Edward 1er (*Edouard 1er* on signs) has two front turrets, a gray-slate roof with third-story rooms peeking out through dormer windows, and a lovely pool. Your hostess, Madame Six, converted the château from an abandoned private residence to the present beautiful hotel. Nine bedrooms are found in the main building and the remaining four in a wing stretching off to one side. The main château rooms enjoy the old surroundings—a sitting area tucked into a turret round or the character and charm of old beams and interesting ceiling angles and pitches. The hall and stairway are hung with lovely paintings. The four less expensive rooms in the newer wing are also attractive but more standard in appointments and size. On the first floor an attractive, intimate bar offers a place to mingle and for taking breakfast you can choose between the breakfast room or your guestroom. The château sits surprisingly close to the Rue Saint Pierre, set back behind its own hedge. *Directions:* Travel south on D710 from Siorac, southwest at Belvès on D53, then 17 km to Monpazier.

HÔTEL EDWARD 1er
Hôtelier: Mme Six
5, Rue Saint Pierre, 24540 Monpazier, France
Tel: 05.53.22.44.00, Fax: 05.53.22.57.99
13 rooms, Double: 500F–1000F
Breakfast: 65F per person
Open April 1 to November 11
Credit cards: all major
No restaurant, pool
Non-smoking rooms, handicap rooms
Region: Dordogne, Michelin Map 235
www.karenbrown.com/franceinns/hoteledward.html

Domaine de la Tortinière, built in 1861, has a most impressive exterior, an inviting interior, and charming hosts in Madame Olivereau-Capron and her son Xavier. Xavier explained that his mother did not want a hotel with a museum, atmosphere, but rather the feeling of a home with a blend of contemporary and traditional decor with modern and antique furniture. In the drawing room old paneling painted in soft yellows combines with modern sofas and tables and traditional chairs to create a very comfortable room. Bedrooms continue in the same vein with a pleasing blend of traditional and contemporary, and are found in the main château, the adjacent pavilion, and a little cottage by the entrance to the property. In autumn the surrounding woodlands are a carpet of cyclamens, while in summer the heated swimming pool and tennis courts are great attractions for guests. The Domaine de la Tortinière remains a favorite in terms of accommodation, welcome, and charm and its dining room is exceptional. Several times a year the château offers cooking courses that serve as an introduction to regional cuisine. Instruction includes preparation of complete menus and you can dine with the owners in their châteaux. *Directions:* The château is located just off N10, on D287 leading to Ballan-Miré, 2 km north of Montbazon, 10 km south of Tours (follow signposts for Poitiers).

DOMAINE DE LA TORTINIÈRE
Hôteliers: Denise & Xavier Olivereau-Capron
Les Gués de Veigné
37250 Montbazon, France
Tel: 02.47.34.35.00, Fax: 02.47.65.95.70
E-mail: domaine.tortiniere@wanadoo.fr
21 rooms, Double: 530F–1450F
Breakfast: 85F per person
Open March 1 to December 20, Credit cards: MC, VS
Restaurant, pool, tennis, rowing boat, handicap rooms
Region: Loire Valley, Michelin Maps 232, 238
www.karenbrown.com/franceinns/domainedelatortiniere.html

An intimate, romantic castle from the age of Napoleon III, the Château de Puy Robert is set in its own beautiful park, just 2 kilometers from the famous prehistoric Lascaux caves. This pretty cream-colored-stone castle with its turrets and gray roof houses 15 guestrooms. The rest of the rooms are found in a nearby newly constructed annex. The bedrooms in the main château are more intimate, particularly those that have a turret incorporated into their living space. Those in the annex are spacious and enjoy either a terrace or patio that overlooks the grounds and the lovely pool. The Parveaux Family also owns the fabulous Château de Castel Novel, and their years as professional hôteliers show in the way they run this hotel. Guestrooms are all well appointed, many are decorated in pastel florals, and all enjoy the quiet of the setting. The large dining room prides itself on local cuisine—some of the finest France has to offer. The grounds are immaculate, geraniums overflow from terra-cotta pots, pink impatiens fill the borders, the lawn is mowed to perfection, and well kept tables and chairs invite you to repose in the leafy shade. *Directions:* From the town of Montignac follow D65, which leads directly to the gates of the château.

CHÂTEAU DE PUY ROBERT
Hôtelier: Albert Parveaux
Directeur: Vincent Nourrisson
Route de Valojoulx, 24290 Montignac, France
Tel: 05.53.51.92.13, Fax: 05.53.51.80.11
E-mail: chateau.puy.robert@wanadoo.fr
38 rooms, Double: 710F–1860F
Breakfast: 95F per person
Open May 1 to October 15
Credit cards: all major
Restaurant closed Monday & Wednesday lunch, pool
Region: Dordogne, Michelin Map 239
www.karenbrown.com/franceinns/chateaudepuyrobert.html

The Château de Montreuil, across from the Roman Citadel in the charming fortified town of Montreuil, is a beautiful building with soft-yellow walls accented by green shutters and topped by a red-tiled roof. Set behind its own wisteria-hung wall within the town, the château has meticulous grounds with brick paths winding to numerous niches. The reception area is intimate and cozy with beautiful old beams and leads to a lovely bar area with orange-and-tan-striped chairs clustered around wooden tables. The dining room is very elegant, with cream linen and crystal set against a backdrop of soft gray and blue, handsome copper pieces, and silk flower arrangements giving splashes of color. Off the dining room a glassed-in salon overlooking the gardens opens onto a terrace where breakfast is offered in warm weather. Guestrooms are all upstairs. First-floor rooms are more traditional in decor, with beams and old parquet and tile floors. Favorites are number 1 with a lovely old wood canopy, weathered brick floors, a large bathroom under a dramatic copper ceiling, and views of the front grounds, and number 3 overlooking the back garden, a lovely corner room with old wood paneling, twin beds, and a separate sleeping alcove off the bathroom. Second-floor rooms are refurbished, but retain an "old" atmosphere. *Directions:* At the heart of Montreuil, opposite the Roman Citadel.

CHÂTEAU DE MONTREUIL
Hôteliers: Lindsay & Christian Germain
4, Chaussée des Capucins
62170 Montreuil sur Mer, France
Tel: 03.21.81.53.04, Fax: 03.21.81.36.43
E-mail: chateau.de.montreuil@wanadoo.fr
14 rooms, Double: 1010F–1200F
Breakfast: 80F per person
Open February to December
Credit cards: all major
Restaurant closed Monday October to May
Region: Pas de Calais, Michelin Map 236

Standing at the entrance to the village, Les Muscadins is an eye-catching sight with its green-shuttered windows and terrace hung with a profusion of deep-red geraniums. With just eight guestrooms, Les Muscadins is intimate and enjoys a lovely restaurant. Edward Bianchini, an American, came to France never expecting to open a hotel, fell in love with the property, and negotiated its purchase within an hour of having first seen it—love at first sight. A hallway winds from the reception area to the guestrooms that look either over the rooftops of the village, out to the ocean, or back onto the walls of the old village. Rooms are comfortable, not large, but fresh in their recently refurbished decor—fabrics are attractive and well chosen. The restaurant, decorated in ochres and beige, is extremely attractive and Edward Bianchini's menu is very reasonable in price and offers an excellent selection. In warm months, guests dine on the terrace and enjoy vistas that almost seem a painting of the surrounding landscape. The true *Muscadins*—loyalists of the king who were in constant search of the good life—would have enjoyed this country hotel. Charming and accommodating, Les Muscadins is also well located—one can walk from the hotel's doorstep to the heart of the village. *Directions:* Take the Cannes/Mougins exit off A8 and continue in the direction of Mougins. Take the *voie rapide* to the Avenue Mougins/Nôtre Dame de Vie exit, turn left, and continue to the old village.

LES MUSCADINS
Hôtelier: Edward W. Bianchini
18, Blvd Georges Courteline, 06250 Mougins, France
Tel: 04.92.28.28.28, Fax: 04.92.92.88.23
E-mail: muscadins@alcyonis.fr
8 rooms, Double: 900F–1400F
Breakfast: 60F per person
Open December 6 to October 31
Credit cards: all major
Restaurant closed Tues in winter, non-smoking rooms
Region: Provence, Michelin Map 245
www.karenbrown.com/franceinns/lesmuscadins.html

One of our favorite destinations in France has drawn one of the country's finest chefs, Alain Ducasse, to offer fine dining matched with fine accommodation. Just outside the pilgrimage village of Moustiers, the 17th-century La Bastide is set in extensive grounds boasting a lovely pool and pasture of grazing horses. Nine new rooms, five of which are situated in three newly built cottages on the estate, enable even more guests the wonderful experience of La Bastide. Two of the original guestroom remain favorites: The Aviary, *La Volière,* is decorated in a strong yellow floral motif and plays on the theme of its previous use as an aviary and The Raspberry Room, *La Framboise*, enjoys views looking back to Moustiers and a decor in rich colors of deep raspberry and cream both in the fabric theme and the color selected for the bath. In addition to the accommodation and the renowned cuisine guests can also partake in truffle hunts, pottery and painting classes and can have an insight into the evening menu by accompanying chef Benoit Witz to the local markets. Just off the first-floor landing, whose wall niches display an array of antique cooking implements, is a maze of rooms set for dinner. From a room reminiscent of a library to a cozy little romantic alcove, the selection is both attractive and varied, and the food guaranteed to please. Dinner is also served in the garden on balmy evenings. *Directions:* Located on a small country road off the road that connects Riez to the Sainte Croix lake.

LA BASTIDE DE MOUSTIERS
Hôtelier: Alain Ducasse, Directeur: Dominique Potier
La Grisolière, 04360 Moustiers Sainte-Marie, France
Tel: 04.92.70.47.47, Fax: 04.92.70.47.48
E-mail: bastide@izm.fr
12 rooms, Double: 100F–1750F
Breakfast: 80F per person
Open all year, Credit cards: all major
Restaurant, pool, handicap room
Region: Provence, Michelin Map 245
www.karenbrown.com/franceinns/labastidedemoustiers.html

A lovely painted relief of grapevines along the top edge of the building and its pretty soft-pink-washed façade dressed with shutters lured me into the bar-reception of Le Relais. Not having discovered it on previous research trips, I questioned how recently it had opened, only to learn that it has existed for almost 50 years and that the present owner herself was born in the hotel! The main entrance to the hotel is just off the street and through the bar. The bar is popular with local residents, filled with conversation and smoke. Off the bar is a charming, simple country restaurant offering meals *en pension*, with wooden tables set with Provençal cloths and faience vases laden with flowers. Guestrooms are quite simple, very basic in decor, but fresh and clean, enjoying modern baths and proper lighting. Serviced by an elevator, the guestrooms are also equipped with direct-dial-phones, alarm clocks, color televisions with British stations, and individual mini bars. This is a hotel that can offer a central location with parking for a very reasonable price. A keyed back entrance is available for guests who do not want to come and go through the more public areas. *Directions*: Located at the heart of the village, on the square by the bridge.

HÔTEL LE RELAIS
Hôteliers: Pierre & Martine Eisenlohr
Place du Couvert
04360 Moustiers Sainte Marie, France
Tel: 04.92.74.66.10, Fax: 04.92.74.60.47
E-mail: le.relais@wanadoo.fr
20 rooms, Double: 400F–500F
Breakfast: 50F per person
Closed December & January
Credit cards: all major
Restaurant closed Thursday off season
Garage: no charge
Region: Provence, Michelin Map 245
www.karenbrown.com/franceinns/hotellerelais.html

Noizay is a quiet town on the north side of the River Loire to the west of Amboise. The Château de Noizay, a lovely hotel tucked into the hillside, played a role in a turbulent period of French history. It was here in 1560 that Castelnau was held prisoner by the Duc de Nemours after a bloody assault in the town. Castelnau was then taken to Amboise where heads were guillotined and then speared and displayed on the balcony of that château. It was the massacre that marked the defeat of the Calvinists. The Château de Noizay entered a new era as a luxury hotel. Fourteen rooms, at the top of the grand central stairway, have been decorated with attractive fabrics and period furniture and each is accompanied by a modern bathroom. From the smallest third-floor rooms tucked under the eaves looking out through small circular windows, to the more dramatic and spacious second-floor bedchambers, accommodations are commodious and quiet. Off the entry, an elegant dining room decorated in a warm yellow and soft blue promises gastronomic cuisine and the wine selection comes from an impressive cellar. The grounds of the château include a lovely forested park, formal garden, pool, and tennis courts. Monsieur Mollard has plans to add an additional four guest suites in the adjacent stables. *Directions:* Cross the Loire river to the north from Amboise, then travel west on N152 for approximately 10 km. Turn north on D78 to Noizay.

CHÂTEAU DE NOIZAY
Hôtelier: François Mollard
Route de Chançay, 37210 Noizay, France
Tel: 02.47.52.11.01, Fax: 02.47.52.04.64
E-mail: noizay@relaischateaux.fr
14 rooms, Double: 550F–1450F
Breakfast: 95F per person
Open mid-March to mid-January
Credit cards: all major
Restaurant, garage: no charge, pool, tennis
Region: Loire Valley, Michelin Maps 232, 238
www.karenbrown.com/franceinns/chateaudenoizay.html

For spectacular sites, the Auberge du Vieux Village d'Aubres is a real winner. Nestled within a stunning small hilltown near Nyons, this rugged stone inn is built on the site of a medieval castle. Its square watchtower remains—a subtle reminder of its colorful past. When you walk out to the spacious terrace behind the hotel, you are treated to the awesome view the castle enjoyed from its strategic defensive position—from its perch in the sky, the hotel looks out to a valley enclosed by a ring of hills. On a lower terrace is a swimming pool where the same view is captured through towering pine trees. The dining room (with a non-smoking section for the convenience of guests) is especially attractive, exuding a country flavor with tables set before tall windows and wooden chairs with rush seats. However, when the weather is warm, no one wants to eat inside, so tables are set outdoors on the terrace, again with an incredible view. There is a large variety of bedroom styles, but most have the benefit of a balcony or terrace. In the ones I saw, the decor was simple. Madame Colombe said that each is different in size, ambiance, and what is offered in the way of views, terraces, etc. Prices, of course, reflect this variety. *Directions*: Heading north on A7 from Avignon, take the Bollène exit (19) and continue east on D94 to Nyons. Go through Nyons and turn north on D94. Watch on your left for the walled town of Aubres, which is 3 km from Nyons.

AUBERGE DU VIEUX VILLAGE D'AUBRES
Hôtelier: Mme Mirelle Colombe
26110 Nyons-Aubres, France
Tel: 04.75.26.12.89, Fax: 04.75.26.38.10
E-mail: auberge.aubres@wanadoo.fr
22 rooms, Double: 450F–1100F
Breakfast: 52F per person
Open all year
Credit cards: all major
Restaurant closed Wed & Thurs noon, pool
Region: Provence, Michelin Map 245

Obernai is one of Alsace's larger towns, enchanting with a pedestrian-only core and many shops opening on to cobbled streets. A river cuts through the town's center from which horse and carriage rides are available. Located across from an expanse of park and just a ten-minute walk from town, Le Parc has grown over the past 40-odd years from a small hotel to a very deluxe, four-star hotel, thogh it is still under the same family concern and management. We were most impressed by the public rooms and the meticulous attention to detail. Hallways are attractive with lovely carpets, heavy pine stairways, and handsome doors to each guestroom. Although there are 57 bedrooms, they are each individual in decor and handsomely appointed. In addition to the standard rooms, there are five apartments, two duplexes, and a number of conference rooms. Open only for lunch, the Stube is a charming Bavarian-style restaurant with pine furnishings and local specialties. The more formal "gastronimique" restaurant is pricey and offers evening meals. Having been disappointed by other hotels whose charming public areas contrast dramatically with their modern guestrooms, we were pleased to find a property where service and comfort of accommodation were equal. *Directions:* Obernai is located 32 km southwest of Strasbourg. From the D392 travel 3 km east on D426. The hotel is just on the outskirts of town.

HÔTEL LE PARC
Hôteliers: Monique & Marc Wucher
169, Rue Géneral Gouraud
67210 Obernai, France
Tel: 03.88.95.50.08, Fax: 03.88.95.37.29
E-mail: leparc@imaginet.fr
57 rooms, Double: 650F–1400F
Breakfast: 75F per person
Open all year, Credit cards: all major
Restaurants, courtyard parking, pools, handicap room
Region: Alsace, Michelin Map 242

After spending the day visiting the elegant châteaux of the Loire Valley, there is nothing more inviting than retiring to your château in the evening, and we have yet to find a château-hotel that we enjoy more than Domaine des Hauts de Loire. Built as a grand hunting lodge in the 19th century for the Count de Rostaing, the ivy-covered château is framed by tall trees and reflected in a tranquil lake where swans glide lazily by. To complete the attractive picture are acres of woodland with inviting forest paths, tennis courts, and a swimming pool. The beautiful salon sets a mood of quiet elegance and it is here that guests gather for drinks and peruse the tempting dinner menu. The restaurant is gorgeous, with soft-pastel linens, silver candlesticks, china, and silver dressing every table. During our stay we were very impressed by the professional, friendly staff and attentions of Madame and Monsieur Bonnigal. Whether you secure a room in the château or the adjacent timbered wing, each luxurious room accompanied by a spacious modern bathroom is delightful. Reader feedback only reaffirms the superlatives we lavish on this magnificent château. *Directions:* Onzain is located northeast of Tours traveling 44 km on N152. From Onzain follow signs for Mesland and Herbault for 3 km to the hotel.

DOMAINE DES HAUTS DE LOIRE
Hôteliers: Marie-Noëlle & Pierre-Alain Bonnigal
41150 Onzain, France
Tel: 02.54.20.72.57, Fax: 02.54.20.77.32
E-mail: hauts-loire@relaischateaux.fr
35 rooms, Double: 700F–2450F
Breakfast: 100F per person
Open February 15 to December 1
Credit cards: all major
Restaurant, pool, tennis, handicap room
Region: Loire Valley, Michelin Map 238
www.karenbrown.com/franceinns/domainedeshautsdeloire.html

Plaisance (located about 30 minutes from the Paris CDG airport) is a heavenly spot to begin or end your holiday in France. Better yet, spend both your first *and* last nights here—plus a few more. Relax in total luxury and be pampered by charming Françoise Montrozier—for a fraction of the cost of a hotel in Paris. Plaisance is an adorable, ivy-covered, 13th-century stone cottage, accented by white shutters and a walled garden with lush lawn and beautifully manicured beds of flowers. In the main house there is one large bedroom elegantly decorated in a color scheme of peach and a second smaller bedroom with wood paneling. But splurge and request the deluxe room across the courtyard. This gorgeous room sets all standards for luxury and refinement. The room is decorated in pretty tones of pink and rose—a color scheme repeated from the beautiful fabric on the headboards to the sofa, lampshades, drapes, and carpet. The bathroom (like the one in the main house) is incredibly splendid, with fixtures of superb quality. Breakfast, a masterpiece of perfection, displays once again Françoise's (formerly of Maxim's in Paris) passion for excellence. This lodging is truly superb! *Directions:* Located about 20 km northeast of Paris CDG. From the airport take D401 to Dammartin-en-Goele, then D64 to Othis where you follow signs to Beaumarchais. Go straight and watch for the Chambre d'Hôte sign on the right. Ask to be sent a map.

PLAISANCE
Hôtelier: Madame Françoise Montrozier
12 Rue des Suisses, Beaumarchais
77280 Othis, France
Tel: 01.60.03.33.98, Fax: 01.60.03.56.71
3 rooms, Double: 690F–790F, 1 apt: 890F
Breakfast: included
Table d'hôte dinner by reservation
Closed February 15 to 28, Credit cards: none
No restaurant: family-style menu, non-smoking rooms
Region: Île de France, Michelin Map 237
www.karenbrown.com/franceinns/plaisance.html

For connoisseurs of fine wines, a visit to France without visiting the Médoc would be quite unthinkable. This region of France not only produces superb wines, but is also fascinating to see—there are endless vineyards etched with vibrant red roses and sumptuous châteaux attesting that wine production is indeed a most lucrative business. The Château Cordeillan-Bages is located in the heart of the most beautiful part of the Médoc, and even if you are not in the least interested in wine, you cannot help being captivated by the beauty and warmth of this small hotel. Perfectly tended flower gardens and a lush lawn front the hotel, while rows of meticulously groomed grapevines stretch to each side. This classic 17th-century beauty has a fairy-tale perfection, with stone walls of beautiful creamy yellow, a gently sloping roof, and round turrets. From the moment you step inside, you are surrounded by an aura of being a guest in a private home. The mood seems to be one of an English manor, with beautiful fabrics, subdued colors, soft lighting, an abundance of handsome antiques, fabric walls, beautiful carpets, and bouquets of fresh flowers. This is a luxurious property and reflects excellent taste and understated elegance throughout. As an added bonus, the staff is extremely gracious and the meals served in the beautiful dining room are excellent. *Directions:* From Bordeaux take D1 to Castelnau-de-Médoc, then continue north on N215 to St. Laurent where you turn east on D206 to Pauillac.

CHÂTEAU CORDEILLAN-BAGES   **New**
Directeurs: Alain Rabier, Marx Thierry
L'École du Bordeaux
Route des Châteaux, 33250 Pauillac, France
Tel: 05.56.59.24.24, Fax: 05.56.59.01.89
E-mail: cordeillan@relaischateaux.fr
25 rooms, Double: 950F–1195F
Breakfast: 80F–100F per person
Closed Dec 15 to Jan 31, Credit cards: all major
Restaurant closed Mon lunch & dinner, Sat lunch
Region: Médoc, Michelin Map 233

Several years ago Even O'Neill gave up a high-powered career to purchase his aunt's 15th-century manor-house hotel. His deep love for his new home shows in every aspect of his solicitous management of the Manoir de Vaumadeuc. All the rooms have been renovated and redecorated under Even's direction, ushering in a new era of freshness and elegant style to the ancient medieval surroundings. In spite of the thick stone walls and huge walk-in fireplaces, the feeling throughout is light, airy, and very comfortable. Under the eaves are several lovely bedrooms with modern bathrooms. Pleasing floral fabrics, paintings, and antiques lend a luxurious, yet personalized atmosphere. We particularly liked our large paneled bedroom but, for a deluxe room, found the bathroom rather small due to the physical limitations of a renovated 15th-century manor. Also, for the price, were disappointed with cheap bathroom amenities such as plastic throw-away cups and piecemeal soaps. There are also two cottage-style bedrooms located in the carriage house which are smaller and cozier than those in the manor. The library with its tall bookcases is a delightful, elegant room. During the summer season most guests opt to dine at the Manoir—their menu is limited and expensive but they do have an appreciative, captive clientele as other restaurants involve quite a journey. Busy raising four boys, Carol is rarely present, but Even graciously manages it all! *Directions:* From Plancoët, take D768 towards Lamballe for 2 km. Go left on D28 for 7 km to the village of Pléven. Go through the village to the Manoir de Vaumadeuc on the right.

MANOIR DE VAUMADEUC
Hôteliers: Carol & Even O'Neill
Pléven, 22130 Plancoët, France
Tel: 02.96.84.46.17, Fax: 02.96.84.40.16
14 rooms, Double: 590F–1100F
Breakfast: 50F per person, Open Easter to January
Credit cards: all major, handicap room
Restaurant closed in low season, except by arrangement
Region: Brittany, Michelin Map 230
www.karenbrown.com/franceinns/manoirdevaumadeuc.html

A reader wrote to tell us that we absolutely must include Les Hospitaliers in our book. He was absolutely right—Les Hospitaliers is a gem, set in one of France's romantic, picture-perfect little villages nestled in the hills of northern Provence. Although this charming hotel is of fairly new construction, you would never know it because the old and new are blended so harmoniously. Simple furnishings provide a homey, comfortable, uncontrived ambiance. While the rooms are extremely attractive, at Les Hospitaliers the view is king—rightly so, because the setting is breathtaking—and all rooms are positioned to take advantage of the scenery. The most stunning vista is from the terrace, which stretches to the old walls of the village. From this perch there is almost a 360-degree view of the valley bound by wooded green hills. On a lower terrace sits a large swimming pool lined with mosaics and decked with old Roman stones. When the weather is mild, most guests dine outside, while on chilly days, meals are served in a handsome dining room with stone walls, beamed ceiling, and casement windows. Wherever you dine, the food is delicious, with plenty of produce from the garden and wines from the huge wine cellar. *Directions*: Exit the A7 at Montélimar Sud or Montélimar Nord. Follow white signs toward Dieulefit. About 8 km after passing La Bégude de Mazenc, you come to Le Poët-Laval—the hotel is in the perched medieval village on the hill to your left.

LES HOSPITALIERS
Hôtelier: Bernard Morin
26160 Le Poët-Laval, France
Tel: 04.75.46.22.32, Fax: 04.75.46.49.99
22 rooms, Double: 380F–880F
Breakfast: 50F per person
Open March 3 to November 15
Credit cards: all major
Restaurant, pool
Region: Provence-Drôme, Michelin Map 245

La Ferme d'Augustin is tucked into the rolling, tree-studded hills between the colorful old port of Saint Tropez and Ramatuelle, a romantic medieval hilltown. The owners carefully preserved its rustic ambiance when they renovated this lovely old farm and converted it into a hotel. The guestrooms are clustered about the property in various farmhouses connected by fragrant, flower-lined paths. Ivy, wisteria, and climbing roses soften the exterior of the typical stone buildings with heavy, red-tiled roofs that dot the park-like grounds. The first building you encounter houses the reception area, lounges, and dining room. The lounges are attractively decorated with yellow slipcovered chairs and sofas, a few accents of antique furniture, and bouquets of fresh flowers. Just off the main lounge is a cozy nook whose focus is a fireplace flanked by benches softened with red-and-yellow provincial-print cushions. The dining room is in a glass-enclosed veranda overlooking the forest. There is a large swimming pool snuggled on a terrace shaded by a towering row of cypress trees and brightened by beds of colorful flowers. *Directions.* Leaving Saint Tropez, follow signs for Ramatuelle, and watch very carefully for hotel signs to the left, which will include La Ferme d'Augustin. The hotel is on Route de Tahiti, a dead-end road that ends at Tahiti beach.

ROMANTIK HOTEL LA FERME D'AUGUSTIN
Hôtelier: Mme Jacqueline Vallet
Route de Tahiti
83350 Ramatuelle–Saint Tropez, France
Tel: 04.94.97.23.83, Fax: 04.94.97.40.30
46 rooms, Double: 720F–1800F
Breakfast: 75F per person
Open March 20 to October 20
Credit cards: all major
Restaurant, pool
Region: Provence, Michelin Map 245

Le Clos Saint Vincent is set in a vineyard on the Alsatian wine route. On the outskirts of the town of Ribeauvillé watch for the sign that directs you up a small road which winds through the vineyards to the hotel. Positioned high on the hill, the hotel looks out over marvelous views of surrounding vineyards of the Alsatian Valley and across to the Black Forest in Germany. The bedrooms are individually identified by a different flower or fruit pattern. Ground-floor bedrooms benefit from a small partitioned patio where one can lounge and enjoy a drink and the panoramic view before dinner. (Each room is equipped with its own mini bar.) The patio is an ideal picnic spot if you decide to pack a light supper of fruit, a crusty baguette and local cheese. The restaurant is very well known for its wine and regional menu. Depending on the weather, tables are set either indoors in a glass-enclosed room or on the surrounding outdoor terrace. Breakfast, a basket piled high with croissants, brioche and an assortment of toasted breads, is served with fresh-squeezed juice, café and the morning paper in the privacy of your room or in the cheerful dinette. *Directions:* Located outside of the village of Ribeauvillé to the northeast. Travel the *Route du Vin* in the direction of Bergheim and follow signage to Le Clos.

LE CLOS SAINT VINCENT
Hôtelier: Chapotin Family
Route de Bergheim
68150 Ribeauvillé, France
Tel: 03.89.73.67.65, Fax: 03.89.73.32.20
E-mail: closvincent@aol.com
15 rooms, Double: 725F–1000F
Breakfast: included
Open mid-March to mid-November
Credit cards: VS
Restaurant
Region: Alsace, Michelin Map 242

Set on a corner just below the hospital at the edge of town, this charming inn is easy to spot with its lower portion colored in a wash of soft yellow and the top a mix of sienna and rough timber. Two sisters converted this lovely, centuries-old home into an *auberge* offering the region's most charming accommodation. An arched doorway beckons you into the reception whose exposed walls of stone are dramatically softened by handsome fabrics hanging at the windows. The salon, an intimate, cozy place to settle with chairs set round the open fireplace, was once the forge and a pot hangs just above the old well. The breakfast room—once the old *cave*—has tables set with cheerful linens. A wide rope tethered to the wall eases the climb up the circular stair to the bedrooms and rough-hewn doors set in hallways of old plaster and timbered beams guard the guestrooms. Anselme II is a lovely, spacious room on the first floor whose twin beds are decked in rich fabrics of rusts, golds and yellows, and harvest patterns of corn and wheat. Another flight up, Ulrich V is a delightful corner room with red-check print at the numcrous windows and a handsome print of beiges and greens on the bed and in the fabric canopy over the bed. Beams, wainscoting, and lots of sunlight make this a true favorite. An enchanting town set right on the *Route de Vin*, Ribeauvillé is an ideal base from which to explore the region, and this inn's accommodation matches the region's charm and appeal. *Directions:* The village of Ribeauvillé is located 19 km north of Colmar via N83 and D106.

HOSTELLERIE DES SEIGNEURS DE RIBEAUPIERRE
Hôteliers: Marie Madeleine & Marie Cecile Barth
11, Rue du Château
68150 Ribeauvillé, France
Tel: 03.89.73.70.31, Fax: 03.89.73.71.21
10 rooms, Double: 650F–950F
Breakfast: included
Open March 1 to December 31
Credit cards: all major
No restaurant, non-smoking rooms
Region: Alsace, Michelin Map 242

The village of Riquewihr is encircled by a tall wall and surrounded by vineyards. Within the walls the narrow pedestrian streets are lined with ancient brick-and-timber houses built to produce wine on the ground floor while the family lived upstairs. Riquewihr is an idyllic little town and the Hôtel l'Oriel is ideally situated for using as your base to explore the Alsace wine region. On a narrow side street, the hotel occupies a 450-year-old building. Guests have a large breakfast room and a small sitting area and recently added in the cellar is an inviting wine salon and bar. Steep stairs and narrow corridors lead to the guestrooms, which overlook either the narrow street or a tiny central courtyard (it's not a place for large suitcases). Bedrooms are all very nicely decorated and outfitted with TV and phone. We particularly liked the rooms on the first floor (second floor for Americans) with their windows overlooking the narrow street. Serge and Sylviane are a charming, handsome couple and wonderful hosts. They are happy to recommend restaurants in the village for dinner. *Directions:* Riquewihr is just south of Ribeauvillé. At the entrance to the town turn right, park in the first available parking space beneath the wall, and walk back to the first entrance through the wall. The hotel is on your right after 50 meters. The Wendels will provide you with a map so that you can drive your car to the hotel to unload luggage before parking it in a car park.

HÔTEL L'ORIEL
Hôteliers: Serge & Sylviane Wendel
3, Rue des Ecuries Seigneuriales
68340 Riquewihr, France
Tel: 03.89.49.03.13, Fax: 03.89.47.92.87
E-mail: oriel@club-internet.fr
19 rooms, Double: 380F–490F
Breakfast: 54F per person
Open all year, Credit cards: all major
No restaurant, wine bar
Region: Alsace, Michelin Map 242
www.karenbrown.com/franceinns/hotelloriel.html

The Domaine de la Rhue is exceptional, offering comfort and elegance in a beautiful country setting. Just 45 minutes by footpath from the pilgrimage site of Rocamadour, the Domaine de la Rhue offers accommodation in converted stables in the shadow of its regal, ivy-clad château. The talented and caring owners, Christine and Eric Jooris, first opted to farm the land but the soil was too poor so they decided to offer accommodation within the stone walls of the stables which they gutted, retaining the old character by preserving the weathered beams and implements. There are guestrooms in the main stable and a few in an outlying building, elegant in their simplicity, with fresh whitewashed plaster and rough beams complemented by fine wood furnishings and rich, muted fabrics. Rooms are individual in decor and priced strictly on their size. Two of the rooms in the stable enjoy their own entrance off the garden and a garden sitting area. A few rooms have a kitchenette and those in the side house are almost like small apartments. The main room at the center of the inn sits behind large glass doors and is very inviting with various groupings of chairs set on old stone floors and warmed by a large open fireplace. In the morning, breakfast is prepared by Eric and Christine assists guests with their journeys. *Directions:* From Rocamadour take the D673 in the direction of Brive then continue towards Brive on the N140. After 1 km, turn left on a small road to Domaine de la Rhue.

DOMAINE DE LA RHUE
Hôteliers: Christine & Eric Jooris
46500 Rocamadour, France
Tel: 05.65.33.71.50, Fax: 05.65.33.72.48
E-mail: domainedelarhue@rocamadour.com
14 rooms, Double: 380F–680F, Breakfast: 45F per person
Open March 30 to October 18, Credit cards: MC, VS
Hot air balloon rides of the canyon: 750F per person
No restaurant, pool
Region: Dordogne, Michelin Maps 235, 239
www.karenbrown.com/franceinns/domainedelarhue.html

The Au Moulin de la Gorce, set in rolling farmland, is a 16th-century mill that has been converted to a lovely countryside hotel and a superb restaurant. In the various buildings clustered along the edge of a quiet pond and brook are luxurious, antique-furnished bedrooms. The wallpapers and materials chosen for the decor are sometimes overbearing, but the rooms all have private baths and are very comfortable—a few open onto a grassy terrace. The restaurant, intimate in size, is romantically furnished in soft pastel tones. Tables are set before a lovely fireplace and the restaurant's atmosphere is surpassed only by the unusually beautiful presentation of each course. The care and attention to detail that the Bertranet family strive for is evident throughout. There are currently only six rooms in the mill, but the Bertranets have built an additional four in an adjacent building. Continuing in the family tradition, the Au Moulin de la Gorce is now managed by their daughter, Catherine Brénont. Please note that the family asks that overnight guests take one meal a day at the hotel. *Directions:* La Roche l'Abeille is located 32 km to the southeast of Limoges. From Saint Yrieix la Perche travel on D704 northeast out of town in the direction of Limoges, 10 km, and then turn right and travel 2 km to La Roche l'Abeille.

AU MOULIN DE LA GORCE
Hôteliers: Mme & M Sarl Jean Bertranet
  & Catherine Brénont
87800 La Roche l'Abeille, France
Tel: 05.55.00.70.66, Fax: 05.55.00.76.57
E-mail: moulingorce@relaischateaux.fr
10 rooms, Double: 750F–1300F
Breakfast: 75F per person
Closed December & January
Credit cards: all major
Restaurant, garage: no charge
Region: Sud-Limousin, Michelin Map 233

During the Middle Ages the Château d'Isenbourg was the cherished home of the prince bishops of Strasbourg and was more recently owned by wealthy wine-growers. On the hillside above the town of Rouffach, the château is still surrounded by its own vineyards. There are forty bedrooms, nine of which are modern additions that overlook either the vineyards, the wide plain of Alsace, or the castle park. A number of rooms are exceptionally elegant with massive, hand-painted ceilings. Room 2 is an especially beautiful apartment and room 14 is also impressive in its furnishings. The kitchen is the domain of the château's remarkable chef, Didier Lefeuvre. You can savor a delicious meal and fine Alsatian wines appropriately in the vaulted 14th-century wine cellar or on the panoramic terrace. An open-air luncheon is offered in summertime. An outdoor and indoor swimming pool, whirlpool, sauna, fitness room, and tennis court are welcome additions. Note: After 25 years the management of this lovely hotel has just changed. I visited this past spring while the Dalibert family was still in residence, and although they advised me of their departure, they did not know who would be taking over. I look forward to meeting Mme Meitinger and would welcome any feedback from our readers. *Directions:* Travel 15 kilometers south from Colmar on the N83 in the direction of Cernay. Exit at Rouffach *Nord*. The Château d'Isenbourg is just to the north of town.

CHÂTEAU D'ISENBOURG
Directeur: Inge Meitinger
68250 Rouffach, France
Tel: 03.89.78.58.50, Fax: 03.89.78.53.70
E-mail: isenbourg@wanadoo.fr
40 rooms, Double: 900F–2100F
Breakfast: 90F or 140F per person
Open mid-March to mid-January
Credit cards: all major
Restaurant, pools, tennis
Region: Alsace, Michelin Map 242

Beyond the ruins of a medieval arched gateway, the Hôtel de la Pélissaria nestles at the foot of the village of Saint Cirq Lapopie, which cascades down the hillside high above the River Lot. This delightful inn is enhanced by its artistic owners, the Matuchets. Fresh and simple in its decor, the inn has whitewashed walls contrasting handsomely with dark-wood beams and sienna-tile floors. Thick stone walls and shuttered windows frame the idyllic scene of the village and the river. An attractive couple, Marie-Françoise and François are wonderful with their guests and enjoy sharing their home. Although they no longer have a restaurant, there are a number of small restaurants within walking distance and they are very pleased to offer recommendations. François's talents are entertaining guests with a wonderful sense of humor and with music—a piano and stringed instruments decorate the intimate salon and his own recordings playing in the background stage a romantic mood. Saint Cirq Lapopie is truly one of France's most picturesque villages: with only a handful of year-round residents, this hamlet of steep, narrow, winding cobbled streets, sun-warmed tile roofs, mixture of timber and stone façades, and garden niches is a postcard-perfect scene. It is wonderful to find an inn that so perfectly complements the beauty of this hamlet. *Directions:* Saint Cirq Lapopie is located 33 km east of Cahors (D653 and D662).

HÔTEL DE LA PÉLISSARIA
Hôteliers: Marie-Françoise & François Matuchet
Saint Cirq Lapopie
46330 Cabrerets, France
Tel: 05.65.31.25.14, Fax: 05.65.30.25.52
10 rooms, Double: 400F–700F
Breakfast: 50F per person
Open April 1 to November 2
Credit cards: MC, VS
No restaurant, small pool
Region: Lot, Michelin Map 235
www.karenbrown.com/franceinns/hoteldelapelissaria.html

Just outside the medieval town of Saint Emilion on the road to Libourne, you find the Château Grand Barrail sitting majestically amongst the vineyards. Its cream-stone façade and silver-gray turrets are impressive against a sea of green vines. For *al fresco* dining, the terrace patio bows outward and overlooks an expanse of green lawn—an ideal spot to linger over lunch or dinner on a warm day. The restaurant is elegant and the chef has perfected a menu to complement some of the world's finest wines. Six bedrooms and three suites are found in the main château, with seventeen bedrooms and two suites in the new residence, which has been juxtaposed to the château to extend it. The guestrooms are spacious and handsomely decorated in rich tones of beiges, burgundies, greens, and gold and set under old beams. Some have turrets and all have lovely vineyard views. The château also has a wine-tasting room where private wine tastings can be arranged. Spend the afternoon on the terrace or by the swimming pool or take an afternoon stroll through the vineyards to your famous neighbor Château Figeac. *Directions:* From Saint Emilion follow D243 in the direction of Libourne.

CHÂTEAU GRAND BARRAIL
Hôtelier: Friedrich Gross
Directeur: Patrick Freiburghaus
Route de Libourne
33330 Saint Emilion, France
Tel: 05.57.55.37.00, Fax: 05.57.55.37.49
E-mail: hotel_ch@grand-barrail.com
28 rooms, Double: 1150F–3200F
Breakfast: 100F per person
Open all year except three weeks in February
Credit cards: AX, MC
Restaurant, pool, helipad, wine-tasting, handicap room
Region: Bordeaux, Michelin Map 234
www.karenbrown.com/franceinns/chateaugrandbarrail.html

The wine town of Saint Emilion was dressed with banners, filled with music and laughter, and visited by all the dignitaries of the region on a warm day in late September to begin the *vendange*—the grape harvest. The day was captivating and we fell in love with the town. Crowning a hillside with vistas that stretch out to the surrounding vineyards, medieval Saint Emilion has traditionally been considered the capital of the Bordeaux wine region. The Hostellerie Plaisance opens onto the square, in the shade of the church, and over the centuries its walls have echoed the church bells commemorating the start of the grape harvest. Staying here, you couldn't be more central to the activity and the town's events. The hotel has only 16 rooms, modern in their comfort and decor and many with views extending out over vineyards and tiled rooftops. The dining room is lovely and extremely popular with travelers and businessmen, with tables set against windows whose views appear to plunge over the valley. Service is gracious and accommodating. The Plaisance is the place to stay in town and Saint Emilion is the most charming town of the Bordeaux wine region. *Directions:* Saint Emilion is located 39 km east of Bordeaux. Take N89 east to Libourne and then travel on D936 in the direction of Bergerac. Saint Emilion is signposted to the north off D936.

HOSTELLERIE PLAISANCE
Hôteliers: Samira & Louis Quilain
Place du Clocher
33330 Saint Emilion, France
Tel: 05.57.55.07.55, Fax: 05.57.74.41.11
E-mail: hostellerie.plaisance@wanadoo.fr
16 rooms, Double: 590F–1400F
Breakfast: 60F per person
Closed January
Credit cards: all major
Restaurant
Region: Bordeaux, Michelin Map 234

Saint Jean Cap Ferrat is an engaging and picturesque port village on one of France's most exclusive residential peninsulas just a few kilometers from Nice and Monaco. Nestled above the harbor, overlooking a maze of yachts, sits La Voile d'Or, a hotel that is larger than those we usually recommend but, having looked at many of Saint Jean Cap Ferrat's hotels, we found this to be the very nicest, and, although expensive, good value for money. La Voile d'Or is a member of Concorde hotels and offers the warm welcome, polished service, and elegant decor that we expect of members of this prestigious group. We particularly enjoyed the airy restaurant with its wonderful cuisine. *Au port* the activity and scenes of the Mediterranean village are framed by floor-to-ceiling glass windows—the marina with its many yachts and fishing boats is simply a part of the hotel's decor. Inside, soft Provençal pastels and countryside furnishings create a relaxed atmosphere. A gorgeous pool on a peninsula below the hotel and restaurant is surrounded on three sides by the sparkling blue water of the Mediterranean. *Directions:* Just west of Nice, take the Avenue Semeria off the N98 in the direction of Saint Jean Cap Ferrat. Signposts will direct you to the port where a one-way street will take you up to the La Voile d'Or located just above the marina.

LA VOILE D'OR
Hôteliers: Jean & Isabelle Lorenzi
06230 Saint Jean Cap Ferrat, France
Tel: 04.93.01.13.13, Fax: 04.93.76.11.17
E-mail: voiledor@calva.net
45 rooms, Double: 1100F–3500F
Breakfast: included
Open March 15 to October 20
Credit cards: AX
Restaurant, garage, pool
Non-smoking & handicap rooms
Region: Riviera, Michelin Map 245

While strolling through the quaint pedestrian area of Saint Jean de Luz, we just happened to spot La Devinière, a small inn which looked so enticing that we just couldn't resist peeking inside. The exterior is painted white, with cute red shutters accented by bright red geraniums in windowboxes. There is a recessed entryway laced with green ivy with an extra marvelous whimsical touch—where the "real" ivy ends, an artist has painted a delicate trail of ivy continuing around the arched entrance. What a pleasant surprise to walk through the double French doors and discover that the hotel is as pretty inside as out! You come first into a small parlor doubling as a reception area and just beyond is a charming lounge filled with country antiques. A wall of bookshelves, a grand piano, a fireplace, and leather sofas make the room as cozy as can be. Another surprise is that the hotel has its own cute little tea room, *L'Heure du Thé*, opening off the reception area (it also has a separate door opening out to the street). Tea, of course, is served here, but this room also doubles as a breakfast room each morning. For a deluxe hotel choice in Saint Jean de Luz, the Hôtel Parc Victoria just can't be surpassed, but if your budget dictates less expensive accommodation, La Devinière makes an excellent alternative choice. *Directions*: Located on the Rue Loquin, a pedestrian street that runs perpendicular to the beach, behind the casino.

LA DEVINIÈRE   **New**
Hôtelier: M. Carrere
5, Rue Loquin
64500 Saint Jean de Luz, France
Tel: 05.59.26.05.51, Fax: 05.59.51.26.38
8 rooms, Double: 600F–750F
Breakfast: 50F per person
Closed mid-November to mid-December
Credit cards: none
No restaurant, tea room
Region: Basque, Michelin Map 234

This stately gingerbread Victorian (Napoleon III if you're French) home sits in a manicured garden in a lovely residential suburb of the picturesque seaside town of Saint Jean de Luz. Roger Larralde purchased the home to prevent an apartment complex from being built next to his family's holiday home, and converted the building into a jewel of a hotel. The entrance hall with its displays of 1930s glassware leads to the spacious living room graced by delicate Victorian furniture. Here guests help themselves to drinks from the honor bar and contemplate the menu offered by the teeny little restaurant found just across the garden, in the romantic little pavilion beyond the swimming pool. The bedrooms are all decorated with beautiful antiques, many from the art deco period, and complemented by lovely fabrics and immaculate marble bathrooms. If you are looking for a romantic hideaway, ask for one of the two luxurious suites on the grounds. From the front gate it is just a two-minute walk to the beach and a ten-minute stroll into town—a tremendous advantage in summer when the narrow streets are clogged with cars. *Directions:* Leave the A63 at *Saint Jean de Luz Nord*, then turn right at the fourth light signposted *Quartier du Lac*. The hotel is on the right.

HÔTEL PARC VICTORIA
Hôtelier: Roger Larralde
Directeur: Richard Perodeau
5 Rue Cepé
64500 Saint Jean de Luz, France
Tel: 05.59.26.78.78, Fax: 05.59.26.78.08
E-mail: parcvictoria@relaischateaux.fr
12 rooms, Double: 1100F–1850F
Breakfast: 85F per person
Open March 15 to November 15
Credit cards: all major
Restaurant closed Tuesday, pool
Region: Basque, Michelin Map 234
www.karenbrown.com/franceinns/hotelparcvictoria.html

La Chapelle Saint Martin is a small gray-washed manor resting on a velvet green lawn. Although there is very little exterior ornamentation (even the shutters are painted to blend with the façade), the interior decor is very ornate and detailed. Colorfully patterned wallpapers, complementing carpets, paintings hung in heavy gilt frames, lavish chandeliers, tapestries, and miniature statues decorate the rooms of the hotel. Known for its restaurant, La Chapelle Saint Martin serves meals in three elegant, small dining rooms. The setting and service are formal, with lovely porcelain, crystal, china, and silver used to enhance the presentation of owner, Chef Gilles Dudognon's masterful creations. La Chapelle Saint Martin is only a few minutes from Limoges, a city famous for its porcelain. Although many guests venture from Limoges for dinner, the manor does have rooms to accommodate overnight guests. The bedrooms are decorated with the same flavor as the restaurant and public rooms. Very spacious, the bedrooms all have private baths and look out onto the hotel gardens and greenery. The surrounding farmland and two ponds complete the story-book atmosphere of La Chapelle Saint Martin. *Directions:* From Limoges take N147 signposted Poitiers to D35 signposted Saint Martin du Fault. The hotel is 12 km from Limoges.

LA CHAPELLE SAINT MARTIN
Hôtelier: Gilles Dudognon
Saint Martin du Fault
87510 Nieul, France
Tel: 05.55.75.80.17, Fax: 05.55.75.89.50
E-mail: chapelle@relaischateaux.fr
13 rooms, Double: 590F–1500F
Breakfast: 75F per person
Open February 12 to December 31
Credit cards: AX, VS
Restaurant closed Mon, pool, tennis, park, lakes
Region: Limousin, Michelin Map 233
www.karenbrown.com/franceinns/lachapelle.html

La Colombe d'Or is located opposite the main square at the gates to the fortified town of Saint Paul de Vence. The hotel is attractive and elegant in its rustic ambiance: antiques, worn over the years to a warm patina, are placed on terra-cotta floors set under rough wooden beams before open fireplaces, walls are washed white and contrasted by heavy wooden doors. Throw pillows, wall hangings, and flower arrangements introduce colors of rusts, oranges, browns, and beiges. The hotel also boasts a fantastic collection of art. In the past, a number of now-famous painters paid for their meals with their talents—and now the walls are hung like a gallery and the reputation of the inn dictates that the value of the art complements the cuisine. The restaurant of La Colombe d'Or is both excellent and attractive. Dine either in the intimacy of a room warmed by a cozy fire or on the patio whose walls are draped with ivy at tables set under the shade of cream-colored umbrellas. In the evening, stars and candles illuminate the very romantic setting. After a day of sightseeing, return to La Colombe d'Or and enjoy its refreshing pool set against a backdrop of aging stone wall and greenery. *Directions:* Saint Paul is 20 km northwest of Nice. From the Autoroute A8, either from Cannes or Nice, exit at Cagnes sur Mer and then travel north on D6 and D7.

HÔTEL LA COLOMBE D'OR
Hôteliers: Mme & M Roux
Place de Gaulle
06570 Saint Paul de Vence, France
Tel: 04.93.32.80.02, Fax: 04.93.32.77.78
26 rooms, Double: 1400F–1650F
Breakfast: 60F per person
Open December 20 to November 2
Credit cards: all major
Restaurant, garage: no charge, pool, handicap rooms
Region: Riviera, Michelin Map 245
www.karenbrown.com/franceinns/hotellacolombedor.html

Perched on a hillside just above the road, La Grande Bastide captures an enchanting view of Saint Paul de Vence, just a few minutes' drive away. There had been a hotel on the site for many years, but in 1995 Brigitte and Georges Laloum bought the property and spent two years in total renovation. Nothing was spared to make this a hotel of outstanding quality—especially for the moderate price. Although not rated as deluxe, this small hotel would certainly make any guest happy. Everything is fresh and pretty, and of excellent quality. You enter into a happy lounge area painted a deep yellow, setting off a collection of original art. This lounge opens onto a balcony overlooking a large swimming pool. Each of the very attractive, individually decorated bedrooms has at least one piece of original art from the Laloums' personal collection. Brigitte is also an artist and has cleverly painted floral designs on the cabinets that hide the small refrigerators in each of the bedrooms. The bathrooms are outstanding, each large and handsomely tiled. What makes this small hotel truly special is the warmth of welcome of your hosts who successfully strive to make everyone feel like a guest in a private home. *Directions*: From the A8, exit at Cagnes sur Mer and travel north on D6 and D7. Before you come to the village of Saint Paul, watch for a sign to La Grande Bastide, which is located on a hill above the left side of the road.

LA GRANDE BASTIDE
Hôteliers: Brigitte & Georges Laloum
Route de la Colle
06570 Saint Paul de Vence, France
Tel: 04.93.32.50.30, Fax: 04.93.32.50.59
E-mail: stpaullgb@lemel.fr
11 rooms, Double: 750F–950F
Breakfast: 60F per person
Open March 15 to November 15
Credit cards: all major
No restaurant, pool, non-smoking rooms
Region: Provence, Michelin Map 245

Le Hameau is an old farm complex set on the hillside just outside the walled town of Saint Paul de Vence. The whitewashed buildings, tiled roofs aged by years of sun, shuttered windows, arched entryways, heavy doors, and exposed beams all create a rustic and attractive setting. The bedrooms of this inn are found in four buildings clustered together amidst fruit trees and flower gardens. Each building has its own character and name: L'Oranger, L'Olivier, Le Pigeonnier, and La Treille. Three of the largest bedrooms have a small room for an infant and a balcony (rooms 1 and 3 have twin beds and room 2 has a double bed). Room 11, with antique twin beds and a lovely view onto the garden, was my favorite. I was very impressed with the quality of this provincial inn. Le Hameau does not have a restaurant, but a delicious country breakfast can be enjoyed in the garden or in the privacy of your room. A lovely new pool with magnificent views of Saint Paul and the Riviera as its backdrop is an inviting spot. Le Hameau is highly recommended as a wonderful inn and a great value. Informed of new ownership as this book goes to press, we have not personally met the Burlandos and would welcome feedback from our readers. This has always been a favorite, in large part due to the previous owner and his attentive welcome. The new owners have written and expressed a commitment to make Le Hameau even more beautiful and comfortable. *Directions:* Saint Paul de Vence is located 20 km northwest of Nice. From the Autoroute A8, either from Cannes or Nice, exit at Cagnes sur Mer and travel north on D6 and D7.

HÔTEL LE HAMEAU
Hôteliers: Lisa & Carmine Burlando
528, Route de la Colle, 06570 Saint Paul de Vence, France
Tel: 04.93.32.80.24, Fax: 04.93.32.55.75
17 rooms, Double: 500F–900F, Breakfast: 65F per person
Open Feb 15 to Nov 16 & Dec 22 to Jan 6
Credit cards: MC, VS
No restaurant, garage: 35F, pool
Region: Riviera, Michelin Map 245
www.karenbrown.com/franceinns/hotellehameau.html

High atop a hill, set against the blue Riviera sky between Cannes and Monaco, the medieval town of Saint Paul de Vence is bounded by tall ramparts. Its narrow streets are lined with little houses and at its very heart you find Hôtel le Saint-Paul. The charming mood is set as soon as you enter the hotel and see the cozy lounge—appealingly decorated in a French country-Provençal theme. Because the hotel is built within the shell of a 16th-century home, the rooms are not large, but each room has recently been tastefully redecorated with new fabrics and antique furnishings and offers every amenity such as air conditioning, beautiful linens, fluffy towels, terry-cloth robes, refrigerator, televisions, and fine soaps. This past year two of the nicest suites, one of which one enjoys a large terrace overlooking the valley, were painted with charming frescoes. For the truly romantic a new suite has also been created with two luxurious bathrooms and a gorgeous view of the valley. Two of our special favorites are a corner room, decorated in pretty Provençal, Pierre-Deux-style print fabrics, and an especially romantic room tucked under the eaves on the top floor with views out over the quaint tiled rooftops. Another bonus: The restaurant has beautiful mural paintings, an interior fountain and serves gourmet meals on the sheltered, flower-decked terrace in the summer. *Directions:* Located 20 km northwest of Nice, exit the A8 at Cagnes sur Mer and go north on the D6 and D7.

HÔTEL LE SAINT-PAUL
Hôteliers: Olivier Borloo & Charles-Eric Hoffmann
86, Rue Grande
06570 Saint Paul de Vence, France
Tel: 04.93.32.65.25, Fax: 04.93.32.52.94
E-mail: stpaul@relaischateaux.fr
18 rooms, Double: 1250F–2700F
Breakfast: 95F per person
Open January 14 to December 8
Credit cards: all major
Restaurant, non-smoking room, handicap room
Region: Riviera, Michelin Map 245
www.karenbrown.com/franceinns/lesaintpaul.html

The Château des Alpilles has been renovated by the Bons to its former state of grandeur with high ornate ceilings, decorative wallpapers, and tall windows draped with heavy fabrics. The public rooms are attractively decorated with period pieces. The sitting room is a stark contrast with its more modern black and white marble and white table and chairs. Upstairs, tiled hallways hung with tapestries lead to the lovely bedrooms. Large armoires, beds, desks, and chairs are arranged easily in the spacious rooms, each with private bath, and make for a very comfortable stay. The corner rooms are especially nice, with four large shuttered windows overlooking the shaded gardens, which are planted with a multitude of exotic species of trees. In addition to the rooms in the main house, La Chapelle is a charming, three-room house set in the grounds, and an adjacent farmhouse accommodates four suites and a family apartment. In summer for a midday meal a barbecue of lamb, beef, pork, or fish and large seafood salads are offered poolside. The Château des Alpilles now also has a more formal restaurant offering a fixed price menu featuring refined, provençal specialties. *Directions:* From Avignon travel south on N570 and N571 to Saint Rémy. Leave town to the west on D31.

CHÂTEAU DES ALPILLES
Hôteliers: Mme Françoise Bon & Mme Catherine Rollin
Route D31, 13210 Saint Rémy, France
Tel: 04.90.92.03.33, Fax: 04.90.92.45.17
E-mail: chateau.alpilles@wanadoo.fr
19 rooms, Double: 1000F–1750F
Breakfast: 68F–95F per person
Open February 15 to November 12, Christmas
Credit cards: all major
Restaurant for hotel guests only, closed Wednesday
Garage: no charge, pool, tennis, sauna, handicap room
Region: Provence, Michelin Maps 245, 246
www.karenbrown.com/franceinns/chateaudesalpilles.html

Fairy-tale in its setting and the luxury of its decor, the Château d'Esclimont is a memorable and convenient choice (only 65 kilometers from Paris) for either a beginning or an end to your countryside travels. Not inexpensive, but well priced for what it offers, the Château d'Esclimont is spectacular. Hidden off a small country road, its private drive winds through handsome gates to expose a stunning château framed by trees and reflected in a beautiful lake graced with swans. Turrets, moats, stone bridges, towers, and sculptured façades create a fanciful world of its regal past. Thirty rooms are located in the main château, all decorated regally with beautifully coordinating fabrics and handsome furnishings. Whether tucked into turret rounds or under the eaves of the third-floor rooms looking out through dormer windows, the accommodations are spacious and equipped with private baths. Also very attractive in their decor and setting, another 23 rooms are found in the Dungeon, the Pavilion des Trophées, and the Trianon—all stately buildings separated from the château by the moat. The Château d'Esclimont has a number of elegant rooms for dining and meetings. Although the hotel often hosts small tours and conferences, guests receive individual attention and excellent service. *Directions:* From Paris take A10 towards Chartres. Exit A10 at Ablis, then take N10 to Essars where you turn towards Prunay (D101) for 6 km to Saint Symphorien.

CHÂTEAU D'ESCLIMONT
Hôteliers: Traversac Family
28700 Saint Symphorien-le-Château, France
Tel: 02.37.31.15.15, Fax: 02.37.31.57.91
E-mail: esclimont@wanadoo.fr
53 rooms, Double: 1000F–3300F
Breakfast: 110F per person
Open all year, Credit cards: all major
Restaurant, pool, tennis, non-smoking rooms
Region: Île de France, Michelin Map 237

Playground of the rich and the famous, Saint Tropez has cobbled streets twisting down the hill, dead-ending at a small harbor lined with enormous yachts. Because these narrow lanes are such a nightmare to navigate in a car, La Maison Blanche makes an excellent choice for a place to stay. It is in the heart of town, yet convenient to the public car park and very easy to find—a real bonus. The hotel faces onto Place des Lices, which is located at the top of the village and handsomely studded with rows of trees. Previously a private home, this delightful manor house has a creamy-white stone façade accented by white shutters and a steep, gray, mansard slate roof. You enter into a cozy, ever-so-pretty lounge with a marble fireplace flanked by twin sofas slipcovered in a cheerful yellow fabric. Colorful pillows on the sofas and fresh flowers enhance the comfortable, homelike charm. A spiral staircase with a white iron railing winds up to the floors where the bedrooms are found. If you feel like a splurge, I highly recommend asking for room 7, tucked up under the eaves. With its steep slanting ceiling and small gabled windows, it oozes romantic charm. *Directions:* When entering Saint Tropez, follow signs to the Place des Lices parking area. La Maison Blanche is at the far end of the plaza, facing the park.

LA MAISON BLANCHE
Hôtelier: M. Gilles Noubel
Place des Lices
83990 Saint Tropez, France
Tel: 04.94.97.52.66, Fax: 04.94.97.89.23
8 rooms, Double: 790F–1680F
Breakfast: 90F per person
Open all year
Credit cards: all major
Restaurant, sauna, garage
Region: Riviera, Michelin Map 245

It is great fun to spend the night right in the heart Saint Tropez to enjoy its magic after the hordes of tourists depart, and it once again assumes its mantle of a sleepy little village. Of course, the enormous yachts moored in the harbor quickly remind you that Saint Tropez is now the playground of the rich and famous. An excellent choice of accommodation is Le Yaca, whose history goes back to 1722 when it was originally built as a private home. During the Impressionist period, it was a favorite meeting place for many famous painters. Since that time it has been "home" to numerous Hollywood celebrities including Tyrone Power, Rita Hayworth, Greta Garbo, and Orson Wells. Today, Le Yaca maintains its romantic heritage. The mood is one of understated elegance and refinement from the moment you step into the alluring lounge with its creamy-yellow walls and chairs upholstered in a pretty paisley fabric. A staircase with marble banister leads up to doors opening to a charming "secret" garden enclosed by high walls draped in greenery. The centerpiece of the garden is its pool, which is dominated by a tall palm tree. From the street you can't see much of the house, but from the back you can enjoy its charm—an intimate, small villa, almost totally draped with lacy ivy, through which crisp white shutters peek. *Directions*: Located in the center of the village, just a few blocks above the church. Signs in the village direct you to the hotel.

LE YACA
Hôtelier: M. F. Huret
Directeur: M. Alistair MacLean
1, Boulevard d'Aumale
83992 Saint Tropez, France
Tel: 04.94.55.81.00, Fax: 04.94.97.58.50
E-mail: hotel-le-yaca@wanadoo.fr
26 rooms, Double: 1100F–2500F
Breakfast: 100F per person
Open Mar to Oct, Credit cards: all major
Restaurant open daily, pool
Region: Riviera, Michelin Map 245

Lucille and Jacques Bon welcome you to their 17th-century farmstead in the Camargue. Jacques' family were farmers who worked the rice fields of this windswept land with its stretches of marsh and wild horses, and he is passionate about the region. Lucille and Jacques' home is covered with vines, shaded by trellises of grapes and wisteria, and decorated by tiled planters overflowing with geraniums. How fortunate that they have restored a wing of their 17th-century *mas* (farmhouse) into a luxurious inn. The guestrooms have rough, exposed, pine beams, and lovely old doors and windows incorporated into their new construction. We particularly appreciated the immaculate modern bathrooms and excellent lighting. The decor in their home marries old wood furniture with crisp white linens, giving a handsome, fresh look. The Bons are an extremely gracious couple. Lucille is pretty and welcoming, Jacques is a handsome, friendly bull farmer with a large white mustache, tall and lean, hardened by years of work and riding. Cowboy, the family dog, is always by their side. Meals are served in a large country kitchen in front of an open fireplace under 19th-century beams, or in summer on the garden terrace. Days are for swimming, horse riding, mountain biking, or visiting the rodeo with the magnificent Camargue bulls and horses. *Directions:* Leave Arles in the direction of Salin de Giraud (D36) for 25 km. Turn left 3 km after Sambuc.

LE MAS DE PEINT
Hôteliers: Lucille & Jacques Bon
Le Sambuc, 13200 Arles, France
Tel: 04.90.97.20.62, Fax: 04.90.97.22.20
E-mail: peint@avignon.pacwan.net
11 rooms, Double: 1195F–2180F
Breakfast: 100F per person
Open March 10 to January 10
Credit cards: all major
Restaurant closed Wed, garage, pool, riding
Region: Camargue, Michelin Maps 245, 246
www.karenbrown.com/franceinns/lemasdepeint.html

Set in the rolling foothills of the Pyrenees, in a picture-book village near the Spanish border, the Hôtel Arraya has captured the tradition and rustic flavor of this Basque region. Long ago the hotel was founded to provide lodgings for pilgrims on the road to Santiago de Compostela. Today it accommodates guests who have fallen in love with this dear inn and return time and again. The Hôtel Arraya is decorated with an abundance of 17th-century Basque antiques and is a comfortable and hospitable village hotel. The entry, lobby, and breakfast nook are charming: cozy blue-and-white gingham cushions pad the wooden chairs, which are set around a lovely collection of antique tables. The restaurant offers regional Basque specialties to tempt you: *ravioles de xangurro*, *agneau aux pochas*, *foie de canard frais*, *poêlé aux cèpes*, *fromages des Montagnes* and *pastiza*, a delicious Basque almond cake filled with cream or black cherry preserve. The bedrooms are all individual in decor and size, and are attractive with their whitewashed walls, exposed beams, and pretty fabrics. The hotel has been in the Fagoagas' family for many generations and guests are welcomed as friends in the traditional way, round the *zizailua* (bench) near the fire. *Directions:* Exit the Autoroute A6 at Saint Jean de Luz. Follow directions to Saint Pée sur Nivelle on N10. After 5 km turn right to the village of Ascain and then take the Col de Saint Ignace to Sare.

HÔTEL ARRAYA
Hôteliers: Mme & M Paul Fagoaga
Directeur: Jean Baptiste Fagoaga
Sare, 64310 Ascain, France
Tel: 05.59.54.20.46, Fax: 05.59.54.27.04
E-mail: hotel@arraya.com
20 rooms, Double: 530F–595F
Breakfast: 50F per person
Open Apr 1 to mid-Nov, Credit cards: AX, VS
Restaurant
Region: Basque, Michelin Map 234
www.karenbrown.com/franceinns/hotelarraya.html

Entirely surrounded by deep forests, Le Hameau de Barboron is less than 12 kilometers from the many activities and fine restaurants of medieval Beaune. Originating in the 16th century as a monastery, the property later became a farm and then a hunting lodge. Guests can still enjoy the thrill of the hunt and participate in a boar hunt. In 1994 Le Hameau de Barboron opened its doors as a small inn with the bedrooms housed in a group of sand-colored stone buildings that used to store grain. Since then the number of rooms has increased to twelve and they have earned a three-star status. Some of the rooms (with lofts in the rafters) accommodate families, others are cozy and all have elegant modern country-style furnishings, beamed ceilings, and views of the tranquil forest in the distance. They all have beautiful modern blue-and-white-tiled bathrooms. Some have parquet floors with a hunting horn motif. Odile and her father also cater to hunting parties and meetings for up to 30 people. Next to the reception area is a great room filled with trestle tables, graced with a high, beamed ceiling and a large fireplace, and lined with hunting trophies. A full breakfast (including freshly baked croissants, cheeses, ham, and juice) is served until noon. To satisfy appetites later in the day, wines, cheeses, and bread are available for purchase. *Directions:* From Beaune, head northwest for 8 km to Savigny-les-Beaune. Turn left in the village at the intersection and follow the signs through the town, up toward the hills. The road narrows to an unpaved, one-lane road. Press on for 3.2 km past farms and through forest to Le Hameau, centered in a large clearing.

LE HAMEAU DE BARBORON
Hôtelier: Odile Nominé
21420 Savigny-les-Beaune, France
Tel: 03.80.21.58.35, Fax: 03.80.26.10.59
12 rooms, Double: 550F–1200F
Breakfast: 65F per person
Open all year
Credit cards: MC, VS
No restaurant, garage: no charge, handicap room
Region: Burgundy, Michelin Map 243

Le Chaufourg is a dream—absolute perfection. The home has been in the Dambier family since the beginning and Georges Dambier has created an exquisite work of art from what was originally a rustic farmhouse dating back to the 1700s. The task of renovation was formidable, but all the ingredients were there: the house, built of beautiful soft-yellow stone, already had charm and its location on a bend of the Isle river is idyllic. Although strategically located in the heart of the Dordogne and conveniently near access roads to all the major sights of interest, once within the gates leading to the romantic front courtyard, you feel insulated from the real world. The exterior of the house is like a fairy-tale cottage with its white shuttered doors and windows laced with ivy and surrounded by masses of colorful flower gardens. Inside, the magic continues. Each guestroom is entirely different, yet each has the same mood of quiet, country elegance, with natural stucco walls of warm honey-beige, stunning antiques, and tones of soft whites and creams. Nothing is stiff or intimidating—just the elegant harmony of country comfort created by an artist. Georges Dambier adds the final ingredient—the warmth of genuine hospitality. *Directions:* From Périgueux take N89 southwest in the direction of Bordeaux for about 32 km to Sourzac (about 3 km before Mussidan). On the right side of the road, you see the entrance to Le Chaufourg.

LE CHAUFOURG EN PÉRIGORD
Hôtelier: Georges Dambier
24400 Sourzac, France
Tel: 05.53.81.01.56, Fax: 05.53.82.94.87
E-mail: chaufourg.hotel@wanadoo.fr
10 rooms, Double: 870F–1550F
Breakfast: 85F per person
Open all year, by reservation only in winter
Credit cards: all major
Restaurant by reservation only, April to November
Children welcome over 10, non-smoking rooms
Region: Dordogne, Michelin Map 233
www.karenbrown.com/franceinns/lechaufourg.html

In a city with many fine hotels to choose from, I always find myself prejudiced by a property that distinguishes itself as a member of the Romantik chain of hotels. The Romantik Hôtel Beaucour was featured on my list to visit, and it did not disappoint. Not only does the Beaucour offer the very professional, yet personalized level of service associated with the chain, its location is excellent and the accommodation is extremely comfortable and well priced. Flags adorn the street-front exterior, and the reception is set back behind the arched entry. I stayed at the Beaucour when traveling on my own and was pleased to be able to just walk across the bridge to the heart of the old district. Convenient and safe, it was nice simply not to have to hassle with public transportation. Be sure to ask about the hotel owner's restaurants, the Maison Kammerzell, Chaine d'Or, and L'Alsace à Table, located nearby for fine regional dining. A breakfast buffet is offered in the public dining room, or you can opt for the luxury of having a Continental breakfast delivered to your guestroom. The rooms are newly furnished and the use of country pines and provincial fabrics is quite attractive. Bathrooms are lovely and modern in their appointments and the plush towels and robes are luxurious. The guest register reflects the greatest praise a hotel can receive—a long list of returning clientele. *Directions:* From the highways, take the *Place de l'Etoile* exit and follow signs to *Parking Austerlitz.* Rue des Bouchers is just across the Ill, south of the Cathedral.

ROMANTIK HÔTEL BEAUCOUR
Hôtelier: Guy Pierre Baumann
5, Rue des Bouchers
67000 Strasbourg, France
Tel: (03) 88.76.72.00, Fax: (03) 88.76.72.60
E-mail: beaucour@pandemonium.fr
49 rooms, Double: 780F–950F
Breakfast: 65F per person
Open all year, Credit cards: all major
Restaurant, parking: 65F per day, handicap rooms
Region: Alsace, Michelin Map 242

Strasbourg is one of our favorite cities, and the charming Hôtel des Rohan sits just around the corner from its magnificent cathedral on a quiet pedestrian street. Nicole and Rolf van Maenen pride themselves on keeping their little hotel in tip-top condition. On the ground floor are the foyer and a traditional salon, hung with tapestries, where breakfast is served. The bedrooms are not very large and are decorated in either traditional or a more country decor with pine paneling. All rooms rented to international guests are air-conditioned and have bath-shower, phone, radio, television, and mini bar. Recently renovated, the bathrooms are lovely and the bedrooms have more queen and king beds "to please our American guests." Breakfast is the only meal served but the staff is delighted to make recommendations for nearby restaurants, which run the gamut from regional to gourmet cuisine. The location is ideal for exploring Strasbourg on foot. The narrow streets are a maze, winding in the shadow of leaning, timbered buildings and in the shade of lacy trees growing beside the river. Shops range from department stores and sophisticated boutiques to souvenir shops. *Directions:* From any direction take the Place de l'Etoile exit and then follow signposts for the cathedral. This will bring you to Place Gutenberg. Facing the cathedral, turn right—the hotel is 100 meters on the right. A private garage is available for guests staying multiple nights. Inquire about parking options.

HÔTEL DES ROHAN
Hôteliers: Nicole & Rolf Van Maenen
17–19, Rue du Maroquin
67060 Strasbourg Cedex B.P. 39, France
Tel: 03.88.32.85.11, Fax: 03.88.75.65.37
E-mail: info@hotel-rohan.com
36 rooms, Double: 410F–795F
Breakfast: 52F per person, Open all year
Credit cards: all major, non-smoking rooms
No restaurant, garage: 80F by prior arrangement
Region: Alsace, Michelin Map 242
www.karenbrown.com/franceinns/hoteldesrohan.html

At the heart of the Loire Valley, Tours is a wonderful city and arrival by train places you within walking distance of its old quarter. The old part of Tours is enchanting with its cobbled streets, timbered houses, and lovely squares encircled with inviting sidewalk cafés. I walked the streets of Tours in search of a charming hotel close to the train station and the old town to recommend for those traveling our train itinerary. I believe I looked at every small hotel in town and recommend the Hôtel du Manoir as the best of what I saw. Just a few blocks from the train station (ten minutes on foot), the entrance to the hotel is off a gated, graveled courtyard. Inside the hotel, the reception area is spotless with marble floors, pretty drapes at the windows and a few clusterings of chairs. Guestrooms are found on the three levels (there is an elevator) and are equipped with good lighting, comfortable beds, televisions, direct-dial phones, attractive fabrics that dress both the beds and the windows, and modern, new bathrooms. The guestrooms for the price range are the best value in town. A 19th-century residence, the Hôtel du Manoir was renovated under the supervision of its owner, Monsieur Schaafsma, who hails from Holland. *Directions:* On foot from the train station turn right for two blocks on Boulevard Herteloup, and then turn left on Rue Jules Simon. (Note: A taxi will take a different route as Rue Jules Simon is a one-way street.) The hotel is located on the corner of Rue Jules Simon and Rue Traversière.

HÔTEL DU MANOIR
Hôtelier: Théodore Schaafsma
2, Rue Traversière
37000 Tours, France
Tel: 02.47.05.37.37, Fax: 02.47.05.16.00
20 rooms, Double: 270F–320F
Breakfast: 30F per person
Open all year
Credit cards: all major
No restaurant, parking: 15F
Region: Loire Valley, Michelin Maps 232, 238

La Bastide de Tourtour is situated on the outskirts of Tourtour, *le village dans le ciel*, and actually guards a position even higher than the "village in the heavens." From its vantage point you can enjoy unobstructed vistas of the surrounding countryside of Haute Provence. The region is lovely and the village, with its cobbled streets, galleries, tempting shops, cozy restaurants, and inviting cafés, a delight to explore. The location of La Bastide de Tourtour is ideal and we are pleased to learn from travelers that the owners have expended some effort and money on refurbishments. A grand circular staircase, with old implements for weaving and spinning on each floor's landing, winds up to the guestrooms. Many of the Bastide's bedrooms have private terraces and enjoy panoramic views (views are a factor in determining rates). The decor and the view vary from room to room. The restaurant is attractive, with tables set under arches and beamed ceilings. When weather permits, tables are set on the terrace. *Directions:* Located 20 km northwest of Draguignan. Leaving Draguignan, follow signposts for Flayosc/Salernes, cross Flayosc, and continue towards Salernes. After 7 km take the road to the right signposted Tourtour.

LA BASTIDE DE TOURTOUR
Hôteliers: M & Mme Lavergne
Directeur: M Barbe
Route Draguignan
83690 Tourtour, France
Tel: 04.94.70.57.30, Fax: 04.94.70.54.90
E-mail: bastide@verdon.net
25 rooms, Double: 530F–1400F
Breakfast: 75F per person
Open all year, Credit cards: all major
Restaurant, pool, tennis, handicap room
Region: Haute Provence, Michelin Map 245

Set on a headland, with garden paths weaving down to a small crescent of golden sand, this large lovely home, Ti Al-Lannec, was opened as a hotel in 1978 by Danielle and Gerard Jouanny. The Jouannys offer a warm welcome rarely found in hotels, so it feels more like staying with friends at the seaside than in a hotel. Each bedroom has a different pretty wallpaper with coordinating drapes and bedspread. Family accommodations have two bedrooms, one for parents and one with bunk beds for children. My favorites were those with *salon en verandah* meaning that each has a small sitting area with doors opening to a tiny balcony so that whatever the weather you can enjoy the fantastic view of sand, ocean, and rocky promontories. The large windows of the restaurant share the same glorious view. The sitting rooms have thoughtfully been equipped with jigsaw puzzles, books, and games to accommodate the interests of the guests and the unpredictable moods of the weather. In the basement is L'Espace Bleu Marine, a complete health center where you can pamper yourself with massages and wraps, work out in the gymnasium, and relax in the solarium, sauna, and large Jacuzzi set in a gazebo overlooking the beach. Children enjoy the outdoor play equipment and giant chess set. *Directions:* From Rennes take N12 to Guigamp and follow signposts for Lannion for 9 km to Trébeurden.

TI AL-LANNEC
Hôteliers: Danielle & Gerard Jouanny
14, Allée de Mezo Guen
22560 Trébeurden, France
Tel: 02.96.15.01.01, Fax: 02.96.23.62.14
E-mail: ti.al.lannec@wanadoo.fr
29 rooms, Double: 700F–1175F
Breakfast: 70F–90F per person,
Open Mar 11 to Nov 12, Credit cards: all major
Restaurant, health center, handicap rooms
Region: Brittany, Michelin Map 230
www.karenbrown.com/franceinns/tiallannec.html

What was once a farm complex now houses a simple, comfortable country hotel and restaurant. The Auberge des Grandes Roches enjoy a setting of 12 acres of parkland, just a few miles inland from the south coast of Brittany. Three buildings cluster around a graveled courtyard and the main building and restaurant open onto a lovely expanse of lawn and garden. The oldest building dates back 600 years and has a roof of thatch continuing to slate. The two-story, ivy-clad main structure houses a charming salon for guests, a cozy breakfast room, and a very attractive country-French restaurant. Twenty guestrooms are divided between the three houses, ranging from very simple to large family suites, their decor also varying dramatically from bright modern colors to the more traditional. They are all comfortable with modern baths, but it is intentional on the part of Monsieur Heinrich to keep some simpler in terms of decor and amenities in order to be able to offer guests a full range of tariffs. Monsieur Heinrich personally showed us around and he implied that while the hotel has always been in his family, one can only guess at the future. He was proud to mention that on their acreage you find the prehistoric standing stone Menhir de Kerangallou, unusual because of its crowning cross. *Directions:* Trégunc is located 5 km east of Concarneau on the D783. Once in Trégunc follow well-placed signs to the hotel on the north side of this small town.

LES AUBERGES DES GRANDES ROCHES   *New*
Hôteliers: M & Mme Heinrich
29910 Trégunc, France
Tel: 02.98.97.62.97, Fax: 02.98.50.29.19
20 rooms, Double: 270F–600F
Breakfast: 45F per person
Closed mid-December to mid-January
Credit cards: MC, VS
Restaurant closed Mon and mid-Nov to mid-Mar
Region: Brittany, Michelin Map 230

Nestled on a picturesque bend of the Dordogne, referred to as the *Cingle de Trémolat*, is the sleepy, tobacco-growing village of Trémolat. Tucked away on a quiet street that leads into the center is Le·Vieux Logis et Ses Logis des Champs. This charming hotel opens up on one side to farmland and has a pretty back garden with a small stream. The Giraudel-Déstord family has lived in this ancient, ivy-covered farm complex for 400 years, and the tradition of welcome and excellence of service seems only to improve with time. Bernard Giraudel-Déstord represents the current generation and he is often about overseeing details in the kitchen and guest quarters. The bedrooms, which have recently been redecorated, are located in various ivy-draped buildings about the property whose tranquil views open onto the freshness of the countryside. Each room has an individual theme for its decor and everything matches, down to the smallest detail. A favorite is decorated in large red-and-white checks on the duvets, the pillows, the curtains, and the canopy on the four-poster bed. The restaurant is in the barn and the tables are cleverly positioned within each of the stalls. The ambiance is romantic and the menu is excellent, offering a tempting selection of regional specialties. *Directions:* Trémolat is located 54 km south of Périgueux. From Périgueux travel south on N139 and at Le Bugue travel southwest on D31 to Trémolat.

LE VIEUX LOGIS ET SES LOGIS DES CHAMPS
Hôtelier: Bernard Giraudel-Déstord
Directeur: Didier Bru
24510 Trémolat, France
Tel: 05.53.22.80.06, Fax: 05.53.22.84.89
E-mail: vieuxlogis@relaischateaux.fr
26 rooms, Double: 840F–1750F
Breakfast: 95F per person
Open all year
Credit cards: all major
Restaurant, garage: no charge
Region: Dordogne, Michelin Map 235

In the middle of a beautiful valley, with mountains towering as high as 1,500 meters on either side, the medieval town of Trigance clings to a rocky spur. The Château de Trigance is found within the walls and ruins of the ancient castle that crowns the village. The restorations and extent of the work involved to prepare this 11th-century fortress as a hotel are fully appreciated after seeing the "before" and "after" photographs. At present there are ten rooms which are tucked behind the ancient fortress's thick stone walls. The accommodation is definitely not luxurious and often a bit austere with beds butted right up against the ancient stone walls, but the setting and atmosphere are unique, with an authentic medieval flavor. You can even reserve a large room in the round tower that overlooks the village. The restaurant is renowned for its fine cuisine. Madame and Monsieur Thomas are in charge of the hotel in its magnificent setting under the warm blue skies of Haute Provence and their personalities enhance the character and attraction of this hillside accommodation. Park on the outskirts of this walled town and Monsieur Thomas or his charming son, Guillaume will greet you. The location of the château is a perfect starting point for touring the spectacular Gorges du Verdon: Pack a picnic and spend a day driving along the canyon at your leisure. *Directions:* From Draguignan take D955 signposted Castellance for 45 km (north) to the hotel.

CHÂTEAU DE TRIGANCE
Hôteliers: Jean-Claude Thomas Family
83840 Trigance, France
Tel: 04.94.76.91.18, Fax: 04.94.85.68.99
E-mail: trigance@relaischateaux.fr
10 rooms, Double: 650F–950F
Breakfast: 75F per person
Open March 24 to November 1
Credit cards: all major
Restaurant
Region: Haute Provence, Michelin Map 245
www.karenbrown.com/franceinns/chateaudetrigance.html

It is always a delight to happen on what I consider an undiscovered gem. The lovely framed entry of La Maison des Chanoines is off a narrow cobbled street that winds up to the crowning château of the beautiful village of Turenne. Madame and Monsieur Cheyroux, as a team, have poured their heart and creativity into the renovation of this very special 16th-century inn. Its gourmet restaurant is set behind a thick, stone archway and tables are intimately set under the arched stone walls and ceiling of the *cave*. Fresh flowers, beautiful copper candlesticks, handsome ceramic jugs, and beautiful china accompany each course. The selection on the menu and wine list is excellent and based on local and regional specialties. With just 16 place settings in the restaurant, it is wise to book ahead. In lovely weather, additional tables are now available outside as the Cheyroux have redone the terrace to accommodate diners. The guestrooms are also limited in number although another three have recently been added across the road. The original rooms are accessed off a small street that winds up behind the restaurant entrance. Guestrooms are a fabulous value, comfortable, simple, and quite charming. Thick-set windows are draped with attractive curtains, beds are comfortable, lighting is good, and bathrooms are spotless and modern. *Directions:* Turenne is located 15 km south of Brive. Take the N20 south then the D158 to the D8 to Turenne.

LA MAISON DES CHANOINES
Hôteliers: Mme & M Cheyroux
Route de L'Eglise
19500 Turenne, France
Tel: 05.55.85.93.43, Fax: none
6 rooms, Double: 340F–500F
Breakfast: 40F per person
Open April 1 to November 5
Credit cards: MC, VS
Restaurant closed Tuesday & Wednesday off season
Region: Limousin, Michelin Maps 235, 239
www.karenbrown.com/franceinns/lamaisondeschanoines.html

A beautiful drive winds up to this lovely, gray-turreted château and the first impression is captivating. The Château de Castel Novel offers refined service and accommodation and, to top it off, the cuisine is superb. This is the country of such delicacies as *foie gras*, truffles, veal, and a delightful variety of mushrooms. The talented chef, who served his apprenticeship in the region and at some of France's finest restaurants, offers you a wonderful menu. Recently air-conditioned throughout, the bedrooms are attractive—I found, as they were shown to me, that each one became my "favorite." One is impressive, if you like to sleep in a turret; another has a pair of magnificent, spiraling-wood four-poster beds; and yet another has twin beds, two balconies, and a lovely view. The Parveaux family has added ten attic rooms in an annex, Le Cottage du Château. These rooms are furnished less luxuriously and do not offer the same wonderful ambiance, but are offered at a reduced rate. Built in the 14th and 15th centuries, the Château de Castel Novel is set in a garden of 15 acres with a swimming pool, tennis courts, and a practice area of three holes for golfers. The hotel is professionally and graciously managed by Albert and Christine Parveaux. *Directions:* Travel 10 km to the northwest from Brive la Gaillarde on D901, in the direction of Objat. Just as you enter Varetz, turn left on D152, where the hotel is signposted.

CHÂTEAU DE CASTEL NOVEL
Hôteliers: Mme & M Albert Parveaux
19240 Varetz, France
Tel: 05.55.85.00.01, Fax: 05.55.85.09.03
E-mail: novel@relaischateaux.fr
37 rooms, Double: 680F–1800F
Breakfast: 90F per person
Open end of May to beginning of October
Credit cards: all major
Restaurant closed Mon, & Thurs lunch, pool, tennis
Region: Dordogne, Michelin Map 239
www.karenbrown.com/franceinns/chateaudecastelnovel.html

Vence is a quaint little town of narrow streets, intriguing passageways, and tempting craft and specialty shops. Look for the largest tree in Vence and there you will find L'Auberge des Seigneurs. This is a delightful inn, located on a quiet side street at the center of Vence. The inn is charming in its decor and country ambiance—heavy old beams are exposed in the ceilings and walls are whitewashed. Copper plates, pans, and bed warmers adorn the walls, Provençal fabrics cover the tables, and lovely antiques decorate every nook and cranny. Wooden doors, rich in their patina, a large stone fireplace, and striking flower arrangements complete a scene in the restaurant and salon that is intimate and cozy. In the evenings the restaurant comes alive, mellow with the soft flicker of candlelight. Diners talk in hushed conversation at clustered tables and Madame Rodi orchestrates excellent and gracious service, tossing salads tableside, pouring wine, and tending chickens grilled on the open fire. Up a creaking stairway are ten delightful, small rooms. Inexpensive in price, the bedrooms are a true bargain—comfortable and simply decorated with pretty country prints. *Directions:* From Nice travel southwest on N98 to Cros de Cagnes and then travel north on D36 to Vence. Vence is located 22 km to the northwest of Nice.

L'AUBERGE DES SEIGNEURS ET DU LION D'OR
Hôtelier: Daniele Rodi
Place du Frêne
06140 Vence, France
Tel: 04.93.58.04.24, Fax: 04.93.24.08.01
6 rooms, Double: 364F–394F
Breakfast: 55F per person
Closed mid-November to mid-March
Credit cards: all major
Restaurant closed Mon, & Tuesday lunch
Non-smoking rooms
Region: Riviera, Michelin Map 245
www.karenbrown.com/franceinns/desseigneurs.html

Looking up from the town of Vence you can see the Château Saint Martin sitting on the hillside on the site of an ancient Templars' castle. The Château Saint Martin, built in traditional style in 1936, stands behind the old drawbridge, tower, and wall which date back to Roman times and give the hotel a feeling of the past, while a beautifully located overflow swimming pool and clay tennis courts provide the pleasures of the present. The accommodation is extremely luxurious and many of the rooms are so large that they are referred to as suites. If you prefer solitude, there are also small Provençal country houses on the estate. A well-known cook is in charge of this most famous kitchen and at his disposal is oil from the 1,000-year-old olive trees. Sample his splendors at tables set on a wide outdoor shaded terrace and enjoy a 100-kilometer vista down to the Côte d'Azur. Indoors, tables set in an elegant restaurant enjoy the same breathtaking panorama. The Château Saint Martin is for those seeking sheer luxury and the finest of service. *Directions:* From the Cagnes sur Mer exit off A8 take D36 to Vence. At Vence follow signs for *Autres Directions,* avoiding the town center. Follow signs for Coursegoules (or Col de Vence or D2) and you find the hotel high above the town about 3 km north of Vence.

CHÂTEAU SAINT MARTIN
Directrice: Mlle Andrée Brunet
Avenue des Templiers
BP 102, 06140 Vence, France
Tel: 04.93.58.02.02, Fax: 04.93.24.08.91
E-mail: st-martin@webstore.fr
34 rooms, 6 bastides
Double: 3000F–4500F
Breakfast: 120F per person
Open December 23 to mid-October
Credit cards: all major
Restaurant, garage, pool, tennis, handicap rooms
Region: Riviera, Michelin Map 245
www.karenbrown.com/franceinns/chateausaintmartin.html

Hôtel le Pontot, a fortified house with a walled flower garden, sits amongst the winding medieval streets of the walled hilltop town of Vézelay. Charles Thum, the American owner, leaves the running of the hotel to the personable Christian Abadie, but he is usually on hand to help unilingual English-speaking guests with their reservations and questions. On warm days guests breakfast off Limoges china, with silver service, at little tables set in the garden; in inclement weather breakfast is served in the elegant blue salon. Curving stone steps lead up to the bedrooms and the comfortable lounge. The traditionally decorated bedrooms are furnished with antiques and have small modern bathrooms. We especially enjoyed the bedroom that contains Monet's easel, and the spacious suite with its blue silk coronet draperies above twin beds. For complete privacy request the suite in the former kitchen: its stone floor, huge fireplace, and old utensils give a rustic feel and you can scramble up above the oven to the extra little bed where the servants once slept. There are some delightful restaurants in the village and guests often dine with Marc Meneau in nearby Saint Père sous Vézelay. *Directions:* Vézelay is located 15 km from Avallon on D957. From the town's main square turn up the hill towards the Basilica and park in the first carport on your left. The hotel is on the left.

RÉSIDENCE HÔTEL LE PONTOT
Hôtelier: Charles Thum
Directeur: Christian Abadie
Place du Pontot
89450 Vézelay, France
Tel: 03.86.33.24.40, Fax: 03.86.33.30.05
10 rooms, Double: 620F–1050F
Breakfast: 65F per person
Open April 20 to October 20
Credit cards: MC, VS
No restaurant, bar service, garage: 50F
Region: Burgundy, Michelin Map 238
www.karenbrown.com/franceinns/hotellepontot.html

Le Prieuré was built as an archbishop's palace in 1322 and became a priory in 1333—now it's a charming hotel at the heart of this inviting medieval village. Ivy clings to its warm stone exterior, green shutters dress its windows, and sun-baked tiles adorn the roof. The hotel has expanded and changed over the years and now has 26 rooms and 10 suites, many of which have lovely terraces, housed in a modern annex. The annex, which might at first disappoint as it doesn't boast the character of old, does enjoy all the welcome, modern comforts. Air conditioning has been incorporated throughout—an appreciated luxury in the hot Provençal summers. Le Prieuré is decorated with beautiful antiques, which add charm and beauty to the ambiance and setting. When blessed with the balmy weather of Provence, dine on the terrace surrounded by foliage and soft lighting in the subtle elegance of a summer night. Marie-France and her son François are your gracious hosts and their presence lends a personal and special touch to the very competent and professional service. *Directions:* Leave Avignon towards Nîmes and immediately after crossing the River Rhône turn right towards Bagnols sur Cèze on D980 for about 2 km. The hotel is in the heart of the village, next to the church.

LE PRIEURÉ
Hôteliers: Marie-France & François Mille
7, Place de Chapître
30400 Villeneuve les Avignon, France
Tel: 04.90.15.90.15, Fax: 04.90.25.45.39
E-mail: leprieure@relaischateaux.fr
36 rooms, Double: 570F–1850F
Breakfast: 90F per person
Open mid-March to November
Credit cards: all major
Restaurant, pool, tennis, non-smoking rooms
Region: Provence, Michelin Maps 245, 246
www.karenbrown.com/franceinns/leprieure.html

Terraced down the hillside with the original domaine as its focal point and center, the Domaine de Rochebois, with its soft, pale stone and gray roof, is elegant and very luxurious. You enter the reception through automatic glass doors and receive a welcome both professional and gracious. The dining room is quietly formal, with grand windows opening onto an outdoor terrace where tables are set in warm weather. There is a cozy English bar and a lovely small, intimate dining room, the Petit Salon, with tables set under beautiful old beams. An elegant staircase winds up to the ten guestrooms found in the pavilion. Extremely spacious and handsome in their decor, the rooms look across the pool to the surrounding property and expansive golf course. Smaller rooms in the pavilion are less expensive but still quite comfortable in size with magnificently appointed bathrooms. The tiled-floor rooms in the side annex are more Italian-Mediterranean in their style and decor, also quite lovely with private balconies and priced according to view. There are four duplexes in the annex which enjoy a first-floor living room, a loft bedroom, and an expanse of private outdoor terrace. Breakfast is served either in a lovely breakfast room off the glassed-in corridor connecting the two buildings or in the guestroom. *Directions:* Located on the D46, 6 km south of Sarlat.

DOMAINE DE ROCHEBOIS
Hôtelier: L. Van de Welle
Directrice: Anne Hillebrand
Route de Montfort, Vitrac, 24200 Sarlat, France
Tel: 05.53.31.52.52, Fax: 05.53.29.36.88
E-mail: info@rochebois.com
40 rooms, Double 890F–2250F
Breakfast: 90F per person
Open mid-Apr to end of Oct, Credit cards: all major
Restaurant, pool, golf, fitness center
Non-smoking rooms, handicap rooms
Region: Dordogne, Michelin Map 235
www.karenbrown.com/franceinns/rochebois.html

Once a Cistercian abbey, the Château de Gilly is surrounded by an expanse of grounds transected by a web of moats, with origins going back to the 6th century. Just north of Beaune, at the heart of Burgundy, the château guards a quiet location near Château du Clos de Vougeot, home of the Chevaliers de Tastevin. You can drive up over one arm of a moat to the entry which was magnificently constructed to blend with two wings of the fortification that date back to the 17th century. Beautifully renovated, the interior of the château is rich in furnishings and comfort. Hung between dramatic beams, handsome tapestries drape the old stone walls. Lofty corridors, dramatic with vaulted ceilings and tile and stone floors lead to ground-floor bedchambers and narrow, steep stairways wind up to rooms tucked under the heavy old eaves and beams. Quality fabrics and incredible 14th- and 18th-century paintings decorate the spacious rooms, and bathrooms have been incorporated with thoughtful modern comforts. Descend to an underground passageway that leads to the magnificent dining room. Dressed in deep-red fabrics, candlelight, crystal, silver, and heavy tapestries, the restaurant is very elegant. *Directions:* Go 22 km north of Beaune on N74. Just before Vougeot, watch for a small road and sign on the right, directing you east to Gilly les Citeaux and the château.

CHÂTEAU DE GILLY
Hôtelier: Traversac Family
Directeur: Fabrice Mercier
Gilly les Citeaux, 21640 Vougeot, France
Tel: 03.80.62.89.98, Fax: 03.80.62.82.34
E-mail: gilly@wanadoo.fr
48 rooms, Double: 700F–2650F
Breakfast: 90F–140F per person
Open March 11 to January 31
Credit cards: all major
Restaurant
Region: Burgundy, Michelin Map 243
www.karenbrown.com/franceinns/chateaudegilly.html

Nestled on the shore of Lake Geneva, the tiny walled medieval village of Yvoire is positively captivating—almost too quaint to be real. Her allure is even more enchanting in summer when every available bit of land is a flower garden and every house draped with red geraniums. Making everything perfect, there is a gem of a small hotel here—the 200-year-old Hôtel du Port which absolutely oozes charm with a stone façade almost totally covered with ivy, brown shutters, and red geraniums spilling out of windowboxes. It is just next to the dock where ferries flit in and out all day, making their circuit around the lake. The main focus of the hotel is its restaurant, which has a summer dining terrace stretching to the edge of the water. Although the majority of guests come just for lunch, for a lucky few there are four sweet bedrooms available. If you want to splurge, request one of the two in front with a romantic balcony overlooking the lake. The moderately sized, spotlessly clean guestrooms are simple and attractive, with built-in wooden furniture and matching drapes and bedspreads. Each has a modern bathroom, air conditioning, telephone, TV, and mini bar. As in so many of our favorite hotels, the gracious owners, Jeannine & Jean-François Kung, are also the managers, always keeping an eye out to be sure the hotel is impeccable in every way. *Directions:* Yvoire is on the south shore of Lake Geneva, 30 km east of Geneva.

HÔTEL DU PORT
Hôteliers: Jeannine & Jean-François Kung
74104 Yvoire, France
Tel: 04.50.72.80.17, Fax: 04.50.72.90.71
4 rooms, Double: 640F–890F
Breakfast: 45F per person
Open March 15 to October 30
Credit cards: all major
Restaurant
Region: Haute-Savoie, Michelin Map 244

323

Regional and Key Map

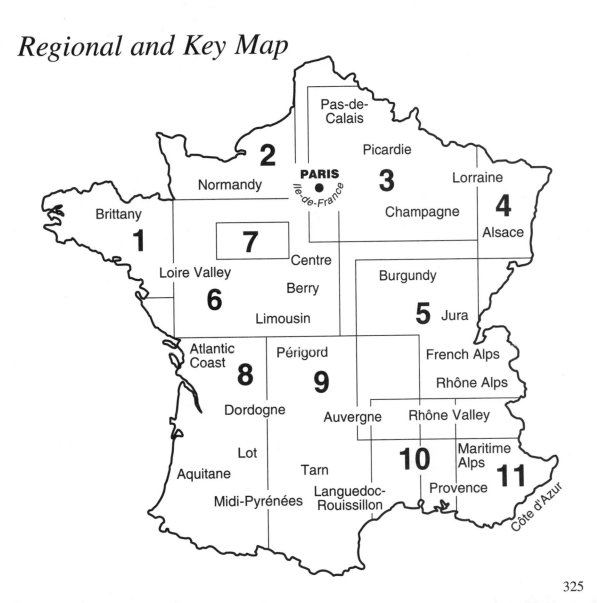

Pas-de-Calais

Picardie

PARIS
Ile-de-France

Normandy

Lorraine

Brittany

Champagne

2

3

4

Alsace

1

7

Centre

Burgundy

Loire Valley

Berry

Jura

6

Limousin

5

Atlantic Coast

Périgord

French Alps

Rhône Alps

8

9

Dordogne

Auvergne

Rhône Valley

Lot

Maritime Alps

Aquitane

Tarn

10

11

Midi-Pyrénées

Languedoc-Rouissillon

Provence

Côte d'Azur

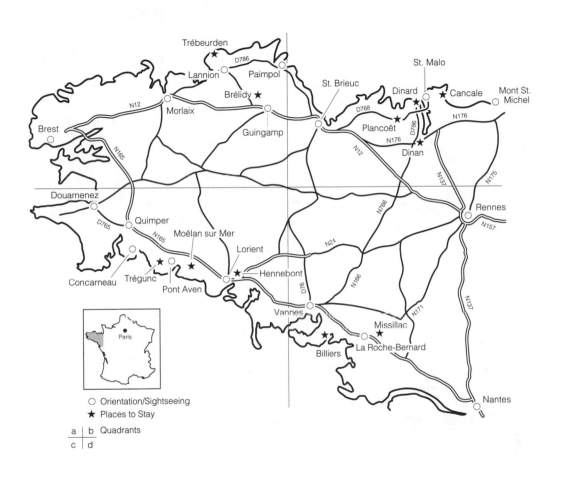

Trébeurden
★
D786
Lannion ○ Paimpol
Brélidy ★ St. Brieuc
St. Malo
Dinard ○ Cancale
★ Mont St.
Michel ○
N12
Morlaix
D768
Plancoët
N176
Guingamp
N176
Dinan ★
N12 N137
N175
Brest
N165
Douarnenez ○
N798
Rennes ○
N157
D765 Quimper ○
N165
Moëlan sur Mer
Lorient ★
N24
N166
Concarneau ○
Trégunc ★
Pont Aven ★
Hennebont
D76
N171
N137
Vannes ○
Missillac ★
Billiers ★
La Roche-Bernard
Nantes ○

Paris

○ Orientation/Sightseeing
★ Places to Stay

| a | b | Quadrants |
| c | d | |

Map 1

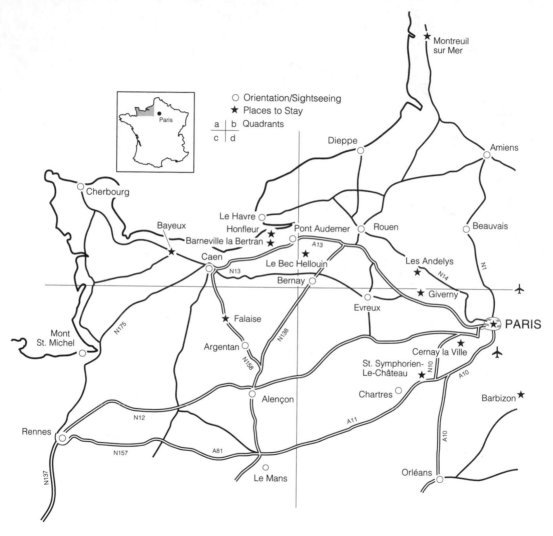

Map 2

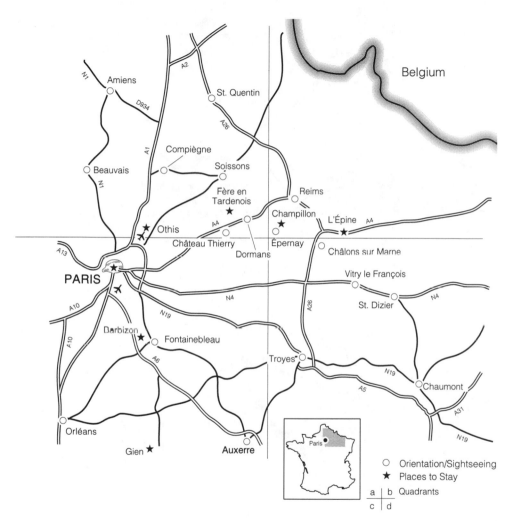

Belgium

N1

Amiens

D934

St. Quentin

A2

A26

A1

Compiègne

Beauvais

Soissons

N1

Fère en
Tardenois

Reims

Champillon

L'Épine

A4

A4

A13

Othis

A4

Château Thierry

Épernay

Châlons sur Marne

Dormans

PARIS

Vitry le François

N4

A26

St. Dizier

N4

A10

Barbizon

N19

A10

Fontainebleau

A6

Troyes

Orléans

N19

Chaumont

A5

A31

Gien

Auxerre

N19

Paris

○ Orientation/Sightseeing

★ Places to Stay

| a | b | Quadrants
| c | d |

Map 3

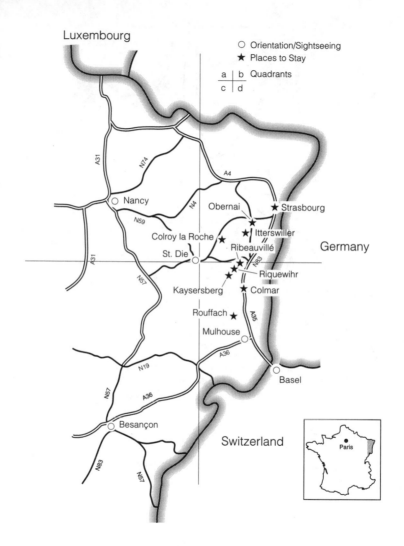

Luxembourg

○ Orientation/Sightseeing
★ Places to Stay

a	b	Quadrants
c	d

A31

N74

A4

○ Nancy

N4

Obernai

★ Strasbourg

N59

Colroy la Roche ★

★ Itterswiller

Germany

Ribeauvillé

A31

St. Die ○

N83

N57

★★

★ Riquewihr

Kaysersberg

★ Colmar

Rouffach ★

A35

Mulhouse ○

A36

N19

Basel ○

N57

A36

Switzerland

○ Besançon

Paris

N83

N57

Map 4

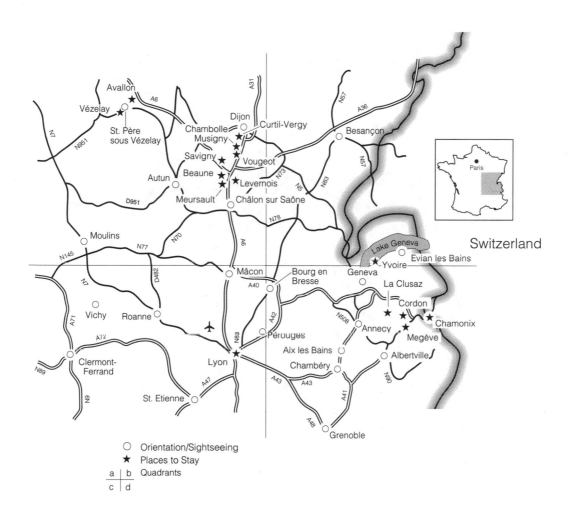

Map 5

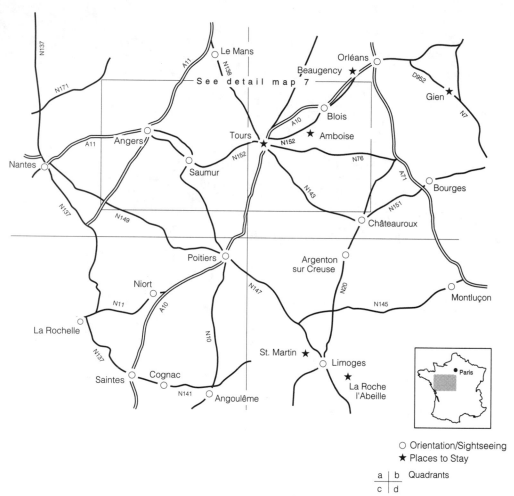

See detail map 7

○ Orientation/Sightseeing
★ Places to Stay

a | b   Quadrants
c | d

Map 6

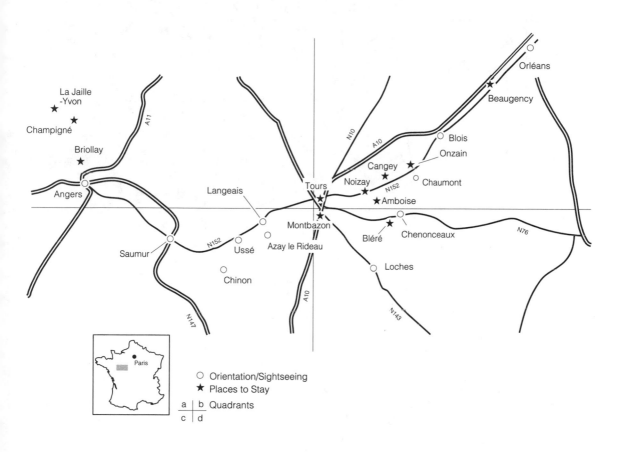

La Jaille
-Yvon ★

Champigné ★

Briollay ★

○ Angers

A11

La Jaille

○ Orléans

★ Beaugency

N10

A10

○ Blois

Onzain

Cangey ★

Noizay ★

Chaumont ○

N152

★ Amboise

Langeais

Tours ★

○ Saumur

N152

○ Ussé

Azay le Rideau ○

Montbazon

Bléré ★

Chenonceaux ○

N76

N147

○ Chinon

○ Loches

A10

N143

Paris

○ Orientation/Sightseeing
★ Places to Stay

| a | b | Quadrants |
| c | d |

Map 7

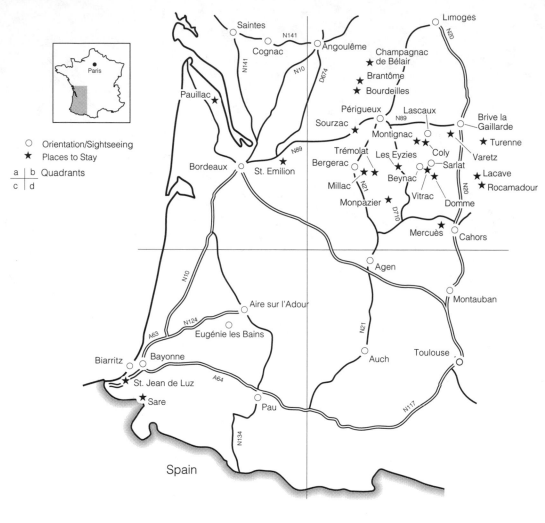

Map 8

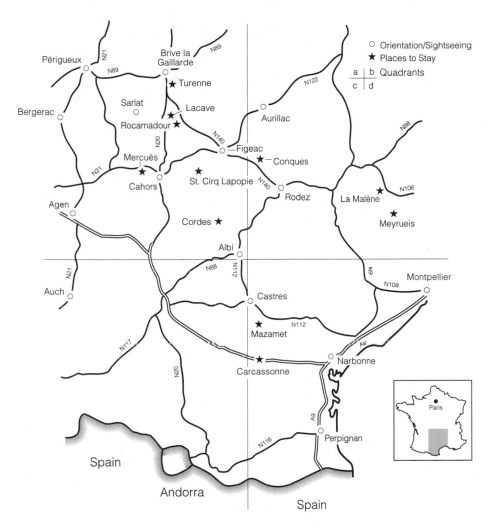

Map 9

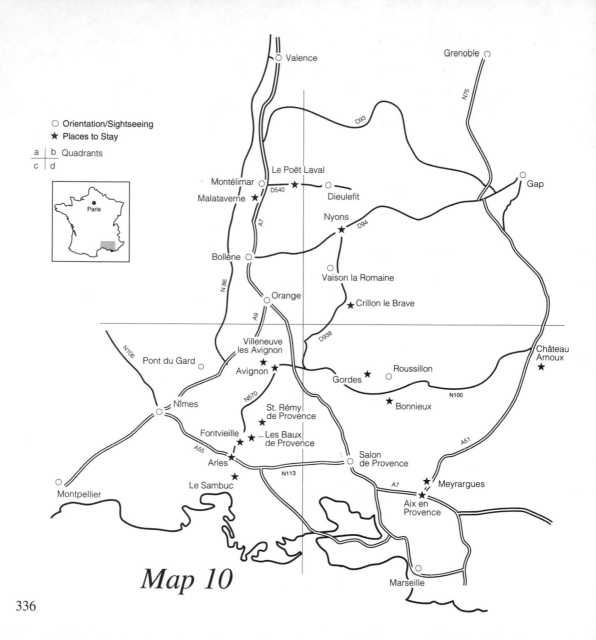

○ Orientation/Sightseeing
★ Places to Stay

a	b
c	d

Quadrants

Paris

Valence ○

Grenoble ○

D93

N75

Gap ○

Le Poët Laval
Montélimar ○ ★ D540
Malataverne ★
Dieulefit ○

Nyons ○
★ D94

Bollène ○

Vaison la Romaine ○
N 86

★ Crillon le Brave

Orange ○
A9

Villeneuve
les Avignon ★
D938

Château
Arnoux ★

N106
Pont du Gard ○
Avignon ★

Gordes ★
Roussillon ○

N570

St. Rémy
de Provence ★

Bonnieux ★

Nîmes ○

N100

Fontvieille ★
Les Baux
de Provence ★
A55

Arles ○
N113

Salon
de Provence ○

A51

Montpellier ○

Le Sambuc ★

A7
Meyrargues ★

Aix en
Provence ★

Map 10

Marseille ○

336

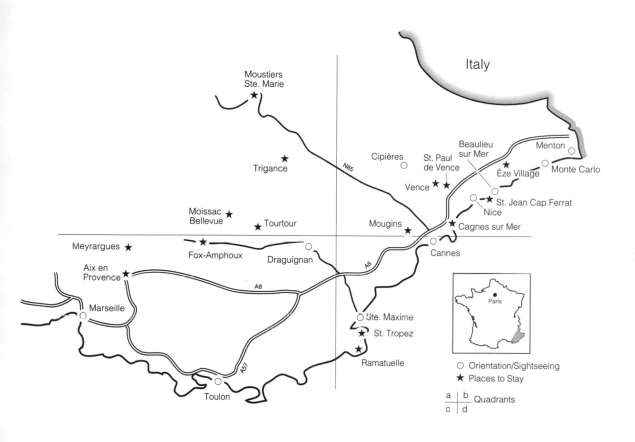

Italy

Moustiers
Ste. Marie ★

Trigance ★

N85

Cipières ○

St. Paul
de Vence ★

Beaulieu
sur Mer

Menton ○

Monte Carlo ●

Èze Village ★

Vence ★ ★

Moissac ★
Bellevue

★ Tourtour

Mougins ★

Nice ○ ★ St. Jean Cap Ferrat

Cagnes sur Mer ★

Meyrargues ★

★ Fox-Amphoux

Draguignan ○

A8

Cannes ○

Aix en
Provence ★

A8

Marseille ○

A57

Ste. Maxime ○

St. Tropez ★

Ramatuelle ★

Toulon ○

Paris

○ Orientation/Sightseeing
★ Places to Stay

a	b	Quadrants
c	d	

Map 11

Index

D

Dambach la Ville, 115
Damery, 122
Deauville, 20
Détroits, Les, 62
Devinière, La, Saint Jean de Luz, 292
Dieffenthal, 115
Dijon, 104
    Musée des Beaux Arts, 104
Dinan, 28
    L'Hôtel d'Avaugour, 28, 224
Dinard, 27
Dinard-Pleurtuit
    Manoir de la Rance, 28, 225
Domaine de la Rhue, Rocamadour, 52, 285
Domaine de la Tortinière, Montbazon, 267
Domaine de Rochebois, Vitrac, 321
Domaine de Rochevilaine, Billiers, 33, 195
Domaine des Hauts de Loire, Onzain, 276
Domaine du Colombier, Malataverne, 252
Domme, 50
    Hôtel de l'Esplanade, 51, 226
    Hôtel de Ville, 51
    Terrasse de la Barre, 51
Donjon, Hôtel, Carcassonne, 64, 206, 139
Dordogne, 137
Dordogne & Lot River Valleys, 45
    Itinerary, 45
    Itinerary Map, 45
Dormans, 123
Driver's License, 5
Driving, 5
Duc de Saint-Simon, Hôtel, Paris (7th), 167

E

Ecrin, Hôtel l', Honfleur, 241
Edward 1er, Hôtel, Monpazier, 266
Eguisheim, 111

Épernay, 121
    Musée du Champagne et de la Préhistoire, 122
Épine, L'
    Aux Armes de Champagne, 227
Esclimont, Château d', Saint Symphorien-le-Château, 300
Esplanade, Hôtel de l', Domme, 51, 226
Eurailpass, 129
Europe, Hôtel d', Avignon, 74, 183, 141
Eyzies, Les, 48, 139
    Font de Gaum, 49, 139
    Hôtel Cro-Magnon, 49, 228, 139
    Les Combarelles, 49, 139
    Musée National de Préhistoire, 49
Eza, Château, Èze Village, 92, 230
Èze Bord de la Mer, 92
Èze Village, 92
    Château de la Chèvre d'Or, 92, 229
    Château Eza, 92, 230

F

Falaise
    Château du Tertre, 231
Familia Hôtel, Paris (5th), 160
Familypass, 129
Faux de Verzy, 121
Fayet Pass, 82
Fer à Cheval, Le, Megève, 255
Fère en Tardenois
    Château de Fère, 232
Ferme d'Augustin, Romantik Hotel la, Ramatuelle, 281
Ferme de la Huppe, La, Gordes, 239
Ferme Saint Siméon, La, Honfleur, 242
Fermes Marie, Les, Megève, 256
Figeac, 57
Fleuray
    Le Fleuray, 204
Fleury, 123
Flexipass, 129
Florac, 61
Font de Gaum, 49, 139

Index

Vougeot
    Château de Gilly, 106, 322
    Château de Vougeot, 106

W

Website, 14
Wine Country—Alsace, 109
    Itinerary, 109
    Itinerary Map, 109
Wine Country—Burgundy, 101
    Itinerary, 101
    Itinerary Map, 101
Wine Country—Champagne, 117
    Itinerary, 117
    Itinerary Map, 117

Y

Yaca, Le, Saint Tropez, 302
Yvoire
    Hôtel du Port, 323

Enhance Your Guides

Online

www.karenbrown.com

- Hotel News
- Color Photos
- New Discoveries
- Corrections & Edits
- Leisure Destinations
- Property of the Month
- Postcards from the Road
- Romantic Inns & Recipes

Become a Karen Brown Preferred Reader

Name _____

Street _____

Town _____

State _____ Zip _____ Country _____

Tel _____ Fax _____

E-mail _____

We'd love to welcome you as a Karen Brown Preferred Reader. Send us your name and address and you will be entered in our monthly drawing to receive a free set of Karen Brown guides. As a preferred reader, you will receive special promotions and be the first to know when new editions of Karen Brown guides go to press.

Please send to: Karen Brown's Guides, Post Office Box 70, San Mateo, California 94401, USA
tel: (650) 342-9117, fax: (650) 342-9153, e-mail: karen@karenbrown.com, website: www: karenbrown.com

SHARE YOUR COMMENTS AND DISCOVERIES WITH US

Please share comments on properties that you have visited. We welcome accolades, as well as criticisms.

Also, we'd love to hear about any hotel or bed & breakfast you discover. Tell us what you liked about the property and, if possible, please include a brochure or photographs. We regret we cannot return photos.

Owner _____ Hotel or B&B _____

Address _____ Town _____ Country _____

Comments:

Your name _____ Street _____

Town _____ State _____ Zip _____ Country _____

Tel _____ E-mail _____ Date _____

Do we have your permission to electronically publish your comments on our website? Yes _____ No _____

If yes, would you like to remain anonymous? Yes ___No ___, or may we use your name? Yes___ No___

Please send report to: Karen Brown's Guides, Post Office Box 70, San Mateo, California 94401, USA
tel: (650) 342-9117, fax: (650) 342-9153, e-mail: karen@karenbrown.com, www.karenbrown.com

KB Travel Service

- ❖ **KB Travel Service** offers travel planning assistance using itineraries designed by *Karen Brown* and published in her guidebooks. We will customize any itinerary to fit your personal interests.

- ❖ We will plan your itinerary with you, help you decide how long to stay and what to do once you arrive, and work out the details.

- ❖ We will book your airline tickets and your rental car, arrange rail tickets or passes (including your seat reservations), reserve accommodations recommended in *Karen Brown's Guides,* and supply you with point-to-point information and consultation.

Contact us to start planning your travel!

800 782-2128 ext. 328 or e-mail: info@kbtravelservice.com

Service fees do apply

KB Travel Service

16 East Third Avenue
San Mateo, CA 94401 USA
www.kbtravelservice.com

is the

Preferred Airline

of

Karen Brown's Guides

auto ⊛ europe.

Karen Brown's

Preferred Car Rental Service Provider

for

Worldwide Car Rental Services
Chauffeur & Transfer Services
Prestige & Sports Cars
Motor Home Rentals

1-800-223-5555

Be sure to identify yourself as a Karen Brown Traveler.
For special offers and discounts use your
Karen Brown ID number 99006187.

TRAVELSMITH®

Need a dual voltage hair dryer, a wrinkle-free blazer, quick-dry clothes, a computer adapter plug? TRAVELSMITH has them all, along with an enticing array of everything a Karen Brown traveler needs.

Karen Brown recommends TRAVELSMITH as an excellent source for travel clothing and gear. We were pleased to find quality products needed for our own research travels in their catalog—items not always easy to find. For a free catalog call TRAVELSMITH at 800-950-1600.

When placing your order, be sure to identify yourself as a Karen Brown Traveler with the code TKB99 and you will receive a 10% discount*. You can link to TRAVELSMITH through our website *www.karenbrown.com.*

*offer valid till December 2000

Seal Cove Inn

Located in the San Francisco Bay Area

Karen Brown Herbert (best known as author of the Karen Brown's guides) and her husband, Rick, have put 22 years of experience into reality and opened their own superb hideaway, Seal Cove Inn. Spectacularly set amongst wild flowers and bordered by towering cypress trees, Seal Cove Inn looks out to the distant ocean over acres of county park: an oasis where you can enjoy secluded beaches, explore tidepools, watch frolicking seals, and follow the tree-lined path that traces the windswept ocean bluffs. Country antiques, original watercolors, flower-laden cradles, rich fabrics, and the gentle ticking of grandfather clocks create the perfect ambiance for a foggy day in front of the crackling log fire. Each bedroom is its own haven with a cozy sitting area before a wood-burning fireplace and doors opening onto a private balcony or patio with views to the park and ocean. Moss Beach is a 35-minute drive south of San Francisco, 6 miles north of the picturesque town of Half Moon Bay, and a few minutes from Princeton harbor with its colorful fishing boats and restaurants. Seal Cove Inn makes a perfect base for whale-watching, salmon-fishing excursions, day trips to San Francisco, exploring the coast, or, best of all, just a romantic interlude by the sea, time to relax and be pampered. Karen and Rick look forward to the pleasure of welcoming you to their coastal hideaway.

Seal Cove Inn • 221 Cypress Avenue • Moss Beach • California • 94038 • USA
tel: (650) 728-4114, fax: (650) 728-4116, e-mail: sealcove@coastside.net, website: sealcoveinn.com

Travel Your Dreams • Order your Karen Brown Guides Today

Please ask in your local bookstore for Karen Brown's Guides. If the books you want are unavailable, you may order directly from the publisher. Books will be shipped immediately.

_____ *Austria: Charming Inns & Itineraries* $18.95

_____ *California: Charming Inns & Itineraries* $18.95

_____ *England: Charming Bed & Breakfasts* $17.95

_____ *England, Wales & Scotland: Charming Hotels & Itineraries* $18.95

_____ *France: Charming Bed & Breakfasts* $17.95

_____ *France: Charming Inns & Itineraries* $18.95

_____ *Germany: Charming Inns & Itineraries* $18.95

_____ *Ireland: Charming Inns & Itineraries* $18.95

_____ *Italy: Charming Bed & Breakfasts* $17.95

_____ *Italy: Charming Inns & Itineraries* $18.95

_____ *Portugal: Charming Inns & Itineraries* $18.95

_____ *Spain: Charming Inns & Itineraries* $18.95

_____ *Switzerland: Charming Inns & Itineraries* $18.95

Name _____ Street _____

Town _____ State _____ Zip _____ Tel _____

Credit Card (MasterCard or Visa) _____ Expires: _____

For orders in the USA, add $4 for the first book and $1 for each additional book for shipment. California residents add 8.25% sales tax. Overseas orders add $10 per book for airmail shipment. Indicate number of copies of each title; fax or mail form with check or credit card information to:

KAREN BROWN'S GUIDES
Post Office Box 70 • San Mateo • California • 94401 • USA
tel: (650) 342-9117, fax: (650) 342-9153, e-mail: karen@karenbrown.com
You can also order directly from our website at www.karenbrown.com.

KAREN BROWN wrote her first travel guide in 1976. Her personalized travel series has grown to thirteen titles which Karen and her small staff work diligently to keep updated. Karen, her husband, Rick, and their children, Alexandra and Richard, live in Moss Beach, a small town on the coast south of San Francisco. They settled here in 1991 when they opened Seal Cove Inn. Karen is frequently traveling, but when she is home, in her role as innkeeper, enjoys welcoming Karen Brown readers.

CLARE BROWN, CTC, was a travel consultant for many years, specializing in planning itineraries to Europe using charming small hotels in the countryside. The focus of her job remains unchanged, but now her expertise is available to a larger audience—the readers of her daughter Karen's country inn guides. When Clare and her husband, Bill, are not traveling, they live either in Hillsborough, California, or at their home in Vail, Colorado, where family and friends frequently join them for skiing.

JUNE BROWN'S love of travel was inspired by the *National Geographic* magazines that she read as a girl in her dentist's office—so far she has visited over 40 countries. June hails from Sheffield, England and lived in Zambia and Canada before moving to northern California where she lives in San Mateo with her husband, Tony, their daughter Clare, their German Shepherd, and a Siamese cat.

BARBARA TAPP, the talented artist who produces all of the hotel sketches and delightful illustrations in this guide, was raised in Australia where she studied in Sydney at the School of Interior Design. Although Barbara continues with freelance projects, she devotes much of her time to illustrating the Karen Brown guides. Barbara lives in Kensington, California, with her husband, Richard, their two sons, Jonothan and Alexander, and daughter, Georgia.

JANN POLLARD, the artist responsible for the beautiful painting on the cover of this guide, has studied art since childhood, and is well-known for her outstanding impressionistic-style watercolors which she has exhibited in numerous juried shows, winning many awards. Jann travels frequently to Europe (using Karen Brown's guides) where she loves to paint historical buildings. Jann lives in Burlingame, California, with her husband, Gene.

Notes